PHYSIOLOGICAL
CORRELATES OF EMOTION

CONTRIBUTORS

MAGDA B. ARNOLD

DALBIR BINDRA

JOSEPH V. BRADY

JAN H. BRUELL

JOSÉ M. R. DELGADO

SEBASTIAN P. GROSSMAN

LYNN J. HAMMOND

HARRY F. HARLOW

MARGARET K. HARLOW

SEYMOUR S. KETY

BEATRICE C. LACEY

JOHN I. LACEY

DONALD B. LINDSLEY

PAUL D. MACLEAN

STUART VALINS

PHYSIOLOGICAL CORRELATES OF EMOTION

Edited by PERRY BLACK

THE JOHNS HOPKINS UNIVERSITY SCHOOL OF MEDICINE
and
FRIENDS MEDICAL SCIENCE RESEARCH CENTER
BALTIMORE, MARYLAND

 1970

ACADEMIC PRESS   New York and London

712934

ACADEMIC PRESS, INC.
111 Fifth Avenue, New York, New York 10003

United Kingdom Edition published by
ACADEMIC PRESS, INC. (LONDON) LTD.
Berkeley Square House, London W1X 6BA

LIBRARY OF CONGRESS CATALOG CARD NUMBER: 78-117105

Second Printing, 1971

PRINTED IN THE UNITED STATES OF AMERICA

CONTENTS

Part 1.   INTRODUCTION

1.   Emotion and Behavior Theory: Current Research in Historical Perspective

DALBIR BINDRA

Part 2.   GENETIC AND DEVELOPMENTAL CORRELATES

2.   Heritability of Emotional Behavior

JAN H. BRUELL

3. Developmental Aspects of Emotional Behavior

HARRY F. HARLOW AND MARGARET K. HARLOW

Part 3. NEUROCHEMICAL AND ENDOCRINE CORRELATES

4. Neurochemical Aspects of Emotional Behavior

SEYMOUR S. KETY

5. Modification of Emotional Behavior by Intracranial Administration of Chemicals

SEBASTIAN P. GROSSMAN

6. Endocrine and Autonomic Correlates of Emotional Behavior

JOSEPH V. BRADY

Part 4. NEUROPHYSIOLOGICAL CORRELATES

7. The Limbic Brain in Relation to the Psychoses

PAUL D. MACLEAN

8. The Role of Nonspecific Reticulo–Thalamo–Cortical Systems in Emotion

DONALD B. LINDSLEY

9. Modulation of Emotions by Cerebral Radio Stimulation

JOSÉ M. R. DELGADO

Part 5. PSYCHOPHYSIOLOGICAL CORRELATES

10. Some Autonomic-Central Nervous System Interrelationships

JOHN I. LACEY AND BEATRICE C. LACEY

11. The Perception and Labeling of Bodily Changes as Determinants of Emotional Behavior

STUART VALINS

12. Conditioned Emotional States

LYNN J. HAMMOND

13. Brain Function in Emotion: A Phenomenological Analysis

MAGDA B. ARNOLD

Contents

LIST OF CONTRIBUTORS

Numbers in parentheses indicate the pages on which the authors' contributions begin.

MAGDA B. ARNOLD, Professor of Psychology, Loyola University of Chicago, Lake Shore Campus, Chicago, Illinois 60626. (261)

DALBIR BINDRA, Professor of Psychology, McGill University, Montreal, 110, P.Q., Canada. (3)

PERRY BLACK, Associate Professor of Neurological Surgery, Associate Professor of Psychiatry, The Johns Hopkins University School of Medicine; Director, Laboratory of Neurological Sciences, Friends Medical Science Research Center, Baltimore, Maryland 21205.

JOSEPH V. BRADY, Professor of Behavioral Biology, Department of Psychiatry and Behavioral Sciences, Johns Hopkins University School of Medicine, Baltimore, Maryland 21205. (95)

JAN H. BRUELL, Professor of Psychology, University of Texas, Austin, Texas 78712. (23)

JOSÉ M. R. DELGADO, Professor of Physiology, Department of Psychiatry, Yale University, School of Medicine, New Haven, Connecticut 06510. (189)

SEBASTIAN P. GROSSMAN, Professor of Psychology, University of Chicago, Chicago, Illinois 60637. (73)

LYNN J. HAMMOND, Assistant Professor of Psychology, Temple University, College of Liberal Arts, Philadelphia, Pennsylvania 19122. (245)

HARRY F. HARLOW, Professor of Psychology, Regional Primate Research Center, University of Wisconsin, Madison, Wisconsin 53706. (37)

MARGARET K. HARLOW, Professor of Psychology, Regional Primate Research Center, University of Wisconsin, Madison, Wisconsin 53706. (37)

SEYMOUR S. KETY, Professor of Psychiatry, Harvard University, Massachusetts General Hospital, Boston, Massachusetts 02114. (61)

BEATRICE C. LACEY, Chairman, Department of Psychophysiology–Neurophysiology, Fels Research Institute, Yellow Springs, Ohio 45387. (205)

JOHN I. LACEY, Senior Investigator, Department of Psychophysiology–Neurophysiology, Fels Research Institute, Yellow Springs, Ohio 45387. (205)

DONALD B. LINDSLEY, Professor of Psychology and Physiology, Member of the Brain Research Institute, University of California, Los Angeles, California 20024. (147)

PAUL D. MACLEAN, Chief, Section on Limbic Integration and Behavior, Laboratory of Neurophysiology, National Institute of Mental Health, Bethesda, Maryland 20014. (129)

STUART VALINS, Associate Professor of Psychology, State University of New York at Stony Brook, New York 11790. (229)

PREFACE

Although the concept of emotion, in varying terminology, dates back to ancient times, it remains somewhat enigmatic to this day. The elusive qualities of emotional phenomena largely account for the difficulty in precise definition. Intuitively, however, men have long recognized that what we call emotion consists of two basic elements: subjective feelings or passions on the one hand, and overt behavioral reactions on the other. Unfortunately, the nature of the problem has frequently confounded attempts at experimental analysis. It is not surprising, then, that the Galenic notion of the emotions circulating in the vascular system was widely held until the nineteenth century. There is, indeed, some truth in this view, but it completely ignored the nervous system!

Within the past century, and particularly in the past few decades, various disciplines have become involved in the study of emotion. The older speculative and descriptive approaches gradually yielded to experiment in both man and animal. Some advances had to await the development of specialized techniques in a number of fields: endocrinology, genetics, neurochemistry, neuro- and psychophysiology, and psychopharmacology. Progress toward an understanding of emotional processes is being made on a multidisciplinary front. Apart from the intrinsic value of this quest, it serves as a stepping-stone to prevention and management of disordered emotional states. Advances in these areas have also given fresh impetus to the age-old interest in mind-body relationships, expressed in modern clinical terms as psychosomatic medicine.

This book is based in part on a conference held in Baltimore on June 14, 1968, on the occasion of the opening of the Maryland State Psychiatric Research Center, under the sponsorship of Friends Medical Science Research Center. The seven papers presented at that conference served as a nucleus for this volume. Six additional contributions were subsequently invited for inclusion, in order to provide a broader interdisciplinary representation. The present volume, directed to readers in the medical and behavioral sciences, reflects the major experimental approaches currently applied to the study of emotion. In a sense, the respective approaches represent working definitions of emotion, each from the viewpoint of a given set of physiological or behavioral parameters. A comprehensive theory of emotion will ultimately have to take each of these "definitions" into account.

ACKNOWLEDGMENTS

The editor wishes to thank Dr. Eugene Brody, Dr. Joel Elkes, Dr. Daniel X. Freedman, and Dr. A. Earl Walker who presided over the various sessions of the original conference. The financial support of the following organizations which contributed to the conference is gratefully acknowledged: Ciba Pharmaceuticals, Summit, New Jersey; Geigy Pharmaceuticals, Ardsley, New York; Hoffmann-La Roche, Inc., Nutley, New Jersey; Knoll Pharmaceutical Company, Orange, New Jersey; The S. E. Massengill Company, Bristol, Tennessee; Merck Sharp & Dohme, West Point, Pennsylvania; Sandoz Pharmaceuticals, Hanover, New Jersey; Smith Kline & French Laboratories, Philadelphia, Pennsylvania; Wallace Laboratories, Cranbury, New Jersey; Wyeth Laboratories, Philadelphia, Pennsylvania. The advice of Thomas E. Hanlon, Dr. Albert A. Kurland, Dr. James E. Olsson, Charles Savage, and Dr. R. W. Von Korff in planning the conference is warmly appreciated. The assistance of Mr. A. Douglas Kirk in arranging the conference proved invaluable. I am especially grateful to Mr. Daniel Mendelsohn, President, and Mr. Richard H. Meacham, Executive Administrator, Friends Medical Science Research Center, for their encouragement and active support in organizing the conference and in the preparation of this volume. Dr. Clinton C. Brown gave helpful advice on several occasions during the editing process. The secretarial duties were competently performed by Mrs.

Phyllis Papi, Miss Sharon Raffensperger, Mrs. Ulla H. M. Martz, and Miss April Steyert. It is a pleasure to acknowledge the collaboration of the staff of Academic Press. The major credit for this volume is, of course, due the contributing authors whose cooperative effort has provided this synthesis of their research and interpretations.

PHYSIOLOGICAL
CORRELATES OF EMOTION

1

INTRODUCTION

EMOTION AND BEHAVIOR THEORY: CURRENT RESEARCH IN HISTORICAL PERSPECTIVE

Dalbir Bindra

INTRODUCTION

In all areas of disciplined inquiry, explanatory ideas have progressed from being animistic and magical to being physicalistic and mechanistic, and from being vague and general to being explicit and refined. This has been the path of science, and man's attempts to understand his own experience, behavior, and accomplishments have come along the same path. Starting with early man's all-embracing concept of soul, philosophers over the centuries proposed a variety of more specific concepts to explain particular types of behavioral phenomena observed in man and animals. These concepts included rational soul, instinct, mind, will, reason, intellect, passion, emotion, appetite, and the like. In the continuous search for more rigorous explanations, these psychological concepts have been examined, modified, discarded, reintroduced, refined, and tested by generations of thinkers, and, more recently, of experimenters. My purpose here is to describe the major ways in which "emotion" has been conceptualized during the modern period of psychology, to indicate the types of experimental investigations that have emerged from the theoretical conceptions, and to set forth my ideas about the place of "emotion" in contemporary behavior theory.

THE PREEXPERIMENTAL PERIOD

The word "passion" was frequently used by early philosophers to connote roughly what in today's common usage is referred to as emotion—the phenomena of fear, anger, courage, jealousy, love, etc. Aristotle (fourth century B.C.) made a distinction between experiences that involve concurrent activity of both soul and body (e.g., sensations, appetites, and passions) and experiences that may involve activity of the soul only (e.g., thinking). This idea that the intellectual or rational experiences and actions are produced by the "spiritual soul" alone, and that actions accompanied by experiences of sensations, appetites, and passions are produced by body and soul together was more explicitly stated and affirmed by St. Thomas Aquinas (thirteenth century). Working within this assumption, Descartes (seventeenth century) directed his attention specifically to the nature of passions. Besides reiterating that every passion experienced by the soul has its bodily counterpart, he emphasized the role of environmental stimulation in the generation of a passion. Descartes also proposed a mechanism by which environmental stimuli create the experienced passions and produce actions. This mechanism may be described as follows. An environmental event or object (e.g., a charging bull), operating through sense organs and nerves (e.g., eyes and optic pathways), creates an impression on the pineal gland. This impression acts immediately on the soul, causing it to see, comprehend, or feel the danger, and, separately, on the animal spirits in the brain and nerves, causing some commotion ("heat and movements") in the heart and blood, and some overt actions (e.g., flight or attack). The animal spirits that cause the bodily commotion also move the pineal gland in a particular way, "fortifying" the comprehension of feeling of danger in the soul in such a way as to convert it into a passion (e.g., fear, courage). Though there are several contradictions and obscurities in his account, Descartes managed to establish conceptual distinctions among passion (of the soul), bodily commotion (activity of the visceral organs), and action (overt movements of the somatic musculature), and to indicate that there is close correspondence among the three.

For about two centuries following Descartes, there was no significant development in theoretical ideas about emotion. Interest in emotional phenomena as worthy of investigation in their own right was rekindled by Darwin's *Expression of Emotions in Man and Animals* (1872). In his comparative survey of emotional "expression" in mammals, Darwin drew attention to emotional behavior—the overt actions—as the biologically significant aspect of emotion, and at the same time pointed to the causal role of stimulus events or situations that typically produce that behavior. William James (1884) brought together the Cartesian attempt at explaining emotional experiences and the Darwinian observations of emotional behavior in animals, and proposed the first explicit psychological theory of emotion. James argued that the perception of an emotional stimulus situation leads directly through "reflex currents" to visceral reactions (e.g., increase in heart rate) and overt muscular actions (e.g., fighting). The "feeling" of these bodily reactions, that is, the arrival of the sensory feedback from these bodily reactions at the cerebral cortex, *is* the experience of emotion. The content or nature of the emotional experience is determined wholly by the particular visceral and overt reactions provoked by the stimulus situation. Thus, in effect, James regarded emotional experience to be a secondary phenomenon, dependent upon visceral and somatic reactions; reversing the common-sense view, he argued that we feel sorry *because* we cry, afraid *because* we tremble. This theory is a significant landmark because it clearly proposed certain relations among three sets of events: emotional stimulus, emotional behavior (both visceral reactions and overt actions), and emotional experience. The earliest experimental investigations of emotion were concerned with studying the relations among these three sets of events. But soon experimental investigations of "emotion" expanded in a variety of directions.

THE EXPERIMENTAL STUDY OF EMOTION

At least four different lines of experimental work developed under the vague rubric, "emotion." These include the study of (a) *emotional experience* (or emotional recognition) as subjectively reported by man and inferred by him in other human beings and animals (e.g., states described as fear, anger, jealousy, love); (b) *emotional arousal*, the changes in internal bodily processes, such as visceral, somatic, and neural functions, produced by environmental stimuli; (c) *emotional action*, the overt environmentally directed response patterns (e.g., attack, withdrawal, growl, smile, approach), and (d) *emotional stimulation*, the particular stimulus features of the physical or social environment that usually provoke one or more of the above three. Consider these four lines of research in turn.

EMOTIONAL EXPERIENCE

James' theory implied that emotional experience is crucially dependent upon the sensory feedback from emotional actions, or emotional arousal, or both. Since it is a common observation that human beings report the same emotional experience (e.g., anger) while displaying a variety of different actions (attack, verbal ridicule, withdrawal from the situation, self-injury), it follows that, if James is correct, there should exist distinctive visceral–somatic reactions (such as changes in heart rate, respiration, muscle tension) corresponding to each different reported emotional experience. But Cannon's (1915) work on visceral reactions showed that there are only two broad patterns of autonomic discharge, one characterized by the (relative) hyperactivity of its sympathetic division and the other by the (relative) hyperactivity of its parasympathetic division. He thus argued that visceral reactions are too diffuse to provide numerous distinctive patterns that would be required to account for the many different emotional experiences reported by human beings—common sense employs scores of different terms to describe emotional experiences. While several investigators (e.g., Arnold, 1945; Ax, 1953; Funkenstein, 1955) have studied the patterns of autonomic reactions accompanying particular kinds of emotional actions, or following particular classes of emotional stimuli, James' suggestion that each emotional experience *depends* solely and critically upon a distinctive set of autonomic reactions has not been seriously revived since Cannon rejected it.

However, the above rejection still leaves tenable the idea that the sensory feedback from visceral reactions plays some part in emotional experience. Though Cannon rejected this idea too, he did not conclusively disprove it. He rejected it on the grounds that emotional *actions* are still present in sympathectomized or vagotomized cats, but this evidence is not critical for the argument that sensory feedback of visceral reactions is necessary for emotional *experience.* The importance of visceral reactions in emotional experience was first clearly demonstrated by experiments in which injections of adrenaline were given to human subjects (Cantril & Hunt, 1932; Marañon, 1924, quoted by Schachter & Singer, 1962). While the injections did not consistently produce any particular emotional experience, the subjects did report a varied set of experiences of "as if" or "cold" emotion. Furthermore, Marañon found that sensitive questions that did not produce any emotion before the injection could do so following the injection; he concluded that "adrenal commotion" places the subject in a situation of "affective imminence." These experiments suggested that the reported emotional experience arises from an interaction of "visceral commotion" and cognition, or *meaning* associated with the stimuli present in the experimental situation.

Schachter and Singer (1962) experimentally studied the nature of the interaction between the sensory feedback from visceral reactions and cognitions provided by the test situation. Manipulating visceral reactions by means of adrenaline injections, and cognitions by means of instructions and social-situational arrangements, they showed that the same visceral reactions (produced by adrenaline) could facilitate the emergence of an experience of anger or euphoria depending on the instructions and the nature of the social situation. But adrenaline by itself, without an "emotional" cognition, was not likely to produce any emotional experience—though it produced the usual visceral reactions. Thus, the change in the pattern of visceral-somatic reactions produced by adrenaline was necessary but not sufficient for producing emotional experience. Clearly, emotional experience emerges as a consequence of some collation of the sensory feedback from visceral-somatic reactions and the cognitions generated by the stimulus situation.

These findings show conclusively that emotional experiences are secondary constructions rather than primary processes. This means that "having" a particular emotional experience (e.g., anger, fear, jealousy, joy, love) is the outcome of a categorizing process that combines a number of separate sensory events into a unitary category or "experience." From this point of view, "recognizing emotion" in others and "experiencing emotion" in oneself may both be regarded as outcomes of the same fundamental process of categorization, with the sole difference that in experiencing emotion one usually obtains direct sensory feedback from one's own visceral reactions, while in judging emotion in others no direct feedback of visceral reaction is available, though indirect cues (e.g., sweating, trembling, vasodilation, change in posture) may be available. Given the knowledge that there is some radical change in visceral reactions (in oneself or in an observed man or animal) the actual category of experience that emerges, or the label of recognition applied, depends on the cognitive factors related to the stimulus situation. The biological significance of this categorizing process must be that it represents an integration of various features of the stimulus situation into a "decision" regarding what the animal whose emotion is being judged is likely to do next. That most mammals are capable of "recognizing emotions" in others is shown by the fact that they can adjust their own actions to the expected actions of others. Recognizing emotion in this sense of predicting the probable future course of action of another animal rests on postural reactions and facial expressions (Darwin, 1872; Andrew, 1963), as well as on complex factors, such as the "normal" (previous) behavior of the animal in similar situations, its age and sex, and the preceding and present stimulus situation (Hebb, 1946). The same threatening gesture on the part of a chimpanzee may be recognized by another chimpanzee as an impending attack or a playful approach depending on who makes the threat, what preceded the threat, and what else is currently going on in the environment. Thus "recognizing emotion" in others or "emotional experience" in ourselves is high-order classification or "summary" of the total situation, giving an indication of what is going to happen next.

My view (Bindra, 1969) is that the classification process involved is one of multidimensional categorization, the process involved in such every-day categories as "a nice day," "a friendly girl," and "an explosive situation." The essential characteristic of such categorization is that several different features (dimensions or elements) are involved in the categorization, and no particular feature may be essential for any category. A girl may be labeled as friendly either because she is approachable and solicitous, or because she is approachable and helpful, or because she is helpful and solicitous; the label "friendly" creates a general expectation that her actions are likely to be unintimidating, unrepelling, and possibly inviting. This means that there cannot be any "core" of an emotional experience (or of emotional label), no distinctive set of bodily reactions that always results in the same "emotion." This is so because emotional experience (e.g., anger, fear, love) represents multidimensional categorization, different instances of the same experience resulting from different combinations of factors. A one-to-one relation between an emotional experience and a particular pattern of bodily reaction would require emotional experience to be a unitary entity. (The process of multidimensional categorization would appear also to be the basis on which we describe some visceral changes, some overt action, and some stimulus situations as "emotional.") This explains why the search for distinctive visceral reactions or patterns of overt actions as correlates of particular emotional experiences was doomed to failure. This also explains why, in psychiatric practice, the same reported emotional experience may have different "contents" in different patients. The nature of cues that typically enter into various categories of experience associated with psychiatric conditions emerges as a problem for further study.

EMOTIONAL AROUSAL

The lack of a relation between distinctive patterns of visceral-somatic reactions and particular emotional experiences or labels does not preclude the possibility that particular emotional *stimuli* can produce characteristic, if not distinctive, patterns of visceral-somatic reactions in individual animals. Indeed it is common knowledge that height makes some people dizzy, a sudden loud noise causes a startle, certain shapes and sounds produce "freezing" in animals, and other shapes and sounds produce excitement and exploration.

This question of the nature of visceral-somatic reactions produced by certain environmental stimuli received considerable attention following the development of instruments for the measurement of autonomic reactions in intact animals. Much of this early work was concerned with isolated measures of autonomic function, such as heart rate, respiration, and galvanic skin response (for a review of the early studies, see Woodworth, 1938, Chapters 12, 13). In the 1940s concepts such as "energy mobilization" or "arousal" (Duffy, 1941; Freeman, 1948) were introduced to describe the general state of body economy produced by changes in bodily functions. However, it was not until the neurophysiological basis of general energy mobilization and alertness was made known to psychologists (Lindsley, 1951, pp. 473-516) that the concept of *arousal* became widely accepted as relevant to discussions of emotional phenomena (Duffy, 1962; Malmo, 1959). Changes in the *level of arousal* of an animal are usually described in terms of measures of visceral reactions (e.g., heart rate or stomach motility), somatic reactions (e.g., muscle tension), and neural reactions (e.g., cerebral activation). When a change in arousal level is brought about by environmental stimuli, rather than by the internal vegetative processes, it is usually referred to as "emotional arousal."

A problem about emotional arousal that has interested many investigators is that of *individual differences* in the degree of arousal change, as well as in the particular pattern of autonomic-somatic changes, produced by particular stimuli (for a review, see Duffy, 1962, Chapters 9, 10, 11). The stimuli used in this work have usually been described as "stress" and include thermal pain stimulation, intense sounds, light flashes, exposure to novel situations, task performance under distraction, talking about sensitive and personally embarrassing matters, and the like. Consistent individual differences in both base levels of various autonomic-somatic measures and in the degree of change in response to a particular stimulus have been found to exist (Schnore, 1957). Another finding of some importance is that the relative degree of change shown in each of a set of autonomic-somatic measures, that is, the pattern of autonomic reactions, remains fairly stable for an individual regardless of the type of stress; this has been termed the principle of "relative response specificity" (Lacey, Bateman & Van Lehn, 1953; Lacey & Lacey, 1958). Group differences in patterns of autonomic–somatic reactivity also exist; thus, under identical testing conditions, operational fatigue patients in the Air Force differ from aviation students (Wenger, 1948), anxiety patients differ from normal subjects (Malmo & Shagass, 1949b), and patients with clinical history of cardiovascular complaints from patients with clinical history of head and neck pains (Malmo & Shagass, 1949a). The existence of such individual differences may be relevant to an understanding of psychosomatic disorders.

The above findings have naturally led to studies of the sources of individual differences in emotional arousal. Two main lines of research have been developed, one concerned with the role of genetic factors (Broadhurst, 1969; Bruell, 1969; see also Chapter 2 in this volume) and one with the role of early experience (Denenberg, 1964) in the determination of individual differences. This is currently an active area of research.

EMOTIONAL ACTIONS

What counts biologically – in terms of survival – is action: response sequences that alter the animal's relation to environmental stimuli. The forms of biologically important, environmentally directed response patterns (e.g., eating, attacking, withdrawing, growling, copulating, nursing the young) vary greatly from species to species but are highly uniform within a species; they are therefore frequently referred to as "species-typical" response patterns. There is no adequate basis for distinguishing between "emotional" and other species-typical patterns, but it has become customary to regard the responses that appear to be provoked primarily by environmental stimulation (e.g., attack, withdrawal, avoidance, growling) as "emotional," and the responses that appear to be provoked primarily by the internal state of the animal (e.g., eating, drinking) as "motivational." Copulation, especially in the female, and nursing the young, both of which are somewhat ambiguous in this respect, are classified as emotional by some authors and motivational by others.

While emotional actions are to some degree dependent upon emotional arousal and emotional recognition, their exact form is determined primarily by the nature of emotional stimuli and the motor patterns typical of the species. The study of emotional actions has thus concentrated on attempts to define the type of emotional responses elicited by certain specified kinds of ("emotional") stimuli and to unravel the specific factors that determine their exact form and occurrence. Several different experimental questions have been studied.

Watson (1919) described what he called three innate patterns of emotional response in the human infant: rage, fear, and love. He also specified the stimuli that produce these responses: rage is elicited by restriction of movement; fear by loss of support and loud sound; and love by gentle tactual stimulation of the skin. Watson's work led to a series of observational studies of the development of patterns of emotional response in the human young (for a review, see Young, 1943, Chapter 4). Some studies of the facial expressions of adult men and women were also carried out during the 1920s and 1930s (for a review, see Woodworth, 1938, Chapter 11). Much of this early work was carried out as an attempt to determine the precise response correlates of particular emotional experiences, reported or presumed. Understandably, this work produced negative or inconsistent results; for, as we have seen, any given emotional experience is essentially a multidimensional categorization and cannot be related, in a one-to-one relation, with any specific autonomic or postural reactions. More recently, facial expressions have been studied in and of themselves, not as indicators or "expressions" of emotional experience, (see Woodworth & Schlosberg, 1954, Chapter 5). These studies have produced fairly consistent results, and tend to show that facial expressions may be classified along two dimensions: attention–rejection and pleasantness–unpleasantness.

Another line of experimental work is concerned with the analysis of the factors that play a part in the development of emotional responses in various species. The types of responses that have been extensively studied include aggressive responses, such as attack, fighting, temper tantrums (Hebb, 1945; Conner, Levine, Wertheim, & Cummer, 1969; Melzack, 1954), fearful responses, such as withdrawal and avoidance (Hebb, 1946b; Melzack & Scott, 1957; Bronson, 1968), and affectional responses, such as preferences for certain objects, places, and persons (Harlow & Zimmermann, 1959; Scott, 1962; Hinde & Spencer-Booth, 1968). Some investigators are concerned primarily with early social experience (Eisenberg, 1969; Kaufman & Rosenblum, 1967) and others with cultural factors (Bandura & Walters, 1963, pp. 364–415).

A third type of research is concerned with neural organization underlying various species-typical emotional responses. Cannon's experimental and clinical observations led him to propose that the thalamic area of the brain was crucially involved in emotional responses. This prompted studies directed at defining the exact location of "emotional brain," its neural connections, and its precise functional significance (Bard, 1934, pp. 264–311; 1950). However, in retrospect it appears that the lesion technique, employed by these early investigators, was too crude to answer the questions posed. The introduction of the technique of electrical stimulation of particular brain sites has led to substantial progress in understanding the neural mechanisms of emotional responses. This work is too extensive to be reviewed here; interested readers are referred to the recent review by Glickman and Schiff (1967), as well as to the work of Flynn and his associates (Levison & Flynn, 1965; MacDonnell & Flynn, 1966), and Delgado (1964).

EMOTIONAL STIMULI

Emotional responses are produced by an interaction of emotional stimuli and the species-typical neural organizations which are excited by those stimuli. Thus there cannot be any definition of emotional stimuli independent of certain specified "emotional responses," nor a definition of emotional responses independent of some specified "emotional stimuli." The stimuli that usually are called emotional stimuli are those that in a given species typically evoke responses described as fearful, aggressive, affectional, etc. Two broad types of studies of emotional stimuli are possible. First, the investigator might select a carefully defined emotional-response pattern (e.g., crouching, attack) and then ask the question: What range of stimuli can elicit that pattern under a given set of physiological and other conditions? While the stimulus *objects* that produce various emotional responses are known in general terms, the precise stimulus features, in terms of sensory analysis, that are critical in eliciting the responses, are only beginning to be discovered. Ethological workers have been especially active in determining the precise stimulus features that serve as "innate releasers" of "instinctive acts." This literature, reviewed by Hinde (1966), is concerned mainly with submammalian species. In mammals, psychologists have studied the range of stimuli effective in eliciting copulation (Beach, 1942), maternal retrieval of the young (Beach & Jaynes, 1956), fear (Bronson, 1968; Hebb, 1946b; Melzack, 1952), and aggression (Levison & Flynn, 1965). But, so far, we have hardly any reliable knowledge about the precise stimuli that are important in the social and sexual life of man.

In the second type of study possible in connection with emotional stimuli, the investigator might select a carefully defined stimulus pattern, or a combination of stimuli, and determine what kinds of responses are elicited by it under varying organismic conditions (i.e., the immediate neural correlates of the internal biochemical milieu). Studies that fall in this category include those of the responses of animals to emotional stimuli under the effects of hormones (Conner, Levine, Wertheim, & Cummer, 1969) and drugs (Herr, Stewart, & Charest, 1961).

EMOTION AND BEHAVIOR THEORY

Parallel to the various kinds of experimental work under the general rubric of "emotion," there has been an interest in defining the concept of emotion theoretically and finding an appropriate place for it in general behavior theory. Three different approaches have been taken, one aimed at specifying a unique "emotional process," another advocating the use of the concept as an intervening variable defined in reference to observable stimulus and response events, and the third regarding emotional phenomena as the outcome of the same general behavioral processes that produce other behavioral phenomena, such as those of perception and motivation.

The earliest theoretical formulations in psychology were characterized by a tendency to link particular types of behavioral phenomena, such as those of perception, motivation, and emotion, to a unique set of faculties or processes, such as "cognition," "conation," and "emotion." In the context of emotion, this practice of aligning particular classes of behavior to particular explanatory concepts meant that emotional phenomena were regarded as a distinct class of behavior, which was to be accounted for by a unique "emotional process." This unique process was conceived as: (a) a "feeling" of bodily changes produced by the perception of an "exciting fact" (James, 1884); (b) a set of visceral reactions (Wenger, 1950); (c) the neural impulses originating in the thalamus as a consequence of release of cortical inhibition (Cannon, 1927); (d) an evaluation in the brain of incoming sensory stimulation that results in an "emotional attitude," which in turn initiates nerve impulses that produce "emotional expression" (Arnold, 1950); (e) activation produced by increased activity of the brain stem reticular formation (Lindsley, 1951, pp. 473–516); (f) disruption of ongoing phase sequences by the disturbance of timing of neuronal activity in the cerebrum (Hebb, 1949);

(g) a disturbed affective state (Young, 1961); (h) a part of the motivational processes (Leeper, 1965), and so on. A review of these and other conceptions of a unique emotional process may be found in a recent paper by Goldstein (1968). None of these views has gained general acceptance. The primary reason for this is undoubtedly that a single process cannot account for the wide variety of phenomena and experimental data that have come to be included under the label of emotion. Furthermore, it is hard to imagine that there would exist a unique "emotional process" as the basis for emotional phenomena which cannot be clearly separated from other behavioral phenomena, such as those of perception and motivation. Arguments that emotion should not be regarded as a unique process or as a distinct class of behavior have been put forth by Duffy (1941, 1948).

The second approach, which advocates use of the concept of emotion as an intervening variable, linking certain stimulating or antecedent conditions with certain responses, arises from the common-sense view that emotion stirs up and goads animals into action. It is this conception that McDougall (1908) put forth in his doctrine of instincts. He regarded the "emotional impulse" or striving as the entity that links the stimuli received to the actions executed. Brown and Farber (1951) have suggested that the concept "emotion" should be used as an intervening variable, and, within the framework of Hull's (1943) behavior theory, they have shown how "frustration" can serve as a useful intervening variable. However, they fail to show how "emotion" as an intervening variable is different from other intervening variables (e.g., drive, arousal) that may be used to explain any particular behavioral phenomenon. Thus, like the first approach, the intervening-variable approach also suffers from the assumption that there is a unique "emotional process," as well as from a lack of specification as to what distinguishes emotion from other processes or intervening variables.

I favor the third approach which seeks to explain emotional phenomena of all types without reference to "emotion" as a theoretical concept. A working assumption, being increasingly accepted by psychologists, is that there exist a few key processes which play a part in all behavioral phenomena. Thus, the processes that produce phenomena described as "emotional" are considered to be no different from those that produce behavior described as "motivational" or "perceptual." None of the presumed fundamental processes is peculiar to emotional phenomena, or motivational phenomena, or perceptual phenomena. Working in terms of this approach, I have recently proposed a set of concepts that could be used to explain and study a wide variety of emotional–motivational phenomena, but whose use need not be restricted to this class of phenomena.

My view, elaborated elsewhere (Bindra, 1969), may be summarized as follows: Whatever the historical reasons that led to the distinction between "emotional" (e.g., attacking, withdrawing, seeking contact) and "motivational" (e.g., eating, drinking, copulating) species-typical actions, the most common justification offered currently seems to concern the roles of internal (physiological state) and external (environmental) events. Emotional actions have generally been thought to be caused by environmental stimulation, and motivational actions are thought to be caused by the physiological state ("drive"). This criterion is now known to be invalid.

The view that is emerging from the current neurophysiological and behavioral studies of species-typical actions, both "emotional" and "motivational," is that the occurrence of any species-typical action depends crucially upon an interaction between environmental events and the prevailing organismic state. For example, electrical stimulation of hypothalamic "feeding sites" leads to eating or drinking actions only in the presence of appropriate environmental objects (food or water), and the electrical stimulation of hypothalamic "aggression sites" leads to an attacking action only in the presence of a particular kind of attackable object. Both a particular *organismic state* and a particular class of *incentive stimulus* are necessary for the elicitation of emotional or motivational species-typical action patterns. The control exerted by the organismic state on emotional actions is demonstrated by the marked effects that hormonal levels and drugs can have on aggression, anxiety, and depression in the absence of any changes in incentive stimuli. The control exerted by incentive stimuli on motivational actions is demonstrated by the marked effects that changes in incentive objects have on eating, copulation, and maternal behavior in the absence of any changes in the organismic state of the animal.

In view of the above considerations, I have suggested (see Figure 1) that we use the term *central motive state* to describe the processes that are crucial, but not sufficient, determiners of emotional and motivational phenomena. A central motive state is best described as a set of neural processes arising from the interaction or combination of a certain type of organismic state and a certain class of incentive stimuli. The interaction results in a change in the functional state of the neural systems involved in a particular class of species-typical action. The changed neural state alters the excitability of certain groups of neurons in both afferent and efferent

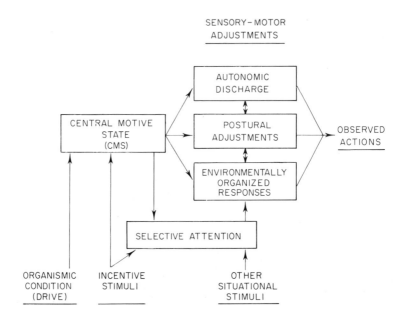

Fig. 1. Schematic diagram of the hypothetical interrelations of the postulated central motive state with (a) internal organismic conditions and environmental incentive stimuli, and (b) sensory and motor mechanisms involved in the organization of actions.

pathways. Apart from producing certain autonomic and somatic "preparatory" adjustments (e.g., salivation, postural changes, muscular tenseness), the changed neural state serves two other functions. It produces *selective attention* for a certain class of incentive stimuli and creates a *response bias* in favor of a certain class of species-typical actions. Table 1 shows how a single concept may be used to replace the pairs of concepts used in the traditional discussion of "emotion" and "motivation." Further, the new concepts are meant to be relevant to an understanding of all behavioral phenomena, not only those labeled "emotional" or "motivational."

SUMMARY

Serious experimental study of emotion started when William James (1884) posed the problem of emotional phenomena as one involving four sets of events, emotional experience, visceral–somatic changes or emotional arousal, emotional actions, and emotional stimuli, and suggested that emotional experience is a *consequence* of bodily (visceral and overt) reactions. Four lines of research have developed since then. Experiments on *emotional experience* have shown it to be dependent upon an interaction of the "emotional" stimulus situation and felt visceral changes. It appears that the process of identifying particular emotional experiences in oneself, and of "recognizing emotions" in someone else, is one of multidimensional categorizing; there is no distinctive core of an "emotion," such as fear, anger, or love. This explains why studies of *emotional arousal* have failed to find distinctive visceral–somatic patterns for different emotions. Current work on emotional arousal is concerned with the problem of genetic and experiential sources of individual differences in the pattern and intensity of visceral–somatic reactions. Investigations of *emotional actions* are concerned with the neural organization of species-typical emotional responses, and the situational and social factors important in their development. Experiments on *emotional stimuli* are concerned with identifying the precise stimulus features that elicit an emotional response under a given set of organismic conditions (internal milieu), and the way in which the efficacy of the stimuli changes with changing organismic conditions (e.g., with hormones and drugs).

In behavior theory, the older approaches that sought to define a distinctive emotional process as the basis of emotional phenomena have failed. A new approach that would attempt to interpret all behavioral phenomena in terms of a few fundamental neuropsychological processes is suggested, and is illustrated by the concept of *central motive state*, which is shown to be useful in understanding both emotional and motivational phenomena.

TABLE 1

Some Suggested Common Terms to Replace the Separate Terms Traditionally Used in Discussions of Emotion and Motivation

Common term	"Emotion" term	"Motivation" term
Central motive state (CMS)	Emotion or emotional state	Motive or motivational state
Incentive stimulus (unconditioned)	"Natural" emotional stimulus	"Natural" or primary reinforcing stimulus
Conditioned incentive stimulus	Conditoned emotional stimulus	Conditioned reinforcing or incentive-motivational stimulus
Physiological or organismic condition	Emotional predisposition	Drive

ACKNOWLEDGMENT

The preparation of this paper was supported by Grant MH-03238-08 from the United States Public Health Service (National Institute of Mental Health) and Grant APT-74 from the National Research Council of Canada.

REFERENCES

Andrew, R. J. Evolution of facial expression. *Science*, 1963, **142**, 1034-1041.
Aquinas, St. Thomas, 13th Century; see Reeves, J. W. *Body and mind in Western thought*. Harmondsworth: Penguin Books, 1958.
Aristotle, 4th Century B.C.; see Reeves, J. W. *Body and mind in Western thought*. Harmondsworth: Penguin Books, 1958.
Arnold, M. B. Physiological differentiation of emotional states. *Psychological Review*, 1945, **52**, 35-48.
Arnold, M. B. An excitatory theory of emotion. In M. L. Reymert (Ed.) *Feelings and emotions: The Moosehart symposium*. New York: McGraw-Hill, 1950. Pp. 11-33.
Ax, A. F. The physiological differentiation between fear and anger in humans. *Psychosomatic Medicine*, 1953, **15**, 433-442.
Bandura, A., & Walters, R. H. Aggression. In *Child psychology, sixty-second yearbook of the national society for the study of education*. Chicago: University of Chicago Press, 1963.
Bard, P. Emotion I. The Neuro-humoral basis of emotional reactions. In C. Murchison (Ed.), *Handbook of general experimental psychology*. Worcester: Clark University Press, 1934.
Bard, P. Central nervous mechanisms for the expression of anger in animals. In M. L. Reymert (Ed.), *Feelings and emotions: The Mooseheart symposium*, pp. 211-237. New York: McGraw-Hill, 1950.
Beach, F. A. Analysis of the stimuli adequate to elicit mating behavior in the sexually inexperienced male rat. *Journal of Comparative Psychology*, 1942, **33**, 163-207.
Beach, F. A. & Jaynes, J. Studies of maternal retrieving in rats: III. Sensory cues involved in the lactating female's response to her young. *Behaviour*, 1956, **10**, 104-125.
Bindra, D. A unified interpretation of emotion and motivation. *Annals of the New York Academy of Sciences*, 1969, **159**, 1071-1083.
Broadhurst, P. L. Psychogenetics of emotionality in the rat. *Annals of the New York Academy of Sciences*, 1969, **159**, 806-824.
Bronson, G. W. The development of fear in man and other animals. *Child Development*, 1968, **39**, 409-431.
Brown, J. S., & Farber, I. E. Emotions conceptualized as intervening variables—with suggestions toward a theory of frustration. *Psychological Bulletin*, 1951, **48**, 465-495.
Bruell, J. H. Genetics of emotional behavior in mice. *Annals of the New York Academy of Sciences*, 1969, **159**, 825-830.
Cannon, W. B. *Bodily changes in pain, hunger, fear and rage*. New York: Appleton, 1915.
Cannon, W. B. The James-Lange theory of emotions: a critical examination and an alternative theory. *American Journal of Psychology*, 1927, **39**, 106-124.
Cantril, H., & Hunt, W. A. Emotional effects produced by the injection of adrenalin. *American Journal of Psychology*, 1932, **44**, 300-307.

Conner, R. L., Levine, S., Wertheim, G. A., & Cummer, J. F. Hormonal determinants of aggressive behavior. *Annals of the New York Academy of Sciences,* 1969, **159,** 760-776.

Darwin, C. *The expression of emotions in man and animals.* London: Murray, 1872.

Delgado, J. M. R. Free behavior and brain stimulation. *International Review of Neurobiology,* 1964, **6,** 349-449.

Denenberg, V. H. Critical periods, stimulus input, and emotional reactivity: A theory of infantile stimulation. *Psychological Review,* 1964, **71,** 335-351.

Descartes, R. 17th Century; see Reeves, J. W. *Body and mind in Western thought.* Harmondsworth: Penguin Books, 1958.

Duffy, E. The conceptual categories of psychology: A suggestion for revision. *Psychological Review,* 1941, **48,** 177-203.

Duffy, E. Leeper's "Motivational theory of emotion." *Psychological Review,* 1948, **55,** 324-328.

Duffy, E. *Activation and behavior.* New York: Wiley, 1962.

Eisenberg, J. Social organization and emotional behavior. *Annals of the New York Academy of Sciences,* in press.

Freeman, G. L. *The energies of human behavior.* Ithaca, New York: Cornell University Press, 1948.

Funkenstein, D. H. The physiology of fear and anger. *Scientific American,* 1955, **192**(5), 74-80.

Glickman, S. E., & Schiff, B. B. A biological theory of reinforcement. *Psychological Review,* 1967, **74,** 81-109.

Goldstein, M. L. Physiological theories of emotion: a critical historical review from the standpoint of behavior theory. *Psychological Bulletin,* 1968, **69,** 23-40.

Harlow, H. F., & Zimmermann, R. R. Affectional responses in the infant monkey. *Science,* 1959, **130,** 421-432.

Hebb, D. O. The forms and conditions of chimpanzee anger. *Bulletin of the Canadian Psychological Association,* 1945, **5,** 32-35.

Hebb, D. O. Emotion in man and animal: An analysis of the intuitive processes of recognition. *Psychological Review,* 1946, 53, 88-106. (a)

Hebb, D. O. On the nature of fear. *Psychological Review,* 1946, **53,** 259-276. (b)

Hebb, D. O. *The organization of behavior.* New York: Wiley, 1949.

Herr, F., Stewart, J., & Charest, M. P. Tranquilizers and antidepressants: A pharmacological comparison. *Archives Internationales de Pharmacodynamie et de Therapie,* 1961, **134,** 328-342.

Hinde, R. A. *Animal Behaviour.* New York: McGraw-Hill, 1966.

Hinde, R. A., & Spencer-Booth, Y. The study of mother-infant interaction in captive group-living rhesus monkeys. *Proceedings of the Royal Society,* B, 1968, **169,** 177-201.

Hull, C. L. *Principles of behavior.* New York: Appleton, 1943.

James, W. What is emotion? *Mind,* 1884, 9, 188-204.

Kaufman, I. C., & Rosenblum, L. A. Depression in infant monkeys separated from their mothers. *Science,* 1967, **155,** 1030-1031.

Lacey, J. I., Bateman, D. E., & Van Lehn, R. Autonomic response specificity: An experimental study. *Psychosomatic Medicine,* 1953, **15,** 8-21.

Lacey, J. I., & Lacey, B. C. Verification and extension of the principle of autonomic response-stereotypy. *American Journal of Psychology,* 1958, **71,** 50-73.

Leeper, R. W. Some needed developments in the motivational theory of emotions. In D. Levine (Ed.), *Nebraska Symposium on Motivation,* pp. 25-122. Lincoln, Nebraska: University of Nebraska Press 1965.

Levison, P. K., & Flynn, J. P. The objects attacked by cats during stimulation of the hypothalamus. *Animal Behaviour*, 1965, 13, 217-220.
Lindsley, D. B. Emotion. In S. S. Stevens (Ed.), *Handbook of experimental psychology.* New York: Wiley, 1951.
MacDonnell, M. F., & Flynn, J. P. Control of sensory fields by stimulation of hypothalamus. *Science*, 1966, 152, 1406-1408.
McDougall, W. *An introduction to social psychology.* London: Methuen, 1908.
Malmo, R. B., & Shagass, C. Physiologic study of symptom mechanisms in psychiatric patients under stress. *Psychosomatic Medicine*, 1949, 11, 25-29. (a)
Malmo, R. B., & Shagass, C. Physiologic studies of reaction to stress in anxiety and early schizophrenia. *Psychosomatic Medicine*, 1949, 11, 9-24. (b)
Malmo, R. B. Activation: a neuropsychological dimension. *Psychological Review*, 1959, 66, 367-386.
Marañon, G. Contribution à l'étude de l'action émotive de l'adrénaline. *Revue Francaise d'Endocrinologie*, 1924, 2, 301-325.
Melzack, R. Irrational fears in the dog. *Canadian Journal of Psychology*, 1952, 6, 141-147.
Melzack, R. The genesis of emotional behavior: An experimental study of the dog. *Journal of Comparative and Physiological Psychology*, 1954, 47, 166-168.
Melzack, R., & Scott, T. H. The effects of early experience on the response to pain. *Journal of Comparative and Physiological Psychology*, 1957, 50, 155-161.
Schacter, S., & Singer, J. E. Cognitive, social, and physiological determinants of emotional state. *Psychological Review*, 1962, 69, 379-399.
Schnore, M. M. Individual differences in patterning and level of physiological activity: A study of arousal. Unpublished doctoral dissertation, McGill University, 1957.
Scott, J. P. Critical periods in behavioral development. *Science*, 1962, 138, 949-957.
Watson, J. B. *Psychology from the standpoint of a behaviorist.* Philadelphia: Lippincott, 1919.
Wenger, M. A. Studies of autonomic balance in Army Air Forces personnel. *Comparative Psychology Monographs*, 1948, 19, No. 4(Serial No. 101).
Wenger, M. A. Emotion as visceral action: An extension of Lange's theory. In M. L. Reymert (Ed.), *Feelings and Emotions: The Mooseheart Symposium*, pp. 3-10. New York: McGraw-Hill, 1950.
Woodworth, R. S. *Experimental Psychology.* New York: Holt, 1938.
Woodworth, R. S., & Schlosberg, H. *Experimental psychology.* New York: Holt, 1954.
Young, P. T. *Emotion in man and animal.* New York: Wiley, 1943.
Young, P. T. *Motivation and emotion.* New York: Wiley, 1961.

2

GENETIC AND DEVELOPMENTAL CORRELATES

2

HERITABILITY OF EMOTIONAL BEHAVIOR

Jan H. Bruell

INTRODUCTION

Individual differences in emotionality are universal, and we all are aware of them. Yet, when speaking of emotional behavior of cats or dogs or monkeys, we seldom take note of individuality. This may be unavoidable. Description and communication would become extremely cumbersome if we insisted on speaking all the time about the singular case rather than the statistical average. But we must not forget individuality, and it thus appears appropriate to include a chapter on individual differences in emotionality in a volume devoted, by and large, to what is general about emotional behavior. Though fully aware of the fact that emotional behavior is modified by the life experiences of an individual, I will not consider this source of individual variation here. I will speak exclusively about heritability of emotional behavior, that is, behavioral variation attributable to genetic variation within a population.

The problem is of interest because it touches on a wider question: Is so-called species-typical, instinctive behavior invariable throughout a species, is it genetically fixed? I will not attempt to define emotional behavior—other contributors to this volume have done that—but I will use the term to refer to adaptive responses that are related to self-preservation and preservation of the species: fearing, fighting, fleeing, mating, caring for young. Expression of fear or fighting spirit, and the movement patterns involved in courting and

mating are often quite stereotyped, species-typical. They are instinctive, unlearned, and obviously inherited. The question then is
whether the hereditary material underlying such species-typical
behavior is also stereotyped and fixed. If it were, then any observed
behavioral variation would be *non*heritable.

To clarify these introductory remarks, we must discuss first the
concept of heritability and explain the difference between genetic
determination and heritability of a trait. We will then direct our attention to two methods of demonstrating heritability, selective
breeding and comparisons of inbred strains, and review a selected
number of studies dealing with heritability of emotional behavior in
animals.

HERITABILITY

GENETIC DETERMINATION VERSUS HERITABILITY

It is a common misconception that, by definition, genetically determined traits are also heritable, but this is not so. In the last analysis,
all traits are genetically determined, but whether, in a given population, they are also heritable depends on the evolutionary past of that
population. In order to discuss this important point, we must introduce several ancillary concepts of quantitative genetics.

Suppose we used a test to measure the emotionality of an individual. His test score would constitute his phenotypic value, P. That
value would be due to the testee's genotype (G) and all the environmental forces (E) that had acted upon him:

$$P = G + E \qquad (1)$$

Having obtained phenotypic values for a representative sample of
individuals drawn from a "Mendelian population"[1] we can compute
the variance of phenotypic values, $V(P)$. Since, according to Equation
1, $P = G + E$, the phenotypic variance is composed of genotypic and
environmental variance:

$$V(P) = V(G) + V(E) \qquad (2)$$

[1]In the language of modern genetics the term "population" refers to "Mendelian
population," that is, a "reproductive community of individuals who share in a common
gene pool" (Dobzhansky, 1955). In theory, all members of a species share in a
common gene pool; they form one large Mendelian population. In practice, however,
mostly because of geographic barriers to free interbreeding, species tend to break up
into geographic races and local breeding communities, or demes.

If in Equation 2 we divide both sides by $V(P)$, we obtain

$$\frac{V(G)}{V(P)} + \frac{V(E)}{V(P)} = 1 \tag{3}$$

The fraction $V(G)/V(P)$ is called heritability, or h^2 (Lerner, 1968, p. 141). It denotes the proportion of phenotypic variance that is due to genetic variation in the population.[2] Similarly, the fraction $V(E)/V(P)$, or e^2, denotes the proportion of $V(P)$ attributable to environmental factors:

$$h^2 + e^2 = 1 \tag{4}$$

The proportions h^2 and e^2 are complementary quantities; if one is large, the other is small. In a genetically highly homogeneous inbred population, h^2 would approach zero, and e^2 would tend toward the limiting value of one. On the other hand, in a genetically heterogeneous population, genetic factors may contribute relatively more to phenotypic variation than environmental factors do. In this case, heritability, h^2, could approach the value of one.

Suppose we were to ask, what is the heritability, h^2, of a given trait, say, aggressiveness? It should be obvious that no general answer to this question could be given. The heritability of a trait depends on the population in which we measure it. Heritability is a relative, "population bound," rather than an absolute, universal measure.

The heritability of a trait depends on its evolutionary history. From Equations 2, 3, and 4 it follows that

$$h^2 = \frac{V(G)}{V(P)} = \frac{V(G)}{V(G) + V(E)} \tag{5}$$

Equation 5 shows the dependence of h^2 on $V(G)$: the heritability of a trait reduces to zero when $V(G)$ becomes zero. But what, in a concrete way, accounts for $V(G)$? Consider the simplest case of a trait controlled by a pair of genes at chromosome locus A, and suppose that in the gene pool of a given population there existed two related genes, A_1 and A_2, that can occupy locus A. Since organisms carry genes in pairs, we will encounter in that population three genotypes: A_1A_1, A_1A_2, and A_2A_2. Thus the presence in the gene pool of more than one alternative form of a gene, A_1 and A_2 in our example, is responsible for genotypic variance, $V(G)$.

[2] A more restrictive definition of h^2 is explained by Falconer (1960, p. 135), who also should be consulted for a more precise definition of all other concepts of quantitative genetics that have been mentioned here.

What would be the fate of $V(G)$ if, in a particular environment, phenotypes $A(11)$ and $A(12)$ were inferior to phenotype $A(22)$, that is, if in each generation $A(11)$ and $A(12)$ produced fewer offspring than $A(22)$? Clearly, the proportion of A_1 genes in the gene pool would decrease. In the long run, gene A_1 would disappear entirely from the population. Consequently, only genotype A_2A_2, and its corresponding phenotype $A(22)$, would persist. Genotypic variation, $V(G)$, would have been eliminated from the population by natural selection. Genetically determined phenotypic variation of the trait would cease, the genetic component $V(G)$ of $V(P)$ would drop out: heritability, h^2, would have been reduced to zero. Whatever phenotypic variation of the trait remained in that population would be of environmental origin. But this does not mean that the trait would cease to be genetically determined. In our example the trait most obviously would continue to be affected by gene pair A_2A_2.

It is such reasoning that forces us to distinguish between the genetic determination of a trait and its heritability. The point can be brought out even more clearly by considering species differences. No one seriously doubts that dogs bark and cats meow because they inherited structures that enable them to utter these species-typical sounds. Behavioral differences *between* species are genetically determined. But whether behavioral differences *within* species are due to genetic variation, whether, in other words, they are heritable, cannot be said a priori; this must be established empirically. Several methods have been developed for such empirical tests but only two of them, the methods of selective breeding and strain comparison, have been employed with any frequency in animal studies of emotional behavior. Examples of the two methods follow.

SELECTIVE BREEDING

Hall (1951, pp. 304–329) conducted the first major selective breeding experiment dealing with the heritability of emotional behavior. Hall worked with rats and started his selective breeding program with a sample of 145 animals. The rats were tested singly in a brightly lit, circular enclosure for 2 minutes a day for 12 days. If during a trial an animal urinated or defecated, it was given a score of 1 for that day. The daily scores were added so that, after 12 days of testing, the maximum D score (D for defecation) was 12. In the original sample, D scores ranged from 0 to 12. High-scoring (H) "emotional" rats and low-scoring (L) "nonemotional" rats were mated assortatively: H × H and L × L matings were performed, to initiate an emotional and a nonemotional strain of rats. In succeeding generations the highest scoring animals of the emotional strain were interbred. In the nonemotional strain the animals scoring lowest were selected for breeding.

The results of Hall's selective breeding experiment were quite conclusive. In the original sample ($N = 145$), the mean D score was 3.86 (S.D. 3.54). After 12 generations of selective breeding the mean D score of 47 "emotional" rats was 10.40 (S.D. 2.18), and the mean score for 31 "nonemotional" rats was 1.65 (S.D. 2.53). These findings can be interpreted in one way only:

In the parental population of Hall's study, emotional defecation must have been heritable: the gene pool of that population must have contained several related or "allelic" forms of genes affecting "emotional" behavior, e.g., alleles D_1 and D_2. Could it have been different? Hall selected from a parental population rats of low emotionality (L), and highly emotional rats (H); these originated the two strains bred by him. Suppose then that the selected rats, L and H, did not differ genetically; suppose they all were of type D_1D_1, and suppose that the observed difference between L and H animals was due solely to differing environmental influences to which these selected animals happened to have been exposed. Had that been the case, all descendants of the selected animals also would have had to be D_1D_1 homozygotes, and we would have to explain why, as the results would seem to indicate, environmental forces "conspired" to lower the D score of descendants of L animals while raising the scores of the progeny of H animals. A genetic interpretation of Hall's results is clearly simpler. Any successful selective breeding experiment can be interpreted in an analogous way: successful selection always points to the heritability of the selected trait in the population from which the founders of the selectively bred lines were drawn.

COMPARISONS OF INBRED STRAINS

The heritability of a quantitative trait can be established by other methods. Most popular among them is the method of strain comparison, and it has often been used to establish the heritability of emotional behavior. Bruell (1965), for example, studied what might be called the "timidity" of 11 strains of inbred mice. More than 1500 mice were tested in a "tunnel emergence test." The animals were placed singly in a narrow 8 in. tunnel that opened into a rectangular, lighted box with an open top. The time the mouse spent in the tunnel before emerging into the center of the open box was measured. Differences between strains were highly significant. Mice belonging to some strains entered the open box only after long delays, or not at all, while mice of other strains moved out of the tunnel and into the open as soon as they were released. Thus, some strains were timid and others were not, and we can conclude that in the ancestral population from which the tested mouse strains descended, timidity was heritable. Let us consider in some detail the reasoning that leads to this particular conclusion.

What is an inbred animal and how does one produce an inbred strain? An organism carrying alike genes at most chromosome loci, e.g., A_2A_2 B_1B_1 C_3C_3, is said to be inbred. Members of a given inbred strain carry the same homozygous gene pairs at most chromosome loci, e.g., they are all of genotype A_3A_3 B_2B_2 C_4C_4, or they are all of type A_1A_1 B_3B_3 C_1C_1. Members of different strains are likely to differ at some loci with regard to the alleles they carry at them, e.g., one strain may carry at locus A two A_1 alleles, while another strain carries at the same locus two A_3 alleles.

Inbred strains are produced by the systematic intermating of close relatives, usually siblings. Two founder animals are chosen and mated. Their young are mated brother to sister. In the next generation one again forms brother–sister pairs, and so on for many generations. Consider the genetic consequences of such mating practices. Suppose the two founder animals were both A_1A_2 heterozygotes. Such a pair would produce $\frac{1}{4}$ A_1A_1 and $\frac{1}{4}$ A_2A_2 homozygotes, and $\frac{1}{2}$ A_1A_2 heterozygotes. If these siblings were mated at random, 1 out of 16 matings would be between A_1A_1 homozygotes. Clearly, only A_1A_1 offspring could issue from such $A_1A_1 \times A_1A_1$ matings in the next and all subsequent generations of these particular brother–sister lines; the A_1 allele would become "fixed" in these families. Similarly, $\frac{1}{16}$ of the original sibling matings would be between A_2A_2 homozygotes; these matings would produce lines in which the A_2 allele was fixed. A proportion of the original matings would not be between homozygotes. For example, $\frac{1}{2} \times \frac{1}{2} = \frac{1}{4}$ of all matings would be between A_1A_2 heterozygotes. However, among their offspring one would obtain $2 \times \frac{1}{16} = \frac{1}{8}$ matings between homozygotes. In time, systematic inbreeding would inevitably lead to the elimination of heterozygosity at the A locus: the A_1 allele would become fixed in one group of brother–sister lines, and the A_2 allele in another. Homozygosity would be achieved not only at one locus, the A locus in our example, but at most if not all chromosome loci. It can be shown mathematically that after 24 generations of brother–sister matings over 99% of all loci would carry homozygous gene pairs (Green, 1966, pp. 11–22). However, it should be noted that one cannot predict which allele of a gene would become fixed in which strain, as such inbred brother–sister lines are called. Within strains, genetic variance, $V(G)$, comes to approach zero, but since during inbreeding different alleles become fixed in different strains, genetic variance persists between strains (Falconer, 1960, p. 49).

With this background, we can return to our study of timidity in 11 inbred strains of mice. The observed significant differences between strains can be attributed to the fixation in those strains of different, though unknown, sets of genes that affect timidity. These allelic genes must have existed in the gene pool of the population (or populations) from which the founders of our strains were drawn. During inbreeding the alleles were dispersed among the strains thus creating strains displaying varying degrees of timidity. The observed strain differences provide prima facie evidence for genetic variance, $V(G)$, in the ancestral base population. But this is only another way of saying that the trait studied in these strains was heritable in the populations from which they descended.

DOMESTIC BREEDS AND GEOGRAPHIC RACES

Selective breeding and inbreeding have one thing in common: genes drawn from an ancestral gene pool are dispersed into "selected lines" in one case, brother–sister lines in the other. An ancestral Mendelian population is split into several smaller populations, and gene flow between populations is prevented by human interference. It should be obvious that the selective breeding and inbreeding methods described here are only extreme forms of breeding practices man has imposed on some animal species since prehistoric times, creating in the process the many breeds of domestic animals we know today. In nature geographic barriers often impede free gene flow between populations of a species, a circumstance that eventually tends to give rise to races with distinct gene pools, and ultimately splits one species into many. While selectively bred animals and recently created inbred strains provide us with some of the best evidence for the heritability of behavioral traits, breeds of domestic animals, geographic races of wild animals, and recently evolved closely related species contribute to our knowledge of heritability of behavior.

ILLUSTRATIVE RESEARCH

The literature dealing with inheritance of emotional behavior is quite extensive and cannot be reviewed adequately in a short chapter. The best we can do is to summarize the findings of a few selected studies. We have already spoken about heritability of fearfulness and timidity. In the situations we described, animals were placed singly into an essentially novel and presumably fear-arousing situation. In this section our examples will deal with social behavior: we will speak about genetics of agonistic behavior, hereditary roots of affectionate behavior, and heritability of sexual behavior.

Agonistic Behavior

The term "agonistic behavior" refers to patterns of behavior displayed by an animal in situations of conflict with another animal. In dogs, for example, the term subsumes such diverse responses as growling, barking, biting, running away, or rolling on the back and yelping. It is a matter of common observation that breeds of dogs differ in their agonistic behavior. Some breeds are known for their aggressiveness, others for their docility. There can be little doubt that these breed differences were brought about by centuries of more or less conscious selective breeding by man (Scott & Fuller, 1965).

In many parts of the world cock fights are an ancient spectator sport. Again, there can be little doubt that game breeds of fowl have been consciously selected for their pugnacity, though the historic record of these efforts is lost. Recently Guhl, Craig, and Mueller (1960) produced by selection an aggressive and a nonaggressive line of chickens. The parental population consisted of hybrids obtained by crossing two breeds of White Leghorns. Two methods for determining the relative aggressiveness of individuals were used: one gave weight to the rank of the selected individual in a peck-order; the other considered the number of his victories in first encounters with opponents. The latter criterion received more weight in the selection of breeding stock. Beginning with the second generation the line selected for high aggressiveness differed significantly from the line selected for low aggressiveness. The ease and rapidity with which selective breeding can split a base population into lines displaying differing levels of aggressiveness was also demonstrated by Lagerspetz (1961). Working with mice, Lagerspetz obtained after only three generations of selection lines of mice that differed significantly in aggressiveness.

During selective breeding, "plus" and "minus" alleles affecting a selected trait are dispersed into "high" and "low" lines by human planning. As discussed above, a similar though unplanned dispersal of trait-enhancing and trait-depressing alleles occurs during inbreeding. Evidence supporting this view was obtained in many studies of agonistic behavior of inbred strains of mice. Lindzey, Winston and Manosevitz (1961), for example, in a study of "social dominance" compared several strains of mice in a situation designed to show which of two mice submitted to the "will" of the other. Mice were trained to run through a narrow tube to a container of food. Some were trained to traverse the tube in one, others in the other direction. On critical trials two mice belonging to different strains were started simultaneously at opposite ends of the tube. Since the tube was too narrow to pass two mice, one of them had literally to "back down." Some strains regularly lost this contest of will when competing with other "dominant" strains.

Geographic races of animals are also known to differ in agonistic behavior. Scott and Fuller (1965) compared several European breeds of dogs with the basenji, an African dog. The basenji was chosen because presumably it was genetically isolated from European breeds of dogs for thousands of years. Most remarkable about basenjis is the fact that one component of agonistic behavior, barking, is almost absent in them. "As a stranger walks by the dog runs at our laboratory, a chorus of barks arises from a group of cocker spaniels and from a nearby group of Shetland sheep dogs. In a pen between, a litter of basenjis look up without opening their mouths" (Scott & Fuller, 1965, p. 274).

Currently, I am studying together with Brubaker two races of house mice, *Mus musculus domesticus* and *M. m. musculus,* brought to this country from Denmark by Selander. The two races differ in many ways, for example, in learning ability, but most noticeable to the "naked hand" is the tendency of *M. m. domesticus* to fight and bite the human handler. *M. m. musculus* is much more tractable. In comparison with *M. m. domesticus,* it is slow and timid and it can be picked up with relative impunity by the unprotected hand of the experimenter (Selander, 1969, pp. 379-390; Bruell, 1970).

AFFECTION

For a long time the terms love and affection were stricken from the vocabulary of psychologists. Today these terms have gained new respectability through the brilliant research of Harlow on the development of several "affectional systems" in rhesus monkeys: the affection of the infant for its mother, of the mother for her infant, of the infant for its peers, and the heterosexual affection of juveniles and adults (Harlow, 1965, pp. 234-265; see also Chapter 3 in this volume). Much of our current knowledge about the development of affection is due to Harlow's work. Research on imprinting, a phenomenon first observed in nidifugous birds, has added to this knowledge. In this case we even have some information about heritability.

Young ducks and geese tend to follow the first moving object they see after hatching. In the wild, of course, this is their parent, but in the laboratory it could be an inanimate object, a foster parent of another species, or the experimenter. The young bird develops a lasting emotional attachment to this first social stimulus; the stimulus is "imprinted" on it.

Hess (1959) studied one aspect of the phenomenon, the early following response, in the laboratory. Ducklings were exposed to and permitted to follow a moving model of a male mallard that uttered a "gock, gock" call. At a later hour the duckling was placed halfway between two duck models: one of these was the male mallard upon which it had been imprinted; the other was a female model which differed from the male in its coloration. The behavior of the duckling in this choice situation was scored on a scale extending from 0% to 100% imprinting. Ducklings received high imprinting scores if they approached the model of the male, followed it, emitted pleasure tones when close to it and distress notes when separated from it. Noting large individual differences in imprintability, Hess asked whether the tendency to be imprinted was heritable. He kept ducklings that had received high imprinting scores and bred them separately from ducklings that were poor imprinters. There was a clear and significant difference in the imprinting behavior of the two groups even in the first generation of selective breeding. The "imprinter" ducklings had imprinting scores more than three times better than those of the "nonimprinter" ducklings. The tendency to form social bonds was shown to be heritable in geese. Similar results were obtained in a study using bantam chicks as subjects. Hess also found that some domestic breeds of chickens were better imprinters than others. "Vantress broilers" were found to be the best imprinters in a study involving 1600 chicks belonging to eight breeds.

SEXUAL BEHAVIOR

The term sexual behavior is applied to a variety of behavior patterns. Common to them is their adaptive function: they lead up to and normally include copulation, thus ensuring reproduction. Natural selection favors the superior reproducer. Individuals whose sexual behavior is inadequate do not contribute to the gene pool of the next generation. This would lead one to expect that in the immense stretches of evolutionary time all alleles affecting sexual behavior adversely would have been eliminated by natural selection. One would expect all variation in sexual behavior to be of environmental rather than genetic origin. One would expect $V(G)$ and h^2 of all forms of sexual behavior to be zero. The facts do not confirm this deduction.

In turkeys wide individual differences exist in frequency of mating: some hens mate 10 times as often as others. After nine generations of selective breeding for high and low levels of mating frequency a seven-fold difference in mating frequency between high and low lines has been attained (Hale & Schein, 1962, pp. 531–564).

Precopulatory behavior of turkeys is also heritable. Females imprinted to humans at hatching would be expected to sexually crouch to man. But, surprisingly, many nonimprinted hens crouch to man as well as to male turkeys. Whether they do or not depends in part on their genotype: 17 of 37 black-wing hens but not one of 44 bronze hens responded in this way to man. Male turkeys often court man but again one observes breed differences: 16 of 24 black-wing males but only 3 of 24 bronze males courted the experimenter in one study (Schein & Hale, 1965, pp. 440–482).

McGill (1965, pp. 76–88) studied sexual behavior in mice recording such quantifiable aspects of the male's mating pattern as the number of seconds elapsing between the introduction of a female and the male's first mount, the number of intromissions preceding ejaculation, the number of seconds from the end of one mount until the beginning of the next, and so on. On 10 of 14 such measures C57BL/6 mice were found to differ significantly from DBA/2 mice. McGill then tested F_1 (C57 × DBA) hybrids. He found that the hybrids resembled one or the other inbred parent on some measures; that their score fell midway between the parental scores on others; and that they scored outside the range bracketed in by the parental scores on still other measures. Obviously various components of the mating pattern of mice are determined by different sets of genes. What interests us here is the fact that even sexual behavior which, for reasons given above, ought not to be heritable, displays a surprisingly high degree of genetic variation.

CONCLUSIONS

We have presented only a few of the many studies that have dealt with heritability of emotional behavior. Had space permitted us to do so, we could have gone on. But our presentation soon would have become quite repetitive since the picture would not have changed substantially. Past studies, with monotonous regularity, have confirmed the heritability of many forms of emotional behavior, and no evidence to the contrary has been found. Thus we must conclude that a large part of the observed phenotypic variation of emotional behavior is a reflection of an underlying genotypic variation. Gene pools of natural populations must harbor a great many allelic forms of genes affecting emotional behavior.[3]

In conclusion, it may be well to point to the fact that the studies we reported dealt with quantitative rather than qualitative differences between individuals. At present there exists no good evidence for heritable qualitative individual differences. Under similar circumstances, all members of a given species display what is essentially the same emotional behavior, though some individuals are propelled into action faster, or with more vigor, or more often than others. The threshold of responses and their amplitude varies, and such variation is heritable, but the basic structure, or plan, or gestalt of emotional reactions remains recognizably the same within any one species. It is for this reason and in this sense that we can properly speak of species-typical emotional reactions. To borrow an expression from comparative anatomy, within species emotional responses are largely homologous; cases of analogous emotional behaviors, that is, responses serving the same function but differing in genetic origin may exist but must be exceedingly rare. Thus even the basenjis, sometimes called the "barkless" dogs of Africa, do bark on occasion; they have not lost one and evolved another, qualitatively different, analogous alarm behavior (Scott & Fuller, 1965).

SUMMARY

All members of a species display essentially the same emotional behavior, but some individuals react faster, with greater vigor, or more frequently than others. Such quantitative differences between individuals are heritable to a degree. This has been shown with regularity in selective-breeding experiments and studies using the method of strain comparison. A small sample of such studies is pre-

[3]How these genes manage to escape "the relentless ravages of natural selection" (Mayr, 1963, p. 215) is a question for students of evolution. We simply note that while in principle genetically determined behavior need not be heritable (see above), in practice it is. Only in inbred strains is $V(G)$ and hence h^2 reduced to zero; but inbred strains are artificial — not natural — populations.

sented in this chapter and the concept of heritability and methods of studying heritability are discussed in some detail.

ACKNOWLEDGMENT

This work was supported by NSF grant GU-1598.

REFERENCES

Bruell, J. H. Mode of inheritance of response time in mice. *Journal of Comparative and Physiological Psychology*, 1965, **60**, 147-148.

Bruell, J. H. Behavioral population genetics and wild *Mus musculus*. In G. Lindzey & D. Thiessen (Eds.), *The mouse as prototype*. New York: Appleton, 1970.

Dobzhansky, T. A review of some fundamental concepts and problems of population genetics. *Cold Spring Harbor Symposia on Quantitative Biology,* 1955, **20**, 1-15.

Falconer, D. S. *Introduction to quantitative genetics*. New York: Ronald Press, 1960.

Green, E. L. Breeding sytems. In E. L. Green (Ed.), *Biology of the laboratory mouse*. (2nd ed.) New York: McGraw-Hill, 1966.

Guhl, A. M., Craig, J. V., & Mueller, C. D. Selective breeding for aggressiveness in chickens. *Poultry Science*, 1960, **39**, 970-980.

Hale, E. D. & Schein, M. W. The behaviour of turkeys. IN E. S. E. Hafez (Ed.), *The behaviour of domestic animals*. London: Bailliere, Tindall and Cox, 1962.

Hall, C. S. The genetics of behavior. In S. S. Stevens (Ed.), *Handbook of experimental psychology*. New York: Wiley, 1951.

Harlow, H. F. Sexual behavior in the rhesus monkey. In F. A. Beach (Ed.), *Sex and behavior*. New York: Wiley, 1965.

Hess, E. The relationship between imprinting and motivation. In M. R. Jones (Ed.), *Nebraska Symposium on Motivation*, pp. 44-78. Lincoln: University of Nebraska Press, 1959.

Lagerspetz, K. Genetics and social causes of aggressive behavior in mice. *Scandinavian Journal of Psychology*, 1961, **2**, 167-173.

Lerner, I. *Heredity, evolution, and society*. San Francisco, Freeman, 1968.

Lindzey, G., Winston, H. D., & Manosevitz, M. Social dominance in inbred mouse strains. *Nature (London)*, 1961, **191**, 474-476.

Mayr, E. *Animal species and evolution*. Cambridge, Massachusetts: Harvard University Press, 1963.

McGill, T. E. Studies of the sexual behavior of male laboratory mice: effects of genotype, recovery of sex drive, and theory. In F. A. Beach (Ed.), *Sex and behavior*. New York: Wiley, 1965.

Schein, M. W. & Hale, E. B. Stimuli eliciting sexual behavior. In F. A. Beach (Ed.), *Sex and behavior*. New York: Wiley, 1965.

Scott, J. P., & Fuller, J. L. *Genetics and the social behavior of the dog*. Chicago: The University of Chicago Press, 1965.

Selander, R. K., Hunt, W. G., & Yang, S. Y. Protein polymorphism and genetic heterozygosity in two European subspecies of the house mouse. *Evolution*, 1969, **23**, 379-390.

3

DEVELOPMENTAL ASPECTS OF EMOTIONAL BEHAVIOR

Harry F. Harlow and Margaret K. Harlow

The unlearned or unconditioned responses which form the ground structure for learned primate social responses are neither the specific, isolated Pavlovian-type unconditioned responses nor the random emitted behaviors advanced by Skinner (1938). The unlearned responses which, modified by learning, build or break adequate primate social adjustments are complex, multivariate, highly organized responses, some of which are relatively late maturing.

MATURATION OF SOCIAL-EMOTIONAL PATTERNS

The three basic social response patterns are affection, fear, and aggression. Under normal or relatively normal environmental circumstances, these social-emotional patterns mature in orderly sequence. Affection appears first, social fear second, and social aggression third. In primates, any environmental manipulation which distorts, disturbs, or denies the orderly sequencing of this trilogy is likely to produce disorder in social-sexual development.

AFFECTION

Infant-Mother and Mother-Infant Affectional Systems. Normally affection of one or more kinds precedes the appearance of social fear and is long antecedent to social aggression. The initial affectional attachment in subhuman primates is to the mother, and in the human child, to the mother or other caretaker usually, but evidence exists that some infants attach initially to persons not their caretakers. We have written extensively of this early attachment as the basis for the infant-mother affectional system and have described its course in relation to the mother-infant or maternal affectional system (Harlow & Harlow, 1962). These two affectional systems are largely complementary and prepare the infant for participation in a more complicated and more complex social environment.

The infant-mother affectional system in rhesus monkeys begins with birth. The neonate is equipped with reflexes that enable it to attach to the fur of the mother (or a dummy) (Figure 1), and move upward on her body until restrained by her arms. This automatically places the infant's face in the vicinity of the mother's breasts. Rooting and sucking reflexes facilitate nursing and, consequently, provide for the infant's most basic physical need for survival. Even primiparous mothers—females giving birth for the first time—generally assist the infant in its movements and provide bodily support.

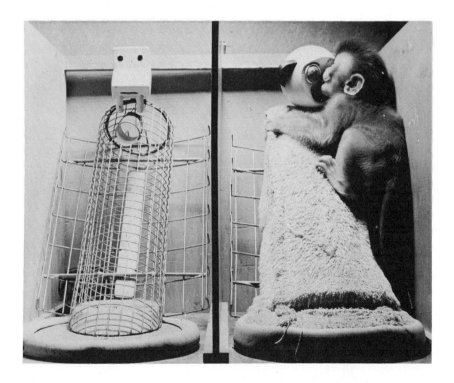

Fig. 1.   Infant attachment reflexes to an artificial mother.

Fig. 2.   Maternal cradling and caressing responses.

In the first 2 to 3 weeks of life the monkey infant's responses to the mother seem to be primarily of this reflex nature, although gradually it gains voluntary control of its various motor responses. Clinging to the mother is a dominant activity in the first 2 months even after the infant has sufficient locomotor skills to walk, run, and climb by itself. We believe that as a consequence of the contact comfort, warmth, and support from the mother as well as from the satisfaction of its nutritional needs, the infant develops an emotional attachment to the mother in the first month or two of life. The attachment seems to strengthen during the next several months.

The mother's cradling, grooming, caressing (see Figure 2), and protection of the infant are evidence of a reciprocal emotional attachment to the baby, perhaps initially elicited by the visual, auditory, and touch qualities of the neonate. That the monkey infant is attractive to monkey females is indicated by the efforts made by preadolescent, adolescent, and adult females to contact every young infant in the group. Moreover, given the opportunity, nonparturient females often adopt infants, indicating that the hormonal changes associated with parturition are not essential to the attachment of mother to infant.

Peer Affectional System. In group-living situations infants show interest in other monkeys, particularly other infants, by the second month of life and attempt to contact them. Any resulting contacts are typically brief at first and begin with unilateral or mutual physical exploration (Figure 3). As the contacts lengthen and merge into play, the infants develop emotional attachments to each other which are positive and affectional in nature. Normally, these attachments to peers begin before fear develops, but the timing is probably not as important for a warmly mothered infant as for an infant raised without a mother or by a rejecting mother. The security derived from the normal mother–infant bond facilitates early peer association and can minimize social fears if peer association is delayed.

We have described this attachment as the infant–infant or peer affectional system and have depicted its course as one that grows while the maternal relationship begins to ebb. That it is separate from the attachment to the mother and not merely a generalization of love originally developed for the mother is suggested in its origins and growth in play. Studies of monkeys that have been deprived of peer associations but not mothering during infancy, or of mothering throughout infancy but not peers (Alexander, 1966) strengthen the proposition that the peer affectional system is separable from the infant–mother affectional system. The peer-deprived infants show wariness of their playmates when exposed to them and do not develop peer ties as strong as those exposed to peers from the first or second month of life. On the other hand, those deprived of mothering develop ties to peers which are by all measures comparable to those of mother-reared infants which were also permitted peer associations (Chamove, 1966).

The universality of peer affection in primates is readily apparent. It starts early in all species of monkeys and apes that have been observed in the field or in laboratories, and it is evident throughout the life-span. At the human level it is more variable in its beginnings because opportunities for associations with agemates vary from family to family and culture to culture. That human infants in the first year of life are generally responsive to each other is clear from

Fig. 3. Early physical exploration in infant monkeys.

research by Bühler (1937) and her associates in Vienna 4 decades ago. Moreover, informal confirmation of the phenomenon in infants by the second half of the first year of life is clear to anyone who sits in a pediatrician's waiting room and watches healthy stranger infants with their mothers. They visually fixate each other and, if held, strain toward the other infant. If in proximity, they tend to reach toward each other and attempt to make physical contact. Smiles and vocalization are common. Furthermore, twins, especially like-sexed twins, generally develop strong early ties to each other which may be so firm that they interfere subsequently with broader social adjustment to peers unless measures are taken to separate them in play situations and in school.

In early infancy the sex of the individuals is relatively unimportant in social interactions — young male and female monkeys or apes play together indiscriminately, and human girls and boys play together without differentiation in the early years of life. Behavioral differences begin to appear in monkeys, however, by the third or fourth month of life, and increase steadily until maturity. Males become progressively more forceful and females develop passivity patterns (see Figure 4 and Figure 5).

Males threaten males and females, while females rarely threaten males but usually confine their threats to other females. There are, of course, exceptional females that dominate some males. Males more and more pursue and females more and more retreat in play. Paralleling this change is also an increasing separation of sexes in play and attachments. Best friends are more often of the same sex although cross-sex friendships also exist. This compares with human children in the age range of 2 to 4 years. Studies of nursery school children (Dawe, 1934) do indicate behavioral differences in the two sexes comparable to those in monkeys and increasing same-sex friendship pairs when the opportunity exists.

In the juvenile period for rhesus monkeys—1 year to 2 years of age—and thereafter, like-sexed friendship pairs and clusters are the rule. Males spend most of their time with males, and females spend most of their time with females. The pattern breaks down in maturity only when the female is in estrus. Then male-female pairs may dominate until estrus is over and the partners return to their own sex groups. At the human level, too, like-sexed friendships predominate in childhood, adolescence, and maturity. Even in mixed-sex social groups, there is frequent clustering of males with males and females with females. The high incidence of male clubs and female clubs further attests to the sexual split which predominates in peer ties. The basis for the separation is doubtless commonality of interests both at the subhuman and human level, and these in turn are based on physiological, anatomical, and physical differences between the sexes. For example, the male primate is larger and stronger in most species than the female, at least from adolescence onward, and better equipped physiologically and anatomically for exertion and physical feats. This probably leads the male to greater participation in large-muscle activities. Cultural influences follow these basic differences and perhaps accentuate them at the human level. Thus the greater athletic potential in boys is culturally reinforced by greater emphasis on athletic achievement in boys than in girls. We would hold that the culture does not originally create sex differences in behavior but merely takes action to maintain, mold, and exaggerate them.

The importance of peer affection cannot be overemphasized. In all group-living primates, attachments between peers are the basis for much of group cohesiveness and the preparation for effective adult social and sexual adjustment. Monkeys learn their sex role and position in the group hierarchy through play. Male and female sexual

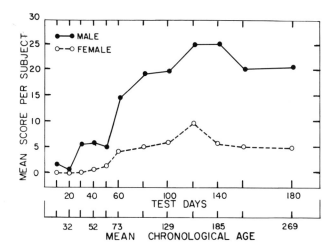

Fig. 4. The development of threat responses. Differences in threat responses of four infant male and four female monkeys.

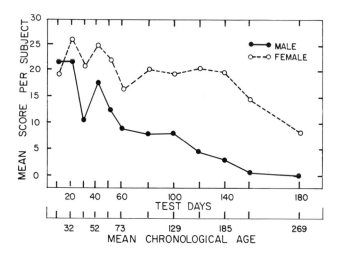

Fig. 5. The development of passive responses. Differences in passive responses of four infant male and four female monkeys.

behaviors begin to differentiate in the third or fourth month of life and progressively specialize by 12 months of age. Most socially reared monkeys display the appropriate sex pattern except for intromission and ejaculation in the male, which is delayed until puberty is achieved in about the fourth year of life (Harlow, Joslyn, Senko, & Dopp, 1966). Most of the learning takes place before social aggression appears toward the end of the first year. Anthropological studies on cultures that permit free sex play in prepubescent children report similar development of sex patterns in childhood.

Fear

In the first 2 months rhesus monkey infants show little or no fear. In the third or fourth month, however, fears begin to become evident (Harlow & Zimmermann, 1959). Unfamiliar objects and places, human beings, objects moving toward them, and unusual or loud noises cause them to screech and cling to their mother if mother is nearby or to screech and run to mother if she is at a distance. Separated from their mother the infants commonly exhibit the crying and self-clasping responses shown in Figure 6. Other monkeys are now a source of fear for infants not permitted prior contact with members of their species, and they may even be wary of monkeys other than their mother if they have been deprived of all social contact except with their mother. On the other hand, infants allowed to associate freely within a group before fear develops usually show fear of

Fig. 6.   Crying and self-clinging by infant separated from mother.

Fig. 7. Social play in young rhesus monkeys.

others only when threatened or hurt. The emergence of fear is at least in part a function of intellectual maturation, for fear requires perception of an object or situation as potentially dangerous. Experience is a factor in determining which objects or situations are in fact strange and/or dangerous.

AGGRESSION

Playful attacks in rhesus monkeys are evident from the beginning of social play and they increase steadily in the first year. Young infants wrestle and roll, sham-bite, and threaten, as seen in Figure 7, but they do not hurt each other even though their tooth development is sufficient to enable them to pierce a peer's skin. From about 10 to 12 months in socially raised rhesus monkeys (Harlow & Harlow, 1965, pp. 287-334) and a little earlier in monkeys reared only with mothers or in individual cages without play opportunities, infants begin to show true aggression toward peers. The socially deprived monkeys may seriously injure each other when placed together, but the socially reared animals show more restraint toward friends and strangers. If threatened, or if the weaker members of their group are threatened, socially-reared monkeys will fight, but they do not display aggression indiscriminately. There is contention for position in a group hierarchy, but as dominance positions are established, relative peace ensues. Monkeys that have been deprived of peer interaction until one-half year of age may as juveniles display uncontrolled aggression toward peers or such incapacitating fear that they do not even defend themselves from aggression. That the fearful are not lacking in aggression is apparent because they may viciously attack young infants that in no way threaten them.

Numerous studies we have conducted at the University of Wisconsin, varying the living conditions for young rhesus monkeys, have led us to conclude that monkeys must develop affectional ties to peers before true social aggression matures. Otherwise they will fail to adjust, either aggressing against peers without cause or yielding to peers and becoming scapegoats.

EFFECTS OF SOCIAL ISOLATION

Isolation starting at birth and continuing until some specified age is a powerful technique for studying maturational processes developing free of learning overlay. Indeed, it is one of the few techniques making it possible to measure the growth and development of complex, late-maturing behavior patterns in any pure or relatively pure form. Two of these complex patterns are fear and aggression, as we have described, and intellectual abilities are also amenable to study by this technique.

Monkeys are taken on the day of birth and enclosed in a stainless steel chamber which provides diffused light, temperature control, and air flow and permits some environmental sounds to filter in. Food and water are provided by remote control, as is cage cleaning. The animal sees no living creature during confinement, not even a human hand. After 3, 6, or 12 months, the monkey is removed from the isolation chamber and placed in an individual cage in the nursery. Several days later it is given its initial experience with age-

Fig. 8. Fear response in 6-month-old monkey taken from total social isolation.

mates: another isolation-reared monkey and two open-cage-reared monkeys. The four are placed together in a playroom equipped with toys and apparatus designed to stimulate activity and play. Play sessions are usually 30 minutes long, 5 days a week, and are provided for 6 months. Eight monkeys were exposed to the 3-month isolation period and four monkeys were isolated for each of the other two time periods.

EFFECTS ON SOCIAL BEHAVIOR

Fear is the overwhelming response upon removal from isolation. The animals are physically healthy but they crouch and appear to be terror stricken by their new environment (Figure 8). The 3-month isolates, however, recover within a few days or at most a few weeks and become active participants in the playroom. At the end of a month they are almost indistinguishable from their control agemates (Griffin & Harlow, 1966).

The 6-month isolates, in contrast, show poor adaptation to each other or to the control animals. Fear dominates their behavior. They cringe when their more normal peers make overtures toward them and they fail to join in the activity. In 6 months of exposure to peers in the playroom they develop only minimal play, and this is primarily nonsocial play, such as individual play with toys or on the apparatus. What little social play occurs is exclusively with the other isolate. When aggressed against by the control animals, they accept the abuse without any effort to defend themselves. For these animals, social opportunities have come too late—fear prevents their developing social interactions and, consequently, affectional ties (Rowland, 1964).

The 12-month isolates are even more severely affected. Although they have reached the age at which aggression normally is present and is evident in the control playmates, they show no evidence of aggression, and even primitive, simple activity play is almost nonexistent. Their behavior presents a picture of apathy and terror (Figure 9), and they crouch at the edges of the room and take the aggression meted out by the controls. We were unable to test them in the playroom after 10 weeks because they were in danger of being seriously injured or killed by their open-cage-reared peers. No social play was

Fig. 9.   Fear responses in 12-month-old monkeys taken from total social isolation.

observed in 12-month isolates in any play session and they exhibited no aggression.

After the conclusion of the playroom experience with open-cage-reared animals, the 6-month and 12-month isolates of the same age were placed together in the playroom. The 6-month isolates, until then devoid of aggressive behavior, almost immediately and viciously attacked the more helpless 12-month group. The results suggest that aggression had matured in these 6-month isolate animals but had been masked by intense fear. Indeed, these animals showed more accentuated aggression as well as fear than monkeys reared under other conditions.

During the next 2 years the 6-month and 12-month total social isolates were raised in standard laboratory cages and then subjected to social tests with strangers. Three types of strangers were paired with them: large, powerful adults, equal-aged normal monkeys, and normal one-year-olds; each pair was housed separately. The 6-month social isolates, now 3 years old, were terrified by all strangers, even the physically helpless juveniles. (To a lesser degree, this was also the case with the 12-month isolates.) But in spite of their terror, the isolates showed uncontrolled aggressive acts. They often engaged in a single suicidal aggression against the large adult males, they were hyperaggressive toward agemates, and they even aggressed against the juveniles — an act essentially never seen in normal monkeys their age. With the passage of time social fears had become more intense and so had social aggression. Time had not ameliorated their asocial and antisocial behaviors but had exaggerated them. The passage of time had in no way initiated positive social behaviors; play was nonexistent, grooming was nonexistent, and sexual behaviors were either nonexistent or totally inadequate (Mitchell, 1968). In human terms these unloved isolate monkeys were in turn totally unloving, distressed, disturbed, and delinquent.

It should be pointed out that we did not give our 6- and particularly our 12-month isolates the maximum possibility of achieving social adjustment during their experience in the playroom, for we had teamed them with monkeys raised in the nursery. These control animals had had no social experience prior to the playroom placement and were themselves deprived and disadvantaged animals. We have frequently referred to them as semi-isolation animals. Fear had matured in the 6-month semi-isolate group prior to their exposure to the total isolates, and both fear and aggression had matured in the 12-month group. These control animals, too, had no affectional ties to counteract fear, or fear and aggression. Although the 6-month semi-isolate group developed play and were active in the playroom, they were probably inferior in their social behavior to equal-aged animals exposed to the playroom at 3 months. We are tentative in this evaluation because the comparison is not entirely satisfactory. These semi-isolates were essentially a play group of two because of the inadequacies of the total isolates, whereas all our early-experience animals had playmates that were able to meet them on equal terms, thus producing four-animal groups. Other studies in this laboratory indicate that four-animal groups provide for more activity and more mature social development than do 2-animal play groups.

Even more deviant were the 12-month animals reared in semi-isolation. They showed the high aggression we have found to be typical of socially deprived animals by 1 year of age. Our total isolates were thus exposed to hyperaggressive peers. Had they been placed with other total social isolates or two socially reared animals, they might have shown less terror and some aggression and made a somewhat different adjustment. Future research is needed to settle this issue.

Even a small degree of social deprivation can have long-term effects on the social behavior of rhesus monkeys. Three groups of monkeys were reared by their mothers from birth but given initial and, thereafter, regular peer experience at 3 weeks, 4 months, or 8 months of age (Alexander, 1966). At a year of age infants in the first group showed greater affiliative behavior than those in the 8-month group. Both the 4- and 8-month groups showed wariness of physical contact throughout the experiment and in a follow-up test a year later. The 8-month group was more extreme than the 4-month group. Aggression was also greater for the delayed-peer-experience groups throughout the experiment and the follow-up, and it was higher in the 8-month than in the 4-month group. We would interpret the results as indicating that the delayed groups were already somewhat fearful of peers on first encounter and therefore formed peer interactions with a more aloof quality than did the monkeys that began their peer relations before fear had matured. When true aggression matured, these peer-delayed groups had weaker peer ties than the early-experience group and consequently exercised less restraint in aggressing toward peers.

Just as some infants have been raised by their mothers but delayed in peer experience, some of our infants have been raised with continuous peer experience but no mothers or only dummy mothers (Chamove, 1966). We have raised groups of two, four, and six monkeys together so that they have had 24-hour-a-day experience living with peers. Groups of two tend in the first weeks of life to form mutual clinging patterns, chest to chest, which persist long after mother-reared infants cease to cling to their mothers. They move about like Siamese twins joined at the chest and engage in little or no play (Figure 10). If the clinging is broken, and one animal attempts to explore an object, the other quickly attempts to resume the clinging. Such behavior persists unless the animals are separately caged. Moreover, if animals reared in this manner are re-paired so that each is given a new partner, mutual clinging resumes without evident concern that the identity of the peer has changed. The fixity of this immature type of clinging can be drastically reduced if pairs are reared together for a fixed period of time and then separately for a time and subjected to successive cycles of alternately living together and living apart.

If four or six animals live together in a cage, they tend very soon to form a "choo-choo" or linear pattern in which one monkey assumes a

Fig. 10. Pair of infant monkeys reared together.

forward position and the remaining animals line up, each clinging to the back of the animal immediately in front (Figure 11). If the forward animal moves without breaking loose, the group usually moves in unison. If the lead animal frees itself, the pattern usually breaks up but re-forms again in short time.

Play is very infrequent in pairs reared together continuously, doubtless because the tight clasp restricts movement and exploration. The larger groups, however, show considerable amounts of play. In one respect these animals, both male and female, raised as groups of four or six are quite precocious—their sexual behavior is perfected early and as adults they breed readily. This contrasts with the absence of sex behavior in male isolates and semi-isolates whose social deprivation is of at least 6 months' duration, and sex inadequacy in the females of these deprived groups.

Still other monkeys have been housed from birth in individual cages with a dummy mother but given 20-min sessions in the playroom with similarly caged peers through the first 9 months or more of

Fig. 11.   Choo-choo pattern of peer-raised monkeys.

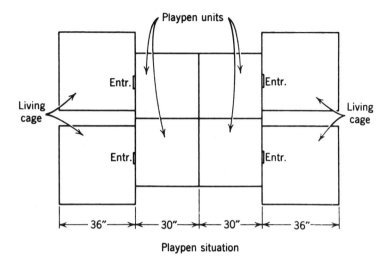

Fig. 12.   Playpen apparatus.

life. Others have been housed in our playpen apparatus (Figure 12) with dummy mothers for 18 months and given 2 hours a day to interact with one peer or, as they grew older, three peers. In the playroom condition the motherless animals have made rapid social adjustments, developing play and affectional attachments that are the equivalent of those or almost the equivalent of real-mother-raised playpen babies. In the playpen situation, which is less stimulating than the playroom for developing active social interactions, the dummy-raised babies initially lagged behind mother-raised playpen babies, but by a year of age they were essentially on a par with them in play, sex behavior, and individual adjustment.

EFFECTS ON SEXUAL BEHAVIOR

One long-term effect of social deprivation which is outstandingly destructive is inadequate sexual behavior, and this has been found in all males and most females reared in social isolation or semi-isolation. That some females survive the semi-isolation conditions and still show some sexual responsiveness is doubtless a function of their easier role in copulation. The separate acts required in copulation begin to appear in young infants but they are not organized into effective patterns in monkeys unless opportunity is provided early for social play, particularly heterosexual social play. Our experience has taught us that monkeys that fail to develop adult-type sex patterns by 12 to 18 months of age are poor risks for breeding in maturity. This is particularly applicable to individuals that show either uncontrolled fear or uncontrolled aggression in the presence of potential mates.

In a study of feral females contrasted with semi-isolate females exposed to selected and proficient breeding males, each female was tested during estrus for 10 hours over a period of 14 months with a total of four different males. The semi-isolate females avoided social proximity and grooming, often engaged in threats and aggression, showed autistic behavior such as self-clutching and self-biting, failed often to present, and failed often to support the male when mounting occurred. Feral females rarely threatened, never aggressed, never showed autistic behavior, and they more often maintained social proximity, groomed, presented, and provided adequate support to the mounting male. Parallel tests were made of feral males contrasted with semi-isolate males exposed to selected, proficient breeding females in estrus over a 14-month period. The deprived males were more inadequate than the deprived females. In contrast with feral males, the semi-isolates groomed less, threatened more, aggressed more (aggression rarely occurred in feral males), rarely initiated any sexual contact, engaged in abnormal sexual responses (feral males rarely did so) and, with one excepting instance, never achieved intromission. Figure 13 shows contrasts in the more complex sexual behaviors of the feral and semi-isolate animals.

The sexual shortcomings of the deprived animals did not result from the loss of any biological sex drive. High arousal was often seen, but it led to combinations of unassociated responses including autistic behaviors, masturbation, and violent aggression, all occurring in frenetic sequences during an elapsed time of but a few seconds. Thus early social deprivation destroyed the monkeys' capability to either receive or initiate adequate sexual responsiveness (Harlow, Joslyn, Senko, & Dopp, 1966).

EFFECT ON INTELLECTUAL DEVELOPMENT

That their social failure is not a consequence of intellectual arrest is evident in the normal learning behavior of the 6- and 12-month isolates when confronted with laboratory learning tests. We have in the course of 35 years of work with monkeys, developed a battery of learning tests that discriminate between species and between ages within species. They also discriminate between monkeys which have been subjected to surgically produced brain damage and

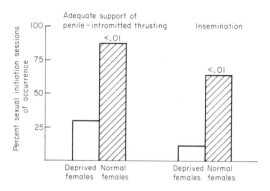

Fig. 13. Sex behavior of normal and socially deprived monkeys. Successful intromissions and inseminations of the females.

normal monkeys. The tests indicate that these isolated animals are intellectually as able as monkeys of the same age raised in open cages provided time is taken to adjust them to the learning apparatus. All monkeys must be adapted to testing, but our isolate animals are more fearful than normal monkeys and take longer to become at ease in the testing situation.

Because these particular isolates had had considerable remote-control exposure to discrimination learning during their confinement, we wanted a more rigorous test of the effects of total isolation on intellectual ability. A new group of five monkeys was confined in the isolation condition for 9 months without learning-test exposure, then adapted to the test apparatus and started on the standard laboratory tests. The study is still in progress, but thus far performance of the isolated monkeys on most learning tests is highly similar to that of open-cage-reared monkeys (Harlow, Schiltz, & Harlow, 1969). They have now completed the learning-set testing, a task which is beyond the capacity of monkeys under 10 months of age, and they are performing at the same level as their controls (Figure 14). We predict that these socially deprived monkeys will show little or no deficit on any of the tests in the battery. Thus it would appear that periods of social isolation which produce permanent social incapacitation in these rhesus monkeys results in no detectable impairment of their learning capabilities to date.

DISCUSSION

Absence of mothering is not insurmountable if peer associations are provided, and there can be peer deprivation for considerable pe-

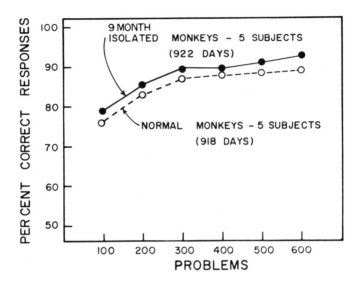

Fig. 14. Learning set performance by isolated and normal monkeys. Six trials were given for each problem; 922 and 918 days refer to the mean age of the respective groups of animals at start of testing.

riods of time if real mothers are provided. Multiple peers, at least three and preferably five (perhaps more but we have no data thus far beyond five), appear to compensate fairly well for lack of mothering although it is likely that animals so reared would show some disadvantage if teamed with animals both mothered and peer-experienced. Similarly, the mother-raised infants without peer experience until 4 or 8 months of age were reasonably well adjusted socially — their greater aloofness and aggression were probably within normal limits and might conceivably provide a competitive advantage in a larger group with more socialized animals.

From an evolutionary point of view there is gain in having two independent affectional systems that can each in part compensate for deficiencies in the other. Mothers vary more in their attachment to infants than infants vary in their attachment to the mother. Monkey mothers denied normal affection early in life may exhibit devastating detachment from their infants and, in many cases, brutality. Human mothers may also exhibit detachment, and some even resort to physical abuse, which pediatricians refer to as the "battered-baby" syndrome, a much more prevalent phenomenon than legal records indicate.

SUMMARY AND CONCLUSION

As the data have accumulated on many groups of infant monkeys subjected to varying rearing conditions, we have come to be impressed by alternative routes monkeys may take to achieve adequate social behavior, which by our criteria would include attachment to peers, control of fear and aggression, and normal sexual patterns. Under the protected conditions of the laboratory, peer socialization and mother-infant socialization appear in large part to be interchangeable in the development of the infant.

Learning is commonly conceived as a process that shapes preestablished, unlearned response patterns. This is only part of the picture insofar as social learning is concerned. One of the most powerful functions of early social learning in primates, and possibly in all mammals and in many other classes of animals as well, is that of developing social patterns that will restrain and check later maturing behaviors having an asocial potential. It is the establishment of positive, learned social patterns before negative, unlearned patterns emerge. It is in this sense an anticipatory form of learning, a check against the inappropriate exercise of negative behavior patterns within the social group while permitting their appropriate expression toward threatening intruders from without.

ACKNOWLEDGMENT

This research was supported by USPHS grants MH-11894 and FR-0167 from the National Institutes of Health to the University of Wisconsin Department of Psychology Primate Laboratory and the Wisconsin Regional Primate Research Center, respectively.

REFERENCES

Alexander, B. K. The effects of early peer-deprivation on juvenile behavior of rhesus monkeys. Unpublished doctoral dissertation, University of Wisconsin, 1966.

Bühler, C. Theoretische Grundprobleme der Kinderpsychologie. *Zeitschrift für Psychologie*, 1937, **140**, 140-164.

Chamove, A. S. The effects of varying infant peer experience on social behavior in the rhesus monkey. Unpublished M. A. dissertation, University of Wisconsin, 1966.

Dawe, H. C. An analysis of two hundred quarrels of preschool children. *Child Development*, 1934, **5**, 139-157.

Griffin, G. A., & Harlow, H. F. Effects of three months of total social deprivation on social adjustment and learning in the rhesus monkey. *Child Development*, 1966, **37**, 533-547.

Harlow, H. F., & Harlow, M. K. Social deprivation in monkeys. *Scientific American*, 1962, **207**, 136-146.

Harlow, H. F., & Harlow, M. K. The affectional systems. In A. M. Schrier, H. F. Harlow, & F. Stollnitz (Eds.), *Behavior of nonhuman primates*. New York: Academic Press, 1965. Pp. 287-334.

Harlow, H. F., & Zimmermann, R. R. Affectional patterns in the infant monkey. *Science*, 1959, **130**, 421-432.

Harlow, H. F., Joslyn, W. D., Senko, M. G., & Dopp, A. Behavioral aspects of reproduction in primates. *Journal of Animal Science*, 1966, **25**, 45-65.

Harlow, H. F., Schiltz, K. A., & Harlow, M. K. Effects of social isolation on the learning performance of rhesus monkeys. In C. R. Carpenter (Ed.), *Proceedings of the 2nd International Congress of Primatology*. Basel: Karger, 1969, Pp. 178-185.

Mitchell, G. D. Persistent behavior pathology in rhesus monkeys following early social isolation. *Folia Primatologica*, 1968, **8**, 132-147.

Rowland, G. L. The effects of total social isolation upon learning and social behavior in rhesus monkeys. Unpublished doctoral dissertation, University of Wisconsin, 1964.

Skinner, B. F. *The behavior of organisms: An experimental analysis*. New York: Appleton, 1938.

3

NEUROCHEMICAL AND ENDOCRINE CORRELATES

NEUROCHEMICAL ASPECTS OF EMOTIONAL BEHAVIOR

Seymour S. Kety

The biochemical aspects of emotional states have been studied and considerable information has been acquired over the past several decades, largely in terms of the peripheral biochemical changes which accompany and feed back into the central emotional state. But an area which is perhaps more interesting, although far more obscure, is the pattern of biochemical changes which take place in the brain in relationship to affective state. This is an area which has not been as well studied and for obvious reasons. It is much easier to examine the excretion of hormones and metabolites in the urine, or the levels of various chemical modulators in the blood than it is to examine the intimate biochemical relationships of neurones in these states. Our data in this area are less complete, our inferences more indirect and speculative, and yet they are equally compelling.

LOCALIZATION OF BIOGENIC AMINES IN THE BRAIN

Much of our speculation revolves about the biogenic amines and their relationship to these states. Quite recently a remarkable contribution was made in Sweden on the basis of earlier work by Eränkö (1955). Dahlström and Fuxe (1964) developed a technique for the histofluorescent demonstration and localization of monoamines in the central nervous system. Not only has it been possible to confirm the presence of these amines in the brain but these workers have been able to demonstrate them in specific neurons and to localize these neurons and their axons to particular portions of the central nervous system (Hillarp, Fuxe & Dahlström, 1966). On the basis of that work it is possible to define the cell bodies of these monoamine-containing neurons in the brainstem reticular formation, the norepinephrine-containing neurons lying laterally, the serotonin-containing neurons largely medially. It is also possible to trace the axons of these neurons containing demonstrable concentrations of serotonin, dopamine, or norepinephrine, as the case may be, to various parts of the brain. High concentrations of these amines occur at the endings of those axons and a large amount of ancillary information permits the inference that these substances are acting as transmitters at specific synapses in the central nervous system.

These axons pass largely into the hypothalamus and the limbic system where their possible relationship to the adaptive response in emotional states can be inferred. It is easy to reason that these axons acting in the hypothalamus control the autonomic nervous system response to stress and initiate the endocrine changes which are known to occur. Their precise role in the limbic system, like the function of that system itself, is less clear, but a wealth of evidence implies a crucial position in affective behavior.

We are, however, also aware of a large network of fine norepinephrine- and serotonin-containing fibers that pass throughout the cerebral cortex where their function is still quite obscure. It is possible to speculate that these amines are involved in arousal and attention. One may further speculate that these amine-containing endings which ramify throughout the cortex have some relationship to learning and the consolidation of memory. It is conceivable that they facilitate the consolidation process and are perhaps responsible for establishing an association between particular memories and their affective component.

BIOGENIC AMINES AND EMOTIONAL STATE

Historical Background

What is the evidence that the system of monoamines in the brain has anything to do with the biological substrate of emotional state? The history of their entrance into this field of study is rather interesting. It can probably be traced back to the discovery of lysergic acid diethylamide (LSD) which, although it has brought about a number of social complications that were unanticipated in 1943, has also been to a large extent responsible for the burgeoning of neurochemical and neuropharmacological interest in the biogenic amines of the brain over the past 20 years.

Shortly after its discovery, it was learned that LSD interacted in some way with serotonin, inhibiting its action on smooth muscle. This started a wave of speculation that serotonin played an important role in the central nervous system, which function, when inhibited by LSD, produced the conceptual, perceptual, and emotional distortions that accompany its administration.

Soon after, reserpine, perhaps the first tranquilizing drug, was found by Shore and his colleagues, working with Brodie in the National Heart Institute, to be associated with a marked depletion of serotonin in the brain (Shore, 1963). This finding was reinforced by the discovery that iproniazid, a powerful excitant, euphoriant, and antidepressant agent, was associated with an inhibition of monoamine oxidase and with an increase in the concentration of serotonin in the brain. Thus, at that time the hypotheses looked simple and clear: serotonin was a hormone which controlled mood. When it was elevated, mood was high; when it was depleted, mood was depressed. However, it was soon found that norepinephrine was also present in the brain and also responded to these drugs — to reserpine with a profound fall in concentration, to iproniazid with an increase in concentration and a potentiation. Consequently, the situation immediately became more complex.

NOREPINEPHRINE

My colleagues, Axelrod (1959), Kopin (1964), Glowinski and co-workers (1965, 1966), Baldessarini (1966), and Schildkraut and Kety (1967), at the National Institute of Mental Health in Bethesda, and my own interest over the past several years, have focused upon norepinephrine — its metabolism and turnover both peripherally and centrally. It is on this amine that I should like to concentrate in this chapter, using it simply as a paradigm of a monoamine in the central nervous system. I should point out that whatever evidence there is for the operation of norepinephrine in emotional states by no means precludes the operation of other amines. The process will likely be seen someday as a complex interaction of several amines at highly specific synapses representing particular pathways.

Stress. A number of studies have indicated that the turnover of norepinephrine in the brain, which is the result of its synthesis on the one hand and its utilization on the other, is facilitated in various emotional states. Maynert and Levi (1964), demonstrated that, when rats were subjected to a severe stress by fairly intense electric shocks to the feet, there was a marked depletion of norepinephrine in the brain. This, however, required severe kinds of stress. More recently, it has been shown that with milder stress, even though the levels of endogenous norepinephrine in the brain may not be changed, a significant increase in the turnover of norepinephrine nevertheless occurs, (Thierry, Javoy, Glowinski, & Kety, 1968). Thus it became clear that stress of this kind somehow induced both the synthesis and utilization of norepinephrine in the brain.

Manipulation of Emotional States in Animals. Coming closer to emotional states, we can refer to the work of Reis and Gunne (1965), who have examined states of rage in cats, induced either by stimulating the amygdaloid nucleus or by appropriate surgical section of the brainstem. In either of these instances when rage occurred, it was associated with a significant decrease in the endogenous levels of norepinephrine in the telencephalon, presumptive evidence that it was released. When, in more recent work, drugs were used which had the ability either of potentiating central norepinephrine or of inhibiting its actions, they found that these drugs had an appropriate effect upon the rage (Reis & Fuxe, 1969). The drugs which inhibited norepinephrine in the brain appeared to block the rage, while those which potentiated norepinephrine facilitated the response and increased its frequency. Thus it seems difficult to deny a role for norepinephrine in the mediation of this kind of emotional behavior.

Other studies in animal behavior have signified the intervention of catecholamines in other affective states as well. The depression which is induced by reserpine in animals can be abruptly terminated by infusing DOPA, the precursor of the catecholamines (Carlsson, Lindqvist & Magnusson, 1957). This experiment does not demonstrate that norepinephrine is necessarily the amine involved, since dopamine, its precursor, is also affected. More sophisticated experiments have recently been performed in which another precursor (dehydroxyphenylserine) is given which bypasses dopamine and increases the concentration of norepinephrine alone (Creveling, Daly, Tokuyama, & Witkop, 1968). This agent does not alleviate the depression, and raises serious doubt whether norepinephrine is in fact the catecholamine involved. Such evidence suggests that dopamine may be the more important catecholamine in the mediation of some behavioral states. Be that as it may, dopamine is the immediate precursor of norepinephrine and although one cannot at present dissect out the respective roles of these two powerful agents, the evidence pointing to the involvement of one or the other or both of them continues to be fairly compelling.

Self-Stimulation Behavior. Stein (1964) used the technique of Olds of self-stimulation in which animals implanted with electrodes in the medial forebrain bundle, or parts of the hypothalamus or septal region will persist in giving themselves mild electric stimulation in these areas for what appears to be some kind of positive internal reward. Stein has investigated the possible role of the catecholamines in this phenomenon. Self-stimulation is found to be promptly inhibited when brain catecholamines are depleted either by reserpine (which is fairly nonspecific) or more specifically by α-methyltyrosine (which blocks the synthesis of catecholamines but not of serotonin). On the other hand, drugs such as amphetamine, or MAO (monoamine oxidase) inhibitors, which should act to increase the concentration of catecholamines at central synapses, serve to facilitate this self-stimulatory behavior. Other behavioral patterns are also disrupted when one disrupts the synthesis of catecholamines in the brain; α-methyltyrosine will not only inhibit self-stimulating behavior but it will also block the conditioned avoidance response.

Drugs and Depression in Humans. A great deal of the evidence which seems to implicate the catecholamines centrally in affective states comes from clinical considerations. It is rather interesting that practically every drug which has been found effective in altering affective states in man has also been found to exert effects upon catecholamines in the brain in a way which would be compatible with the possibility that these amines are involved in the mediation of these states and in the actions of the drugs which affect them (Kety, 1966).

For example, the drugs which cause the loss of catecholamines from the synapse by facilitating their presynaptic release and destruction, such as reserpine, or those, like α-methyltyrosine, which block their synthesis, are associated wih depressive phenomena in man. Reserpine, in a significant proportion of patients who have received it for treatment of hypertension, produces a state of depression which is extremely difficult to differentiate from the clinical form of endogenous depression. Similarly, α-methyltyrosine in humans produces sedation which is followed by a tendency toward hypomania, in some cases, upon its withdrawal.

The drugs which have been found useful in elevating mood and acting as antidepressants have opposite effects upon norepinephrine and perhaps dopamine which are compatible with this general concept. The MAO inhibitors, by blocking the enzyme which destroys these catecholamines, increases their concentration at the nerve endings and presumably in synapses and increase the amount of norepinephrine which is released in the form of the methylated derivatives (Glowinski & Axelrod, 1966). Kopin and Gordon (1963) have indicated, at least in the heart, that these products represent the norepinephrine which is released at the synapse in association with sympathetic activation.

Imipramine, which is perhaps the most potent of the antidepressant drugs, appears to block another form of inactivation of norepinephrine consisting of its reuptake from the synapse (Schanberg, Schildkraut, & Kopin, 1967). By blocking this mechanism, imipramine could increase the concentration of norepinephrine at the synapse and could favor whatever action it has there.

Lithium. This agent, which has been found useful in the treatment of mania and hypomanic states, has actions which are compatible with the hypothesis that it acts by depressing the synaptic concentrations of norepinephrine, either by favoring its destruction presynaptically or by inhibiting its release. The less well-established usefulness of lithium salts in the treatment of depression or in the prevention of recurrence of manic-depressive cycles is not explicable on the basis of this action. The similarity of the lithium ion to that of sodium readily suggests some membrane effect of this substance. This would not account, however, for its highly specific action on only one aspect of neural function. Accordingly it may be worth suggesting a more complex role for lithium ions in ion transport, necessary for the release of norepinephrine or its action on receptors.

Electroconvulsive Shock. By far the most effective treatment for depression in man, however, is not a drug at all but electroconvulsive shock. A number of controlled clinical studies have shown this treatment to be effective in some 80% of patients, a considerably higher efficacy than even imipramine. Yet the mechanism by which electroconvulsive shock may operate to alleviate depression is unknown, and plausible hypotheses to account for this action have rarely been proposed.

A great deal is known about the peripheral effects of electroconvulsive shock but relatively little about its central effects. Moreover, the central effects which have been demonstrated have been largely the acute changes which accompany or follow the convulsive shock and hardly explain its prolonged beneficial effect for weeks after the treatments have been terminated.

During studies regarding the stimulating effect of mild physical stress in rats on the synthesis of norepinephrine in the brain (Thierry, Javoy, Glowinski, & Kety, 1968), the hypothesis presented itself that perhaps electroconvulsive shock acted by producing a persistent stimulation of this synthetic process. This hypothesis was tested by subjecting a group of rats to electroconvulsive shock (Kety, Javoy, Thierry, Julou, & Glowinski, 1967). A rather more rigorous regimen than is used clinically was employed, shocking the animals twice a day for a week. There was a similar group of controls treated in exactly the same way, even to the application of the electrodes except that the shocking current was not turned on. Twenty-four hours after the last shock, both groups of animals appeared quite normal in their behavior and it was at that time that the changes in norepinephrine metabolism which might have been produced were examined. Thus acute changes were not measured; the focus instead was on changes which would persist for at least 24 hours after the shock, when the immediate effects of the shock should be over. There was a significantly increased turnover of norepinephrine in the brains of the shocked animals and this had persisted for at least 24 hours after the last shock. It was possible to infer from the increase in turnover and an increase in the endogenous levels of norepinephrine which was also observed, that there had been a significant stimulation of the synthesis of norepinephrine in the brain.

Our present studies are directed at elucidating the mechanism by which this stimulation of synthesis occurs. Most attempts to demonstrate an increase in the activity of tyrosine hydroxylase, the important enzyme controlling the synthesis of norepinephrine, have not been successful. That is not unexpected since other homeostatic mechanisms exist to permit an increased synthesis of norepinephrine in response to its acute release. On the other hand, chronic stimulation of other adrenergic nerves in the periphery has been shown to induce an increase in the activity of the synthesizing enzyme. Following a regimen of electroconvulsive shocks, the activity of tyrosine hydroxylase in the brain has been found to be moderately but significantly elevated (Musacchio, Julou, Kety, & Glowinski, 1969).

The finding that electroconvulsive shock stimulates the synthesis of norepinephrine in the brain helps to explain two interesting behavioral effects of electroconvulsive shock. After a series of 4 to 7 days of twice-daily electroconvulsive shock in rats, Stein (1962) found that some of his animals showed increased self-stimulatory behavior, which the same investigator later found to be associated with drugs which increased the availability of norepinephrine in the brain (Stein, 1964). Cohen and Dement (1966) found that animals which had been given a course of electroconvulsive shock required less REM (rapid eye movement) sleep than did normal animals. [REM, also referred to as paradoxical sleep, is a phase of sleep which appears to be associated with dreaming in man and which is quite different from the type of sleep which occupies most of the sleeping state. It has been the subject of a great deal of investigation recently (Kety, Evarts, & Williams, 1967)].

It is interesting that electroconvulsive shock seems to substitute for REM sleep. It seems quite possible that REM sleep and electroconvulsive shock have a similar effect in replenishing norepinephrine in the brain by increasing its synthesis. That REM sleep is in fact associated with an increase in turnover of norepinephrine in the brain has now been demonstrated (Pujol, Mouret, Jouvet, & Glowinski, 1968).

The studies on electroconvulsive shock add to the accumulating information regarding the actions of drugs which influence affective state in man to suggest the hypothesis that at least one of these amines, norepinephrine or more broadly catecholamines, is involved in depression and may be involved in the mechanism by which antidepressant drugs or electroconvulsive shock relieve depression.

This is not, as indicated before, to imply that catecholamines are the only substances involved. There is cogent evidence that serotonin is also involved in emotions although the picture is not as clear. There are some suggestions that serotonin and the catecholamines play antagonistic or reciprocal roles in behavior—but much more research is needed to clarify these roles.

COGNITIVE FACTORS

It would be a mistake to conclude that neurochemical factors were the only or even the most important factors mediating affective states. They undoubtedly contribute, but the delicate nuances of affect, its personal and cultural significance, the factors which determine what is pleasurable or rewarding, what causes fear or concern, can hardly be implied by these small molecules operating in the brain. It may involve their action but, in addition, a great superstructure of cognitive function and life experience from which the affective state takes its meaning. These cognitive and social aspects have been the subject of studies by Schachter and Singer (1962); (see also Chapter 11 in this volume). In the case of peripheral epinephrine they showed that the changes induced in mood were to a large extent dependent upon the set of the individual and the social situation, from which they inferred the overriding importance of cognitive factors in the emotional effects of epinephrine acting peripherally.

It is possible to make the same inference with regard to central affective states. The biogenic amines may play the chords of the affective state, but the melody is carried to a large extent by cognitive factors. The whole performance can be best appreciated by an awareness of both the biological and the psychosocial processes.

SUMMARY

It is thus compatible with the anatomical, physiological, pharmacological, and behavioral evidence to suggest the existence of an important neural system, parallel and complementary to the sensorimotor systems, but more sluggish, coarse, and diffuse, and closer to the primitive parts of the brain; one which evaluates experience and the outcome of action in terms of built-in or acquired survival value, which prompts vigilance, determines attention, and integrates adaptive, vegetative, and endocrine behavior, and which reinforces learning and colors recall. Many of the characteristics of the biogenic amines and the correlations with behavior which have been presented, suggest that these substances play crucial roles in such a system.

REFERENCES

Axelrod, J. Metabolism of epinephrine and other sympathomimetic amines. *Physiological Reviews*, 1959, 39, 751–776.

Baldessarini, R. J., & Kopin, I. J. Norepinephrine-H^3 release from brain slices by electrical stimulation. *Science*, 1966, 152, 1630.

Carlsson, A., Lindqvist, M., & Magnusson, T. 3-4 Dihydroxyphenylalanine and 5 hydroxytryptophan as reserpine antagonists. *Nature (London)*, 1957, 180, 1200.

Cohen, H., & Dement, W. Sleep: Suppression of rapid eye movement phase in the cat after electro-convulsive shock. *Science*, 1966, 154, 396–398.

Creveling, C. R., Daly, J., Tokuyama, T., & Witkop, B. The combined use of α-methyltyrosine and threo-dihydroxyphenyl-serine—selective reduction of dopamine levels in the central nervous system. *Biochemical Pharmacology* 1968, 17, 65–70.

Dahlström, A., & Fuxe, K. Evidence for the existence of monoamine containing neurons in the central nervous system. I. Demonstration of monoamines in the cell bodies of brain stem neurons. *Acta Physiologica Scandinavica*, 1964, 62, Supplementum 232, 1–55.

Eränkö, O. The Histochemical demonstration of noradrenalin in the adrenal medulla of rats and mice. *Journal of Histochemistry and Cytochemistry*, 1955, 4, 11.

Glowinski, J., Kopin, I. J., & Axelrod, J. Metabolism of H³-norepinephrine in the rat brain. *Journal of Neurochemistry*, 1965, 12, 25-30.

Glowinski, J., & Axelrod, J. Effects of drugs on the disposition of H³-norepinephrine in the rat brain. *Pharmacological Review*, 1966, 18, 775-785.

Hillarp, N. A., Fuxe, K., & Dahlström, A. Demonstration and mapping of the central neurons containing dopamine, noradrenaline, and 5-hydroxytryptamine and their reactions to psychopharmaca. *Pharmacological Review*, 1966, 18, 727-741.

Kety, S. S. Catecholamines in neuropsychiatric states. *Pharmacological Review*, 1966, 18, 787-798.

Kety, S. S., Evarts, E. V., & Williams, H. L. (Eds.) *Sleep and altered states of consciousness*. Research Publications Association for Research in Nervous and Mental Disease 45. Baltimore: Williams & Wilkins, 1967.

Kety, S. S., Javoy, F., Thierry, A.-M., Julou, L., & Glowinski, J. A sustained effect of electroconvulsive shock on the turnover of norepinephrine in the central nervous system of the rat. *Proceedings of the National Academy of Sciences of the United States of America*, 1967, 58, 1249-1254.

Kopin, I. J. Storage and metabolism of catecholamines: The role of monoamine oxidase. *Pharmacological Review*, 1964, 16, 179-191.

Kopin, I. J., & Gordon, E. K. Metabolism of administered and drug released norepinephrine-7-H³ in the rat. *Journal of Pharmacology and Experimental Therapeutics*, 1963, 140, 207-216.

Maynert, E. W., and Levi, R. Stress induced release of brain norepinephrine and its inhibition by drugs. *Journal of Pharmacology and Experimental Therapeutics*, 1964, 143, 90-95.

Musacchio, J. M., Julou, L., Kety, S. S, & Glowinski, J. Increase in rat brain tyrosine hydroxylase activity produced by electroconvulsive shock. *Proceedings of the National Academy of Sciences (USA)* 63, 1117-1119, 1969.

Pujol, J. F., Mouret, J., Jouvet, M., & Glowinski, J. Increased turnover of cerebral norepinephrine during rebound of paradoxical sleep in the rat. *Science*, 1968, 159, 112-114.

Reis, D. J., & Fuxe, K. Brain norepinephrine: Evidence that neuronal release is essential for sham rage behavior following brainstem transection in the cat. *Proceedings of the National Academy of Sciences of the United States of America*, 64, 108-112, 1969.

Reis, D. J., & Gunne, L.-M. Brain catecholamines: Relation to the defense reaction evoked by amygdaloid stimulation in cats. *Science*, 1965, 149, 450-451.

Schachter, S., & Singer, J. E. Cognitive, social and physiological determinants of emotional state. *Psychological Review*, 1962, 69, 379-399.

Schanberg, S. M., Schildkraut, J. J., & Kopin, I. J. The effects of psychoactive drugs on norepinephrine H³ metabolism in brain. *Biochemical Pharmacology*, 1967, 16, 393-400.

Schildkraut, J. J., & Kety, S. S. Biogenic amines and emotion. Pharmacological studies suggest a relationship between brain biogenic amines and affective state. *Science*, 1967, 156, 21-30.

Shore, P. A. Release of serotonin and catecholamines by drugs. *Pharmacological Review*, 1963, 14, 531-550.

Stein, L. Effects and interactions of imipramine, chlorpromazine, reserpine and amphetamine on self-stimulation: Possible neurophysiological basis of depression. *Recent Advances in Biological Psychiatry*, 1962, 4, 288-308.

Stein, L. Self-stimulation of the brain and the central stimulant action of amphetamine. *Federation Proceedings*, 1964, **23**, 836-850.

Thierry, A.-M., Javoy, F., Glowinski, J., & Kety, S. S. Effects of stress on the metabolism of norepinephrine, dopamine and serotonin in the central nervous system of the rat. I. Modification of norepinephrine turnover. *Journal of Pharmacology and Experimental Therapeutics*, 1968, **163**, 163-171.

5

MODIFICATION OF EMOTIONAL BEHAVIOR BY INTRACRANIAL ADMINISTRATION OF CHEMICALS

Sebastian P. Grossman

INTRODUCTION

Intracranial drug administration has become a popular technique for the study of brain-behavior relationships. The drug-induced facilitation or inhibition of neural function is almost always reversible, and it is often possible to obtain selective effects on functionally related pathways rather than an indiscriminate activation or inhibition of cells within a given geographic location.

In some instances, it is possible to obtain very specific effects by activating or inactivating central chemoreceptors which monitor the extracellular concentration of substances such as sex hormones (Harris, 1958; Hartmann, Endröczi, & Lissák, 1966), glucose (Mayer, 1955), or sodium (Andersson, 1952). Our understanding of appetitive motivational processes has been significantly advanced by recent investigations of these mechanisms (Grossman, 1967, 1969).

We have not, as yet, been as successful in our search for similarly specific chemoreceptor functions which might be related to emotional behavior. The efficacy of mood-altering drugs, such as tranquilizers or antidepressants, suggests, however, that our efforts may some day be repaid. It has been possible to modify an animal's reacto noxious stimulation in various escape–avoidance situations by increasing or decreasing the local concentration of neurohumors, such as acetylcholine or norepinephrine, in restricted portions of the brain. Functionally related pathways appear to maintain their identity in areas of extensive anatomical overlap, at least in part, by employing neurohumoral transmitters which are different from those of other neural mechanisms in the same area. It is consequently often possible to obtain a more selective effect by microinjections of neurohumors or related blocking agents than by electrical stimulation or coagulation. Let me illustrate the usefulness of this technique by some of my own experiments and by related studies from other laboratories. The field, though young, has grown so rapidly in recent years that this review must be illustrative rather than comprehensive.

REGIONAL SITES OF STUDY

AMYGDALA

Electrical stimulation (Ursin, 1960) or lesions (Spiegel, Miller, & Oppenheimer, 1940) in the amygdaloid complex increase emotional reactivity and facilitate rage and attack behavior. Amygdaloid lesions also block the formation of conditioned emotional reactions (Kellicutt & Schwartzbaum, 1963) and interfere with the acquisition of active as well as passive avoidance responses (Horvath, 1963).

When I attempted to investigate these phenomena further by observing the behavioral and electrophysiological effects of local injections of neurohumoral substances, long-term effects became apparent which seem to be unique to this region of the temporal lobe. Carbachol (a parasympathomimetic drug which is not hydrolized by cholinesterase and therefore produces a prolonged excitatory action on cholinergic neurons) was injected into the amygdaloid complex of cats. Even minute doses induced epileptiform seizure activity which gradually spread to other regions of the brain and eventually involved all areas from which recordings were obtained (sensory and motor cortices, frontal lobes, thalamus, hippocampus, septal area, hypothalamus, midbrain reticular formation) (Grossman, 1963). This generalized EEG (electroencephalographic) seizure was accompanied by violent convulsions which appeared similar to the grand mal seizures of epileptic patients. After several hours of uninterrupted seizure activity, the EEG records began to show gradually lengthening periods of more normal, low-amplitude activity, accompanied by a gradual lessening of the convulsions. In the course of the following week, the animals recovered to the point where they could walk and even perform fairly complex visually guided motor responses without noticeable impairment. They maintained adequate nutritional and fluid levels by voluntary intake and resumed normal sleep–activity cycles. However, all animals remained extraordinarily vicious and attacked man as well as other animals without provocation or apparent regard for their own safety. This made handling all but impossible and precluded formal neurological examinations. However, the animals' sensory and motor functions appeared normal; even complex, learned behaviors seemed to be executed without difficulty.

Some of the cats were observed for 5 months. They remained vicious and uncooperative throughout this period in spite of repeated attempts to make them more docile by handling and petting. Abnormal EEG activity also persisted in all areas of the brain. Histological examination of the tissue surrounding the cannula implant failed to show any evidence of abnormal tissue reaction, suggesting that the single application of carbachol may have produced permanent functional changes.

More recently, Belluzzi and Grossman (1969) have found that a single, bilateral injection of carbachol into the amygdala of rats produces similarly permanent changes in avoidance behavior. The injections were followed, almost immediately, by electrical seizure activity which spread apparently throughout the brain. This was typically accompanied by overt convulsive activity. The motor seizures disappeared completely within a few hours, and the abnormal EEG activity also gradually abated. After 24 hours, the animals' EEG and behavior appeared normal. In contrast to the previous observations on cats, there were few signs of viciousness or aggressive behavior. A persisting impairment became apparent only when the animals were placed into a simple one-way avoidance situation. Normal rats learn this problem to perfection in two or three sessions. Animals which received a single injection of carbachol weeks before the first training trial, did not make a single avoidance response during 14 days of training. The inhibitory effects of carbachol appeared entirely reversed when the cholinergic blocking agent, scopolamine, was administered to the amygdaloid complex before each daily training session. This suggests that the long-term effects of carbachol may involve a persisting activation of cholinergic neurons.

Goddard (1969) has recently found that even very small doses of carbachol infused into the amygdala of rats modify the animals' response to punishment. In these experiments, the inhibitory effects of carbachol were seen most dramatically in the CER (conditioned emotional response) and passive avoidance paradigm. These observations indicate that components of the amygdaloid complex may be specifically related to the organism's reaction to punishment. A test of this hypothesis (Margules, 1968) supports this interpretation but suggests that adrenergic as well as cholinergic pathways may be related to this function. Margules demonstrated that injections of norepinephrine into the amygdaloid complex disinhibited punished lever-pressing behavior. He did not, unfortunately, report whether carbachol injections may have produced similar effects as one might predict on the basis of our work. Margules did note that injections of the cholinergic blocking agent, methyl atropine, did not affect punished behavior. This does not, unfortunately, provide a convincing argument against the involvement of cholinergic neurons in the organism's reaction to punishment. The disinhibitory effects of carbachol may reflect an activation of cholinergic neurons which are normally inhibited in the presence of aversive stimulation. Further inhibition of such a system by atropine could not produce noticeable behavioral effects because the animal is already responding at such a low level that further depression cannot become manifest.

It may be of interest, in this connection, that microinjections of phenothiazines and related drugs into the amygdaloid complex did not, in a recent experiment, affect shuttle-box avoidance behavior (Grossman, 1968a). Horovitz and Leaf (1967) similarly reported that chlorpromazine injections into the amygdala did not interfere with mouse killing in rats, whereas comparable injections of imipramine blocked this response entirely.

HIPPOCAMPUS

Damage to the hippocampus has been reported to facilitate (Isaacson, Douglas, & Moore, 1961), have no effect on (Brady, Schreiner, Geller, & Kling, 1954), or depress (Pribram & Weiskrantz, 1957) avoidance behavior. Electrical stimulation of this region typically facilitates or elicits "emotional" responses and related autonomic reactions (MacLean & Delgado, 1953). The latter authors also reported that carbachol injections into the dorsal hippocampus facilitated attack behavior in response to mildly noxious stimuli. In a subsequent investigation, MacLean (1957; see also Chapter 7 in this volume) observed enhanced pleasure and grooming reactions as well as penile erections following carbachol injections into the hippocampus. He suggested that the attack reactions which were seen in the earlier experiments may have been due to the escape of the drug into the ventricle overlying the dorsal hippocampus.

Delgado and Kitahata (1967) have more recently reported that microinjections of local anaesthetics such as xylocaine or phenobarbital into the dorsal hippocampus of monkeys produced a marked decrease in aggressiveness which persisted to some extent for several days. This apparent depression of affect was accompanied by a decrease in the amplitude of spontaneous EEG activity in the hippocampus and a shift in the threshold and pattern of hippocampal after-discharges. The animals' general state of alertness or appetite did not appear to be affected.

SEPTAL AREA

Damage to the septal area of rats, cats, or monkeys commonly produces permanent changes in the animals' reactivity to noxious stimulation and nonreward. The resulting behavioral deficits have been demonstrated in active as well as passive (conflict) avoidance situations (McCleary, 1961; Zucker, 1965), extinction and position-habit reversal tests (Zucker & McCleary, 1964).

My colleagues and I have recently concluded a series of experiments which suggest that the "septal syndrome" may have several distinct components which can be isolated by pharmacological techniques. The observation was made some years ago (Grossman, 1964) that rats did not learn a simple shuttle-box avoidance response when minute quantities of carbachol were injected into the septal area 5 min before each daily training session. A smaller but consistent performance decrement was seen in a lever-pressing avoidance situation when the drug was administered only after the animals had reached asymptotic performance levels. Injections of the cholinergic blocking agent, atropine, into the septal area significantly facilitated avoidance behavior in this experiment.

It has been shown that this atropine facilitation is much more pronounced when the drug is given during acquisition of a two-way shuttle-box avoidance response (Kelsey and Grossman, 1969). A comparison of the effects of septal lesions with those of septal atropine injections showed that the atropine effect, though consistent, was not as large as that of massive lesions. Hamilton, McCleary, and Grossman (1968) found that atropine injections into the septal area of cats produced some, but not all, of the behavioral deficits typically seen following septal lesions. The blockade of cholinergic neurons in the septal region produced passive-avoidance deficits as large or larger than those produced by septal lesions. The drug also significantly increased the number of trials required to obtain extinction of a shuttle-box avoidance response but did not affect behavior in a one-way avoidance situation or a position-habit reversal situation.

Hamilton and Grossman (1969) further observed that the administration of atropine to the septal area of cats produced dramatic inhibitory effects on the acquisition of avoidance responses in a shelf-jumping situation. These paradoxical effects were at least as large as those produced by massive lesions in the septal area (Hamilton, 1968). The same atropine injections significantly facilitated performance during the acquisition of the standard two-way shuttle-box avoidance response. The complexity of the influence of the septal area on avoidance behavior is emphasized by a further experiment with squirrel monkeys (Hamilton & Grossman, in preparation). Carbachol injections into the septal area of monkeys which had just learned to press a lever periodically to avoid painful tail shock (i.e., a Sidman avoidance situation), produced marked inhibitory effects. The same injections facilitated responding when the experiment was repeated after the animals had worked in this situation for 12 months. A reversal of the drug effect was also seen in a shelf-jump avoidance situation. Carbachol injections given during acquisition depressed avoidance behavior. Similar injections, given only a few days later, when the animals had reached asymptotic performance levels, produced small changes in the opposite direction.

It is interesting to note in this connection that microinjections of chlorpromazine and other phenothiazine derivatives into the medial or lateral septal area of rats does not modify shuttle-box avoidance behavior. The administration of these drugs to the medial septal area of monkeys also fails to affect behavior in a Sidman avoidance situation (Grossman, 1968a).

HYPOTHALAMUS AND PREOPTIC AREA

Lesions in the ventromedial portion of the hypothalamus produce complex behavioral effects which include marked changes in food intake (Hetherington, 1941), sexual behavior (Sawyer, 1960), and affective reactivity (Wheatley, 1944). Electrical stimulation of this region tends to inhibit all ongoing activity (Krasne, 1962), although more specific effects on affective behavior have been noted (Hess, 1949). It is not clear, at this time, whether the entire syndrome of behavioral reactions to ventromedial stimulation or damage can be explained in terms of a general shift in affective reactivity as has been suggested (Grossman, 1966a). It seems certain, however, that this portion of the diencephalon is a major way station in the neural circuit which determines the organism's response to noxious stimulation.

A number of investigators (Myers, 1964; Yamaguchi, Ling, & Marczynski, 1964; McPhail, 1968; McPhail & Miller, 1968) have reported that microinjections of carbachol into many portions of the medial hypothalamus and preoptic area increase excitability and induce a "generalized emotional response." This includes a variety of autonomic reactions typical of affective behavior as well as marked overt aggressive or defensive responses. Perhaps the most remarkable aspect of this effect is its apparent lack of anatomical specificity. Since negative placements can be found in the immediate vicinity of positive sites, this lack of anatomic specificity cannot be explained as a result of widespread drug diffusion. Instead, it seems that the diencephalon may contain a very diffuse system of cholinergic fibers and cells which seem to be part of the neural mechanisms which control affective reactions.

It is worthy of note that pathways related to general arousal and sleep appear to follow a similarly diffuse route through the diencephalon. Hernández-Peón and associates (Hernández-Peón, 1962, 1965; Hernández-Peón & Chávez-Ibarra, 1963; Hernández-Peón, Morgan, & Timo-Iaria, 1963a, 1963b) have reported that microinjections of carbachol, acetylcholine, or the cholinesterase inhibitor, eserine, into many points of the diencephalon induced drowsiness or sleep. Other workers have confirmed the observation that acetylcholine injections into the preoptic area and upper hypothalamus elicited sleep but reported opposite excitatory reactions when carbachol was administered to the same sites (Yamaguchi, Ling, & Marczynski, 1964). This excitatory response to carbachol has been seen frequently in my own laboratory in the rat. McPhail and Miller (1968) have recently demonstrated that carbachol injections into a total of 43 points in the diencephalon of cats failed to elicit sleep or drowsiness. Affective defense reactions were seen following carbachol injections into 26 of the 43 points.

It is puzzling to find that carbachol (a parasympathomimetic which is not hydrolyzed by cholinesterase and therefore produces a long-lasting excitatory effect on postsynaptic membranes and generally mimics the effects of acetylcholine at peripheral neuromuscular junctions) should produce opposite effects on arousal when topically applied to the hypothalamus. It is, of course, possible that high concentrations of the drug may produce a long-lasting depolarization of the postsynaptic membrane and thus inhibit rather than stimulate. Another consideration is that differences in the nicotinic action of acetylcholine and carbachol may account for the differential reaction. However, in a number of previous investigations (Grossman, 1960, 1962a, 1962b, 1968b), it has been consistently found that central applications of carbachol produce effects similar to acetycholine, though typically more prolonged and pronounced. Further study of this interesting phenomenon is needed, particularly since a similar dissociation of the acetylcholine and carbachol effects has been reported with respect to their effects on the reticular formation of the lower brainstem (Cordeau, Moreau, Beaulnes, & Laurin, 1963; Yamaguchi et al., 1964).

The work of Olds and associates (Olds & Olds, 1958; Olds, Yuwiler, Olds, & Yun, 1964) indicates that neural pathways which mediate positive affect may be as diffusely represented in the diencephalon as those which mediate the organism's response to noxious stimulation or punishment. Animals pressed a lever in order to administer a small quantity of carbachol to their lateral hypothalami. This self-injection behavior was inhibited when another neurohumor, norepinephrine, was added to the injection.

A more discretely localized portion of the neural systems which mediate affective reactions has been demonstrated in the ventromedial region of the hypothalamus. Bilateral injections of atropine into the ventromedial region reproduced many of the behavioral changes commonly seen after lesions in this area (Grossman, 1966a). The animals overate when the food was fresh and palatable but ate little or nothing of a diet that was quinine-adulterated or made unpalatable by the admixture of roughage. Compared to normal controls, the animals also did not work well for food rewards in a simple lever-pressing situation and stopped responding when shifted to a low-density reward schedule. Surprisingly, similar deficits could be seen when water rewards were used. This suggested that the impairment might not be specifically related to a primary interference with a food-satiety mechanisms as has been generally assumed, but might reflect instead a general shift in affect.

This hypothesis was tested by observing the effects of atropine injections on escape–avoidance behavior in a two-way shuttle box. In the first experiment, atropine facilitated the acquisition and performance of avoidance responses. Subsequently, I have observed an interesting interaction of the drug effect with the intensity of punishment. At shock intensities which are just high enough to produce approximately 40–60% avoidance responses in normal animals, injections of atropine into the ventromedial area facilitate performance. At shock intensities which are high enough to maintain 90–100% avoidance behavior, atropine injections depress responding. This interaction supports my hypothesis, if it is reasonable to assume that an increase in affective reactivity can aid avoidance behavior in situations where the shock-induced affect is relatively low but not in situations where it is high. Sepinwall (1966) has reported a facilitation of avoidance behavior in a Sidman paradigm following carbachol injections into the lateral hypothalamus of rats. There is, as yet, no information to suggest whether this effect might show a drug-shock interaction similar to that seen in our experiments on the ventromedial area.

Margules and Stein (1967) have reported that atropine injections into the ventromedial area depressed the effectiveness of punishment in a lever-pressing situation whereas carbachol injections enhanced it. The hypothesized shift in affect can account for these findings if it is assumed that the resulting change in the reinforcing properties of the food reward are greater than the change in the animals' reaction to punishment. There is, as yet, no direct test of this interpretation.

Margules and Stein noted that the response-suppression produced by chemical stimulation of the ventromedial hypothalamus was antagonized by systemic[1] injections of tranquilizers such as chlordiazepoxide, and suggested that tranquilizers might "exert at least part of their disinhibitory action by blocking the outflow of inhibitory influences from the ventromedial nucleus." Some experimental support for this hypothesis has been obtained (Grossman, 1968a). Microinjections of chlorpromazine and several related phenothiazine derivatives into the ventromedial hypothalamus significantly reduced the frequency of avoidance responses and increased the latency of escape responses in a one-way avoidance situation. The relatively small effects appeared noteworthy because similar injections into the septal area, amygdala, and mesencephalic reticular formation did not produce any changes in escape or avoidance behavior.

THALAMUS

Microinjections of carbachol into the midline or dorsolateral thalamus of rats was found to impair the learning of a simple shuttle-box

---

[1]Systemic injection here implies subcutaneous, intramuscular or intravenous route of drug administration, in contrast to topical injection into specific loci in the brain.

avoidance response (Grossman, Freedman, Peters, & Willer, 1965). Animals which received carbachol injections in the midline thalamus 5 min before each daily training session were significantly retarded but eventually learned the hurdle-jumping response and reached asymptotic performance levels which did not differ significantly from the performance of normal controls. Animals which received carbachol injections into the dorsolateral thalamus never performed an avoidance response in 150 trials and required an additional 150 trials after the discontinuation of the drug treatment to reach normal performance levels. Carbachol injections into either the midline or dorsolateral thalamus did not significantly modify food or water intake of animals deprived for 24 hours, but depressed their rate of responding for food or water rewards in a lever-pressing situation.

Further investigation demonstrated that an atropine-induced blockade of the midline nuclei facilitated the acquisition of avoidance responses and produced asymptotic performance levels which were consistently superior to those of normal rats (Grossman & Peters, 1966). Atropine injections into the dorsolateral thalamus, on the other hand, depressed avoidance behavior during acquisition and at the asymptote of performance. EEG recordings from the site of drug action did not indicate grossly abnormal reactions to either carbachol or atropine in these experiments, suggesting that avoidance behavior may be depressed when the functions of the dorsolateral thalamus are inhibited as well as when they are nonspecifically facilitated. The differential reaction to atropine was also observed in appetitive test situations where all animals had shown qualitatively similar inhibitory reactions to carbachol. Atropine facilitated the acquisition of a brightness discrimination when administered to the midline thalamus, but depressed performance during acquisition and at the asymptote when injected into the dorsolateral region.

CAUDATE NUCLEUS

Microinjections of small doses of carbachol into the caudate nucleus have been reported to inhibit all ongoing behavior, much as low-frequency electrical stimulation of this area does (Hull, Buchwald, & Ling, 1967). The activation of cholinergic neurons did not, however, result in the cortical EEG changes (spindling) which are typically seen after electrical stimulation of the caudate. Higher doses of carbachol, which may have produced more extensive diffusion of the drug, were reported to produce aggressive or defensive reactions, various autonomic responses, and a cortical temperature drop.

Neill and I are currently investigating the effects of drug injections into the caudate nucleus in more formal behavioral test situations. We find that a scopolamine-induced blockade of cholinergic components of the ventral caudate facilitates the acquisition and performance of avoidance behavior in a two-way shuttle box. Comparable scopolamine injections into the dorsal portion of the same nucleus produce marked inhibitory effects. These observations are particularly interesting in view of the fact that lesions in the ventral as well as dorsal caudate produce only depressive effects on avoidance behavior in our test situation. However, scopolamine hydrobromide, given systemically before each daily training session, facilitates avoidance behavior in animals with dorsal lesions but not in animals with ventral damage, suggesting that the two lesions do produce different effects on the organism's response to noxious stimulation.

MIDBRAIN

Small bilateral lesions in the central grey of the midbrain result in an apparently permanent reduction in emotional reactivity (Molina & Hunsperger, 1962). Larger lesions in the mesencephalic reticular formation inhibit the organism's reactivity more completely (Lindsley, Schreiner, Knowles, & Magoun, 1950). Electrical stimulation in the central grey elicits affective reactions in cats (Hunsperger, 1956; Molina & Hunsperger, 1959). Electrical stimulation of the midbrain reticular formation arouses a sleeping animal (Moruzzi & Magoun, 1949) and may facilitate perceptual functions (Fuster, 1957).

Small, implant-produced lesions in the brainstem reticular formation were found to depress avoidance behavior in a shuttle-box apparatus (Grossman, 1966b). Microinjections of carbachol into the same sites produced marked agitation and a further inhibition of avoidance behavior. When the drug treatments were repeated daily, the animals seemed to adjust to the apparent increase in general reactivity and performed significantly better than controls in the avoidance situation.

In another study, the effects of cholinergic stimulation of the midbrain in several appetitive situations were observed (Grossman & Grossman, 1966). Somewhat unexpectedly, small lesions facilitated the acquisition of simple conditioned responses in maze as well as lever-pressing situations. Microinjections of carbachol into the same sites inhibited the acquisition and performance of all appetitive con-

ditioned responses but did not interfere with such overtrained behaviors as feeding or drinking in response to deprivation.

An attempt has been made to obtain some additional information
on this complex reaction to chemical stimulation of the midbrain reticular formation (Grossman, 1968b). Microinjections of carbachol
resulted in a marked hyperreactivity to suprathreshold stimuli of all
sensory modalities without significantly lowering the absolute detection thresholds. Lights, sounds, air puffs, or tactile stimuli of mod-
erate intensity elicited exaggerated startle responses and often attempts to attack the source of stimulation. Repeated presentations
of such stimuli produced little evidence of habituation. The animals appeared frightened (i.e., squealed, urinated, defecated, and
crouched) when placed into an open field or in novel apparatus.

The carbachol-treated animals regulated their fluid and energy
balance throughout the experiment and fed or drank when offered
food or water immediately after carbachol injections. However, their
behavior appeared grossly abnormal in all test situations which required the acquisition or performance of food- or water-rewarded
instrumental responses. Following carbachol injections, the animals
were easily distracted by extraneous stimuli, gave exaggerated startle
and orienting responses to familiar sights and sounds, and explored
familiar apparatus on every trial. This excessive reactivity to "irrelevant" aspects of the environment interfered with the acquisition and
performance of simple brightness discriminations and decreased the
animals' rate of responding for food or water rewards in a two-lever
operant situation.

When the carbachol-treated animals were tested in a two-way
shuttle-box avoidance situation, an interesting interaction between
the drug-induced shift in reactivity and the intensity of the grid
shock became apparent. At high shock intensities, the experimental
animals' exaggerated reaction to the UCS (unconditioned stimulus)
interfered with the simple escape response. They were consequently
exposed to longer and more frequent punishments and developed
excessive conditioned fear reactions to the apparatus which, in turn,
interfered with the acquisition of avoidance responses. When the
intensity of the grid shock was reduced to the point where control
animals avoided on only 40 to 60 % of the trials, carbachol injections
produced facilitatory effects, presumably because the drug-induced
hyperreactivity to noxious stimulation enhanced the effects of the
grid shock without exceeding some maximal level of arousal.

It was of particular interest to find that carbachol injections did not
modify the animals' detection threshold for foot shock (i.e., the inten-

sity required to elicit overt movement) but did lower their aversion threshold (i.e., the shock intensity required to elicit such presumed indices of emotionality as squealing, crouching, defecation).

Atropine injections into the midbrain reticular formation produced relatively small inhibitory effects. The animals moved about less than normal controls and showed none of the emotional behaviors which characterize the carbachol-treated animals in an open field. The animals' lowered reactivity was reflected in a small depression in the rate of lever-pressing for food and water rewards and in a rise in the response latencies in the brightness discrimination situation. In the avoidance experiment, atropine produced shock-intensity dependent effects on behavior which were, in all instances, opposite in direction to those produced by carbachol.

These observations suggest that the midbrain reticular formation may contain a cholinergic component which influences the organism's general level of reactivity. In view of the marked arousal effects of systemically administered catecholamines, it seemed important to investigate the effects on this mechanism of norepinephrine and related substances. Microinjections of norepinephrine into the midbrain reticular formation produced an apparent lowering of reactivity to environmental stimuli, often accompanied by bursts of agitated and seemingly random behavior. The animals responded appropriately to food or water deprivation and consumed normal quantities of food or water when tested immediately after the administration of norepinephrine. Food- or water-rewarded instrumental responses were, however, markedly depressed in all test situations. The effects of norepinephrine on escape–avoidance behavior were shock-intensity dependent and, in all instances, opposite in direction to those seen after cholinergic stimulation. The reduced reactivity of the norepinephrine treated animals seemed to aid performance in the high-shock situation which often induced frantic and uncoordinated behavior in the carbachol experiments. Norepinephrine almost entirely inhibited responding in the low-shock situation.

Microinjections of the adrenergic blocking agent dibenzyline (phenoxybenzamine) did not produce sufficiently gross changes in reactivity or locomotor activity to permit detection by inspection. All formal test situations did show small but consistent behavioral changes opposite in direction to those seen after norepinephrine.

EEG records, obtained from the tip of the cannula implant, did not show consistent drug effects. Recordings obtained from cortical leads did reflect some of the drug-induced changes in overt reactivity. Carbachol injections produced a significant shift towards low-voltage fast activity in the cortical EEG. Norepinephrine, on the other hand, increased the proportion of high-amplitude slow waves. The adrenergic and cholinergic blockers produced only small changes in the predicted direction.

The overall pattern of behavioral and electrophysiological effects suggests that neurons of the brainstem reticular formation which influence the organism's reactivity to the environment may be selectively sensitive to adrenergic as well as cholinergic chemicals. The apparently opposite effect of the two types of neurohumors may be due to excitatory actions on distinct excitatory and inhibitory pathways or to differential drug effects on the same neural mechanisms. Microelectrode studies have shown that the brainstem contains cells which respond to either adrenergic or cholinergic substances or both (Bradley & Mollica, 1958; Bradley & Wolstencroft, 1962, 1965; Salmoiraghi & Steiner, 1963). Inhibitory responses to norepinephrine are most commonly reported, suggesting that the apparently inhibitory effects of this drug in behavioral investigations may be due to an inhibitory action on brainstem neurons. Carbachol may have a stimulating action on the same cells or on components of a complementary excitatory mechanism.

It is important to emphasize, in this context, that these drug effects are peculiar to a restricted aspect of the upper mesencephalon and do not characterize the entire brainstem reticular formation. Cordeau and associates (Cordeau, Moreau, & Beaulnes, 1961; Courville, Walsh, & Cordeau, 1962a,b) have reported that microinjections of epinephrine into the pontine and bulbar reticular formation usually increased the amplitude of evoked potentials and the likelihood of cortical desynchronization. Acetylcholine injections into the same sites produced EEG synchrony and a reduction in the amplitude of cortical potentials.

The picture is further complicated by species differences as well as rather puzzling variations in the reaction to apparently similar drugs. For instance, it has been reported that microinjections of epinephrine into some loci in the mesencephalon produced behavioral as well as EEG arousal. By contrast, acetylcholine injections into the same sites induced behavioral depression and EEG patterns characteristic of REM (rapid-eye-movement) sleep (Cordeau, Moreau, & Beaulnes, 1961; Cordeau, Moreau, Beaulnes, & Laurin, 1962, 1963). Other investigators replicated these observations with the exception that carbachol injections into the same sites produced continuous activation (Yamaguchi, Ling, & Marczynski, 1964). Arousal responses to carbachol injections into the lateral mesencephalic reticular formation have also been reported (Hernández-Peón, Morgan, & Timo-Iaria, 1963a, 1963b). More puzzling yet is a report by Cordeau *et al.* (1961) that the administration of acetylcholine mixed with physostigmine (a cholinesterase inhibitor which should potentiate the action of acetylcholine) to the mesencephalic brainstem produced behavioral as well as EEG arousal, whereas the administration of acetylcholine, by itself, induced sleep.

At least some of these apparently paradoxical observations may be related to a differential action of carbachol and acetylcholine on nicotinic and muscarinic receptor sites. It has been shown that microinjections of oxotremorine, which lacks nicotinic activity but has strong muscarinic actions, produces deep sleep and REM sleep patterns in the cortical EEG (Cordeau *et al.*, 1962). Carbachol, which has strong nicotinic activity, may produce its excitatory effects on arousal by selective activation of nicotinic receptors.

Allikmets, Delgado, & Richards (1968) have reported that infusions of antidepressant drugs, such as chlorprothixene and promazine, into the midbrain of monkeys raised the threshold for the elicitation of affective reactions by electrical stimulation of the affected region. Since the threshold for simple motor responses did not appear to be affected by this procedure, Allikmets and associates interpreted their results as suggesting a selective drug effect on neurons mediating affective reactions.

Microinjections of chlorpromazine and related drugs into the mesencephalic reticular formation of rats did not significantly modify escape or avoidance behavior but did elicit high-amplitude slow waves both cortically and at the site of drug administration (Grossman, 1968a). Baxter (1968) on the other hand, has reported that injections of carbachol into the midbrain of cats elicited such affective reactions as hissing, growling, piloerection, or attack and defense reactions.

Discussion

A number of problems remain to be solved before we can reap the full benefits of intracranial microinjection techniques. The most important of these is the question of rate and extent of drug diffusion. My own experiments have rather consistently shown that the application of small quantities of drugs in crystalline form produces an effective spread which must be smaller than 0.5 to 0.8 mm because positive and negative placements often are found less than 1.0 mm apart. However, larger diffusion patterns can be obtained (MacLean,

1957; Routtenberg, Sladek, & Bondareff, 1968) when larger quantities are administered or when the drugs are injected in solution. It
remains to be seen to what extent diffusion may account for the apparently wide distribution of some of the neural pathways which we
have discussed.

Perhaps equally important is a clarification of the nature of the
drug action itself. Can we assume, a priori, that a cholinomimetic
such as carbachol always produces an excitatory action, even though
the concentrations of the drug are undoubtedly aphysiological, particularly close to the tip of the implant? What is the overall effect of
the gradual dilution of the drug as it diffuses farther and farther from
the point of application? It may turn out that all drugs are in such
high concentrations at the point of administration that the tissue in
the immediate vicinity of the implant is subject to abnormal conditions and may consequently not function normally at all. The behavioral reaction may then be a compound response to this abnormal
condition added to a more nearly normal stimulating or inhibiting
action at some distance from the implant. Microelectrode studies
should help to clarify these important points. All of these questions
are, fortunately, answerable using currently available techniques,
and it is to be hoped that these procedural matters will not be forgotten in the quest for inherently more interesting scientific information.

SUMMARY

Intracranial microinjection techniques have provided a valuable
tool for the study of the immensely complex neural pathways which
mediate affective reactions. In a number of instances it has been possible to reduce the enormous complexity of the behavioral effects of
even localized lesions or electrical stimulation. In others, rather
widely and diffusely distributed neural mechanisms have become
apparent which had, by and large, escaped detection by traditional
approaches. The technique has made it possible to make "functional" lesions and to observe the behavior of the same animal after he
has recovered from this lesion. The relatively long-term effects of
drugs have made it possible to study at some leisure the effects of
stimulation in a particular region of the brain. Most importantly, perhaps, it has become possible to record the electrical activity of stimulated or inhibited neurons as well as that of functionally or anatomically related parts of the brain.

REFERENCES

Allikmets, L., Delgado, J. M. R., & Richards, S. A. Intramesencephalic injection of imipramine, promazine and chlorprothixene in awake monkeys. *International Journal of Neuropharmacology*, 1968, 7, 185-193.

Andersson, B. Polydipsia caused by intrahypothalamic injections of hypertonic NaCl-solutions. *Experientia*, 1952, 8, 157-158.

Baxter, B. L. Elicitation of emotional behavior by electrical or chemical stimulation applied at the same loci in cat mesencephalon. *Experimental Neurology*, 1968, 21, 1-10.

Belluzzi, J. D., & Grossman, S. P. Avoidance learning: long-lasting deficits after temporal lobe seizure. *Science*, 1969, 166, 1635-1637.

Bradley, P. B., & Mollica, A. The effect of adrenaline and acetylcholine on single unit activity in the reticular formation of the decerebrated cat. *Archives Italiennes de Biologie*, 1958, 96, 168-186.

Bradley, P. B., & Wolstencroft, J. H. Excitation and inhibition of brainstem neurons by noradrenaline and acetylcholine. *Nature (London)*, 1962, 196, 840.

Bradley, P. B., & Wolstencroft, J. H. Action of drugs on single neurons in the brainstem. *British Medical Bulletin*, 1965, 21, 15-18.

Brady, J. V., Schreiner, L., Geller, I., & Kling, A. Subcortical mechanisms in emotional behavior: the effect of rhinencephalic injury upon the acquisition and retention of a conditioned avoidance response in cats. *Journal of Comparative and Physiological Psychology*, 1954, 49, 179-186.

Cordeau, J. P., Moreau, A., & Beaulnes, A. EEG and behavioral effect of microinjection of drugs in the brainstem of cats. In *Proceedings of the International Congress of Electroencephalography and Clinical Neurophysiology, 5th, 1961*, Excerpta Medica Foundation, International Congress, 1961, Series 37.

Cordeau, J. P., Moreau, A., Beaulnes, A., & Laurin, C. EEG and behavioral effects of microinjections of drugs in the brainstem of cats. In *International Congress of Physiological Sciences, Proceedings, 22nd Leiden, 1962*, Abstract number 1076.

Cordeau, J. P., Moreau, A., Beaulnes, A., & Laurin, C. EEG and behavioral changes following microinjections of acetylcholine and adrenaline in the brainstem of cats. *Archives italiennes de Biologie*, 1963, 101, 30-47.

Courville, J., Walsh, J., & Cordeau, J. P. Functional organization of the brainstem reticular formation and specific sensory input. *Proceedings of the Canadian Federation of Biological Societies*, 1962, 5, 22. (a)

Courville, J., Walsh, J., & Cordeau, J. P. Functional organization of the brain stem reticular formation and sensory input. *Science*, 1962, 138, 973-975. (b)

Delgado, J., & Kitahata, L. Reversible depressions of hippocampus by local injections of anesthetics in monkeys. *Electroencephalography and Clinical Neurophysiology*, 1967, 22, 453-464.

Fuster, J. M. Tachistoscopic perception in monkeys. *Federation Proceedings Federation of American Societies for Experimental Biology*, 1957, 16, 43.

Goddard, G. V. Analysis of avoidance conditioning following cholinergic stimulation of amygdala in rats. *Journal of Comparative and Physiological Psychology*, 1969, 68 (Monograph).

Grossman, S. P. Eating or drinking elicited by direct adrenergic or cholinergic stimulation of hypothalamus. *Science*, 1960, 132, 301-302.

Grossman, S. P. Direct adrenergic and cholinergic stimulation of hypothalamic mechanisms. *American Journal of Physiology*, 1962, 202, 872-882. (a)

Grossman, S. P. Effects of adrenergic and cholinergic blocking agents on hypothalamic mechanisms. American Journal of Physiology, 1962, **202**, 1230-1236. (b)

Grossman, S. P. Chemically induced epileptiform seizures in the cat. *Science*, 1963, **142**, 409-411.

Grossman, S. P. Effects of chemical stimulation of the septal area on motivation. *Journal of Comparative and Physiological Psychology*, 1964, **58**, 194-200.

Grossman, S. P. The VMH: A center for affective reactions, satiety, or both? *Physiology & Behavior*, 1966, **1**, 1-10. (a)

Grossman, S. P. Acquisition and performance of avoidance responses during chemical stimulation of midbrain reticular formation. *Journal of Comparative and Physiological Psychology*, 1966, **61**, 42-49. (b)

Grossman, S. P. Neuropharmacological analysis of central mechanisms contributing to the control of food and water intake. In C. F. Code (Section Ed.), *Handbook of physiology, alimentary canal*. Baltimore: Williams & Wilkins, 1967. Pp. 287-302.

Grossman, S. P. Behavioral and electrophysiological effects of intracranial microinjections of phenothiazines. *Communications Behavioral Biology*, 1968, **1**, 9-17. (a)

Grossman, S. P. Behavioral and electroencephalographic effects of micro-injections of neurohumors into the midbrain reticular formation. *Physiology & Behavior*, 1968, **3**, 777-786. (b)

Grossman, S. P. The physiological basis of specific and non-specific motivational processes. In W. J. Arnold (Ed.), *The Nebraska Symposium on Motivation*, pp. 1-46. Nebraska: University of Nebraska Press, 1969.

Grossman, S. P., & Grossman, L. Effects of chemical stimulation of the midbrain reticular formation on appetitive behavior. *Journal of Comparative and Physiological Psychology*, 1966, **61**, 333-338.

Grossman, S. P., & Peters, R. Acquisition of appetitive and avoidance habits following atropine-induced blocking of the thalamic reticular formation. *Journal of Comparative and Physiological Psychology*, 1966, **61**, 325-332.

Grossman, S. P., Freedman, P., Peters, R., & Willer, H. Behavioral effects of cholinergic stimulation of the thalamic reticular formation. *Journal of Comparative and Physiological Psychology*, 1965, **59**, 57-65.

Hamilton, L. W. Active avoidance impairment following septal lesions in cats. *Journal of Comparative and Physiological Psychology*, 1969, **69**, 420-431.

Hamilton, L. W., & Grossman, S. P. Behavioral changes following disruption of central cholinergic pathways. *Journal of Comparative and Physiological Psychology*, 1969, **69**, 76-82.

Hamilton, L. W., & Grossman, S. P. Modification of avoidance behavior in monkeys following carbachol injections into the septal area. In preparation.

Hamilton, L. W., & Grossman, S. P. Modification of avoidance behavior in monkeys following carbachol injections into the septal area. In preparation.

Hamilton, L. W., McCleary, R., & Grossman, S. P. Behavioral effects of cholinergic septal blockade in the cat. *Journal of Comparative and Physiological Psychology*, 1968, **66**, 563-568.

Harris, G. W. The reticular formation, stress and endocrine activity. In H. H. Jasper, L. D. Proctor, R. S. Knighton, W. C. Noshay, & R. T. Costello (Eds.), *The reticular formation of the brain*. Boston: Little, Brown, 1958.

Hartmann, G., Endröczi, E., & Lissák, K. The effect of hypothalamic implantation of 17-β- oestradiol and systemic administration of prolactin (LTH) on sexual behavior in male rabbits. *Acta Physiologica Hungaricae*, 1966, **30**, 53-59.

Hernández-Peón, R. Sleep induced by localized electrical or chemical stimulation of the forebrain. *Electroencephalography and Clinical Neurophysiology,* 1962, **14,** 423-424.

Hernández-Peón, R. Central neurohumoral transmission in sleep and wakefulness, *Progress in Brain Research,* 1965, **18,** 96-117.

Hernández-Peón, R., & Chávez-Ibarra, G. Sleep induced by electrical or chemical stimulation of the forebrain. *Electroencephalography and Clinical Neurophysiology Supplement,* 1963, **24,** 188-198.

Hernández-Peón, R., Morgan, J. P., & Timo-Iaria, C. Limbic cholinergic pathways involved in sleep and emotional behavior. *Experimental Neurology,* 1963, **8,** 93-111. (a)

Hernández-Peón, R., Morgane, P. J., & Timo-Iaria, C. Induction of sleep by direct cholinergic stimulation of the brain. *Clinical Research,* 1963, **11,** 177. (b)

Hess, W. R. *Das Zwischenhirn: Syndrome, Lokalizationen, Funktionen.* Basel: Benno Schwabe, 1949.

Hetherington, A. W. The relation of various hypothalamic lesions to adiposity and other phenomena in the rat. *American Journal of Physiology,* 1941, **133,** 326-327.

Horovitz, Z. P., & Leaf, R. C. The effects of direct injections of psychotropic drugs on the amygdalae of rats and the relationship to antidepressant site of action. In H. Brill, J. P. Cole, P. Deniker, H. Hippius, & P. B. Bradley (Eds.), *Neuro-psychopharmacology,* New York: Excerpta Medica Foundation. 1967 (Abstract p. 1042).

Horvath, F. E. Effects of basolateral amygdalectomy on three types of avoidance behavior. *Journal of Comparative and Physiological Psychology,* 1963, **56,** 380-389.

Hull, C. D., Buchwald, N. A., & Ling, G. Effects of direct cholinergic stimulation of forebrain structures. *Brain Research,* 1967, **6,** 22-35.

Hunsperger, R. W. Affektreaktionen auf elektrische Reizung im Hirnstamm der Katze. *Helvetica Physiologica et Pharmacologica Acta,* 1956, **14,** 70-92.

Isaacson, R. L., Douglas, R. J., & Moore, R. Y. The effect of radical hippocampal ablation on acquisition of avoidance responses. *Journal of Comparative and Physiological Psychology,* 1961, **54,** 625-628.

Kellicutt, M. H., & Schwartzbaum, J. S. Formation of a conditioned emotional response (CER) following lesions of the amygdaloid complex in rats. *Psychological Report,* 1963, **12,** 351-358.

Kelsey, J. E., & Grossman, S. P. Cholinergic blockade and lesions in the ventromedial septum of the rat. *Physiology and Behavior,* 1969, **4,** 837-845.

Krasne, F. B. General disruption resulting from electrical stimulus of ventromedial hypothalamus. *Science,* 1962, **138,** 822-823.

Lindsley, D. B., Schreiner, L. H., Knowles, W. B., & Magoun, H. W. Behavioral and EEG changes following chronic brainstem lesions in the cat. *Electroencephalography and Clinical Neurophysiology,* 1950, **2,** 483.

MacLean, P. D. Chemical and electrical stimulation of hippocampus in unrestrained animals. II: Behavioral findings. *AMA Archives of Neurology and Psychiatry,* 1957, **78,** 128-142.

MacLean, P. D., & Delgado, J. M. R. Electrical and chemical stimulation of frontotemporal portion of limbic system in the waking animal. *Electroencephalography and Clinical Neurophysiology,* 1953, **5,** 91-100.

Margules, D. L. Noradrenergic basis of inhibition between reward and punishment in amygdala. *Journal of Comparative and Physiological Psychology,* 1968, **66,** 329-334.

Margules, D. L., & Stein, L. Neuroleptics vs. tranquilizers: Evidence from animal studies of mode and site of action. In H. Brill, J. P. Cole, P. Deniker, H. Hippius, & P. B. Bradley (Eds.), *Neuro-Psychopharmacology.* New York: Excerpta Medica Foundation, 1967.

Mayer, J. Regulation of energy intake and the body weight. The glucostatic theory and the lipostatic hypothesis. *Annals of the New York Academy of Sciences,* 1955, **63**, 15-43.

McCleary, R. A. Response specificity in the behavioral effects of limbic system lesions in the cat. *Journal of Comparative and Physiological Psychology,* 1961, **54**, 605-613.

McPhail, E. M. Effects of intracranial cholinergic stimulation in rats on drinking, EEG, and heart rate. *Journal of Comparative and Physiological Psychology,* 1968, **65**, 42-49.

McPhail, E. M., & Miller, N. Cholinergic brain stimulation in cats: Failure to obtain sleep. *Journal of Comparative and Physiological Psychology,* 1968, **3**, 499-503.

Molina, F. A. de, and Hunsperger, R. W. Central representation of affective reactions in forebrain and brainstem: Electrical stimulation of amygdala, stria terminalis, and adjacent structures. *Journal of Physiology (London),* 1959, **145**, 265-281.

Molina, F. A. de, and Hunsperger, R. W. Organization of the subcortical system governing defense and flight reactions in the cat. *Journal of Physiology (London),* 1962, **160**, 200-213.

Moruzzi, G., and Magoun, H. W. Brainstem reticular formation and activation of the EEG. *Electroencephalography and Clinical Neurophysiology,* 1949, **1**, 455-473.

Myers, R. D. Emotional and autonomic responses following hypothalamic chemical stimulation. *Canadian Journal of Psychology,* 1964, **18**, 6-14.

Olds, J., & Olds, M. E. Positive reinforcement produced by stimulating hypothalamus with iproniazid and other compounds. *Science,* 1958, **127**, 1175-1176.

Olds, J., Yuwiler, A., Olds, M. E., & Yun, C. Neurohumors in hypothalamic substrates of reward. *American Journal of Physiology,* 1964, **207**, 242-254.

Pribram, K. H., & Weiskrantz, L. A comparison of the effects of medial and lateral cerebral resections on conditioned avoidance behavior of monkeys. *Journal of Comparative and Physiological Psychology,* 1957, **50**, 74-80.

Routtenberg, A., Sladek, J., & Bondareff, W. Histochemical fluorescence after applications of neurochemicals to the caudate nucleus and septal area in vivo. *Science,* 1968, **161**, 272-274.

Salmoiraghi, G. C., & Steiner, F. A. Acetylcholine sensitivity of cat's medullary neurons. *Journal of Neurophysiology,* 1963, **26**, 581-597.

Sawyer, C. H. Reproductive behavior. In J. Field, H. W. Magoun, and V. E. Hall (Eds.), *Handbook of Physiology. Vol. II.* Baltimore: Williams & Wilkins, 1960.

Sepinwall, J. Cholinergic stimulation of the brain and avoidance behavior. *Psychonomic Science,* 1966, **5**, 93-94.

Spiegel, E. A., Miller, H. R., & Oppenheimer, M. J. Forebrain and rage reactions. *Journal of Neurophysiology,* 1940, **3**, 538-548.

Ursin, H. The temporal lobe substrate of fear and anger. *Acta Psychiatrica et Neurologica Scandinavica,* 1960, **35**, 378-396.

Wheatley, M. D. The hypothalamus and affective behavior in cats: A study of the effects of experimental lesions, with anatomic correlations. *Archives of Neurology and Psychiatry,* 1944, **52**, 296-316.

Yamaguchi, N., Ling, G. M., & Marczynski, T. J. The effects of chemical stimulation of the preoptic region, nucleus centralis medialis, or brainstem reticular formation with regard to sleep and wakefulness. *Recent Advances in Biological Psychiatry,* 1964, **6**, 9-20.

Zucker, I. Effect of lesions of the septal-limbic area on the behavior of cats. *Journal of Comparative and Physiological Psychology,* 1965, **60**, 344-352.

Zucker, I., & McCleary, R. A. Perseveration in septal cats. *Psychonomic Science,* 1964, **1**, 387-388.

6

ENDOCRINE AND AUTONOMIC CORRELATES
OF EMOTIONAL BEHAVIOR

Joseph V. Brady

INTRODUCTION

The relationship between behavioral and physiological response processes has long provided an important focus for both laboratory and clinical studies of emotion. Although over a half-century has passed since Cannon (1915) and his collaborators provided convincing experimental evidence of endocrine and autonomic participation in emotional response patterns, systematic development of such laboratory models has proceeded slowly and somewhat haltingly amidst a host of behavioral and physiological complexities. Traditionally, research in this area has focused upon classical Pavlovian or respondent conditioning procedures concerned primarily with adjustments of the organism's internal economy (Pavlov, 1879; Cannon, 1915; Gantt, 1944, 1960; Mahl, 1949, 1952; Malmo, 1950, pp. 169–180; Lacey, 1956; Liddel, 1956). More recently, however, reliable methods have been developed for direct analysis of visceral and hormonal processes in relationship to emotional behavior situations involving both respondent and instrumental or operant interactions whereby the organism deals more directly and effectively with the external environment (Wenzel, 1961; Brady, 1967; Perez-Cruet, Tolliver, Dunn, Marvin, & Brady, 1963; Mason, Brady, & Tolson, 1966, pp. 227–248). For the most part, relatively transient visceral changes have been emphasized in such psychophysiological analyses, although a current focus on more durable endocrinological and autonomic effects will be apparent in discussing some of the research to be reviewed in this chapter.

REVIEW OF RECENT PAST STUDIES

Three major groups of laboratory studies emerging over the past two decades provide a background for the psychophysiological analysis of emotion to be presented in this review. First, several research reports have described cardiorespiratory changes which invariably accompany both acute and chronic emotional stress reactions in behavioral conditioning situations. Such autonomic effects as have been described in these studies, however, tend to be confined to specific experimental periods when performance is required and appear in at least some instances to represent physiological responses conditioned to stimuli produced by the instrumental behavior. Reports by Eldridge (1954), Shapiro and Horn (1955), Wenzel (1961), Perez-Cruet *et al.* (1963), DeToledo and Black (1966), and Stebbins and Smith (1964) have described such effects in emotional conditioning situations involving aversive control. Several studies have even reported cardiovascular effects in relationship to instrumental performance requirements with no apparent dependence upon aversive processes (Malmo, 1961; Wenzel, 1961; Berlanger & Feldman, 1962; Hahn, Stern, & McDonald, 1962; Perez-Cruet, Black, & Brady, 1963). Interestingly, more central effects described in emotion-related electrophysiological studies involving behavioral conditioning appear to be characterized by a similar transience, seldom, if ever, enduring beyond the limits of the specific experimental conditions under which they were elicited (Hearst, Beer, Sheatz, & Galambos, 1960; John & Killam, 1959; Porter, Conrad, & Brady, 1959; Ross, Hodos, & Brady, 1962).

The second group of emotion-oriented behavioral experiments have, however, called attention to more durable physiological changes involving visceral-alimentary and endocrinological processes. The production of marked obesity in normal rats by controlling drinking behavior as a shock avoidance response (Williams & Teitelbaum, 1956) and the experimental elevation of alcohol ingestion levels in rhesus monkeys during and for prolonged periods following exposure to shock-avoidance conditioning (Clark & Polish, 1960) represent two of the more dramatic examples of relatively durable behaviorally induced alimentary changes. Endocrinological effects associated with such emotional behavior-conditioning procedures also appear somewhat less transient than similarly induced cardiorespiratory alterations. The systematic analysis of such psychoendocrinological relations has been extensively described in a series of studies which provide at least a partial basis for the psychophysiological approach to be elaborated in the substantive sections of the present discussion (Mason & Brady, 1956; Mason, Brady, & Sidman, 1957; Mason, Brady, Polish, Bauer, Robinson, Rose, & Taylor, 1961a; Mason, Brady, Robinson, Taylor, Tolson, & Mougey, 1961; Mason, Mangan, Brady, Conrad, & Rioch, 1961b; Sidman, Mason, Brady, & Thach, 1962; Mason, Brady, & Tolson, 1966, pp. 227-248). Indeed, an increasing number of reports from other laboratories (Levine & Treiman, 1964; Brush & Levine, 1966) confirm the intimate association between such hormonal and behavioral interactions.

A third group of psychophysiological studies concerned with the relationship between behaviorally induced emotional stress and chronic somatic change involving primarily gastrointestinal and infectious disease processes has emerged most recently and bears on the mediational role of endocrine and autonomic processes in such psychosomatic changes. Laboratory investigations in this area, however, continue to present many difficult problems imposed in large part by the generally irreversible character of the behaviorally produced somatic effects. Sawrey and Weisz (1956), for example, first described a behavioral conflict procedure for producing gastric ulcers in which laboratory rats lived for a period of 30 days in an experimental chamber which required the crossing of electrically charged grids in order for the animals to obtain food and water. Exposure to this conflict was reported to produce a significantly higher incidence of gastric lesions than exposure to comparable periods of food and water deprivation without conflict. Subsequent studies, however, have suggested that interactions involving hunger, fear, shock, weight loss, and even social experience play a significant role in the production of such altered somatic states (Sawrey, Conger, & Turrell, 1956; Weisz, 1957; Conger, Sawrey, and Turrell, 1958; Sawrey, 1961). Indeed, the rather intensive experiences with the production of peptic ulcers in emotionally conditioned rhesus monkeys reported by Brady and collaborators (Brady, Porter, Conrad, & Mason, 1958; Porter, Brady, Conrad, Mason, Galambos, & Rioch, 1958; Brady & Polish, 1960; Polish, Brady, Mason, Thach, & Niemeck, 1962; Brady, 1963) confirm the complexity of the analysis required by such studies. A provocative series of studies, however, on the effects of such behaviorally induced emotional stress upon susceptibility to infectious and other disease processes (Rasmussen, Marsh, & Brill, 1957; Ader & Plaut, 1968; Ader & Friedman, 1965, pp. 457–470) has begun to broaden the scope of investigations in this difficult area, and prospects for future experimental advance appear bright.

SOME CURRENT PSYCHOPHYSIOLOGICAL EXPERIMENTS

The activity of the pituitary-adrenocortical system as reflected in 17-hydroxycorticosteroid (17–OH–CS) levels (Harwood & Mason, 1956) provided the physiological focus for the initial psychoendocrine studies of emotion using the now well-known chair-restrained primate (Mason, 1958) illustrated in Figure 1. Briefly, the primate restraining-chair situation provides for automatic and programmable delivery of food and water, administration of mildly punishing electric shock to the feet, a hand-operated electromechanical lever switch, and presentation of a variety of visual and auditory stimuli to the experimental animal. Blood is obtained from the leg of the monkey or through a chronically indwelling right atrial catheter. Urine samples are collected in a receptacle attached below the seat of the chair. Programming and control of all behavioral procedures are accomplished remotely and automatically with an electromechanical system of relays, timers, counters, and recorders.

The Conditioned "Anxiety" Response

Preliminary studies readily established that neither restraint in the chair following an initial 48-hour adaptation period nor performance of lever pressing for food reward alone on several different schedules of reinforcement produced any significant hormone changes in monkeys maintained for prolonged intervals under such conditions. When, however, emotional behavior conditioning procedures involving electric shock to the feet were superimposed upon such performance baselines, marked elevations in plasma 17–OH–CS levels were observed. One of the basic procedures which produced this adrenal-cortical response is a modification of the Estes-Skinner conditioned suppression technique (Estes & Skinner, 1941); this provides a convenient laboratory model for emotional behavior. Conditioning trials consisting of 5-min continuous presentations of an auditory warning stimulus terminated contiguously with a brief

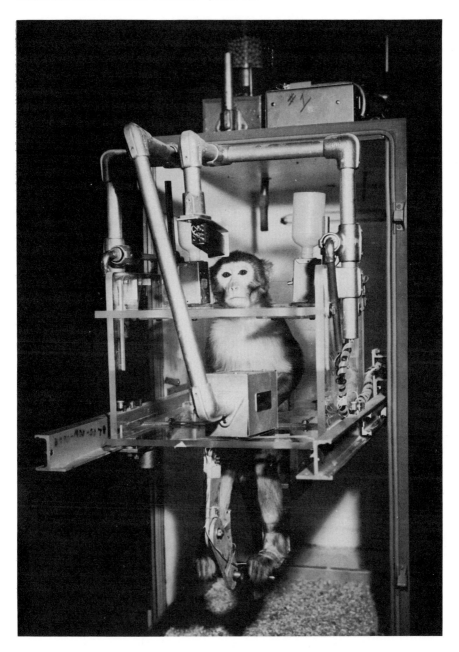

Fig. 1. Rhesus monkey in primate restraining chair (*from* Brady, 1965).

electric shock to the feet are superimposed upon the lever-pressing performance for food on a variable interval schedule of reinforcement. Within a few trials, virtually complete suppression of the lever-pressing behavior occurs in response to presentation of the clicker, as illustrated in Figure 2, accompanied by piloerection, locomotor agitation, and frequently urination and/or defecation.

The development of this conditioned "anxiety" response has been studied in relationship to changes in plasma 17-OH-CS levels occurring during a series of acquisition trials consisting of 30-min lever-pressing sessions with auditory stimulus and shock pairing occurring once during each session approximately 15 min after the start (Mason *et al.*, 1966, pp. 227-248). Seven such conditioning trials were accompanied by the withdrawal of blood samples immediately before and immediately after each 30-min session; 17-OH-CS levels associated with successive stages in the acquisition of the conditioned emotional behavior were determined. Figure 3 shows the corresponding changes in lever pressing and 17-OH-CS throughout the series of seven conditioning sessions.

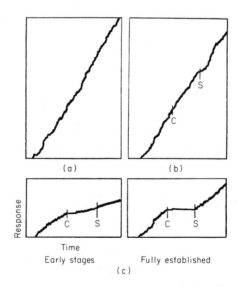

Fig. 2. Conditioned emotional behavior as it appears typically in the cumulative response curve. Clicker introduced at C and terminated by shock at S after 5 min. (a) Typical output during 15-min period. (b) First conditioning trial. (c) Conditioned emotional response (*modified from* Hunt & Brady, 1951).

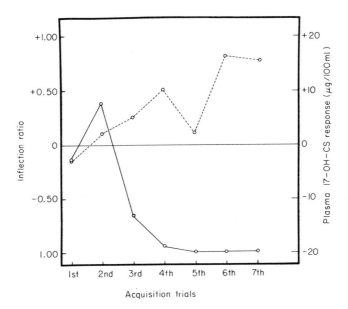

Fig. 3. Changes in plasma 17-OH-CS levels related to emotional conditioning in monkey M-19. Dashed lines are cortico steroid response, solid lines give inflection ratio. The progressive suppression of lever pressing in response to presentation of the auditory stimulus during each successive trial is represented by the lower solid line in terms of an "inflection ratio" which provides a quantitative measure of the conditioned emotional behavior. The upper broken line reflects the progressive increase in 17-OH-CS elevations occurring during each of the seven successive "anxiety" conditioning sessions.

The "inflection ratio" is derived from the formula $(B - A)/A$ in which A represents the number of lever responses emitted during the 5 min immediately preceding introduction of the auditory stimulus, and B represents the number of lever responses emitted during the 5 min presentation of the auditory stimulus. The algebraic sign of the ratio indicates whether output increased (plus) or decreased (minus) during the auditory stimulus, relative to the output during the immediately preceding 5-min interval. The numerical value of the ratio indicates the amount of increase or decrease in output as a fraction (percentage in decimal form) of the output prior to introduction of the auditory stimulus. Complete cessation of lever pressing during the auditory stimulus yields a ratio of -1.00, and a 100% increase a value of $+1.00$. A record showing essentially unchanged output yields a ratio in the neighborhood of 0.00. The ratio thus indicates whether introduction of the conditioned stimulus produced an inflection in the output curve, how much of an inflection it produced, and in which direction (*from* Mason *et al.*, 1966, pp. 227-248. In R. Levine (Ed.) "Endocrines and the Central Nervous System." Copyright, 1966, Williams and Wilkins, Baltimore, Maryland; reprinted by permission).

This relationship between emotional behavior and the activity of the pituitary–adrenal cortical system has been further confirmed in a series of experiments with monkeys in which the conditioned suppression of lever pressing had been previously established. Five such animals were studied during 1-hour lever-pressing sessions for food reward involving alternating 5-min periods of auditory-stimulus presentation and no auditory stimulus, as illustrated in Figure 4. Blood samples, taken before and after several such experiments with each animal, during which no shock followed any of the auditory stimulus presentations, revealed substantial corticosteroid elevations related to the conditioned emotional behavior alone. Figure 5 shows that the rate of this behaviorally induced steroid elevation is strikingly similar to that observed following administration of large doses of ACTH (adrenocorticotrophic hormone) in these animals. Such pituitary–adrenal stimulation, however, appears to cease shortly after termination of the emotional interaction, hormonal levels returning to normal within an hour. When the conditioned "anxiety" response is markedly attenuated by repeated doses of reserpine administered 20-22 hours before experimental sessions, the elevation of 17-OH-CS in response to the auditory stimulus is also eliminated (Mason & Brady, 1956).

THE "HORMONE PATTERN" APPROACH

When measurements of plasma epinephrine and norepinephrine levels were added to the corticosteroid determination in experiments with this conditioned emotional behavior model, the potential contributions of a "hormone pattern" approach to such psychophysiological analyses became evident. Preliminary observations with monkeys in the course of a rather rudimentary conditioning experiment involving a loud truck horn and electric foot shock suggested the differential participation of adrenal medullary systems (epinephrine and norepinephrine) in conditioned and unconditioned aspects of such emotional behavior patterns (Figure 6).

This hormone-pattern approach has been extended in a series of experiments in which concurrent plasma epinephrine, norepinephrine, and 17-OH-CS levels were determined during monkey performance on the alternating 5-min "on," 5-min "off" conditioned anxiety response procedure illustrated in Figure 4. The results summarized in Figure 7 confirm the differential hormone response pattern characterized by marked elevations in both 17-OH-CS and norepinephrine, but little or no change in epinephrine levels.

Observations of autonomic changes related to this same condi-

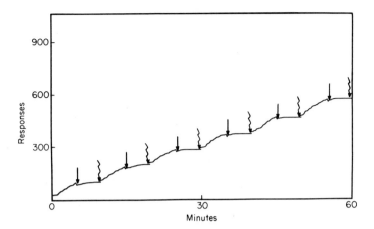

Fig. 4.   Cumulative record of lever pressing with superimposed conditioned "anxiety" response. The straight arrows indicate the onset, and the jagged arrows the termination of each 5-min clicker period. Between clicker periods the lever-pressing response rate is maintained. During clicker presentations, lever pressing is suppressed (*from* Mason et al., 1957).

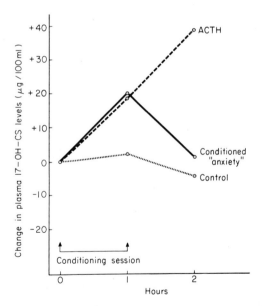

Fig. 5.   Plasma 17-OH-CS response during conditioned "anxiety" sessions (alternating 5-min periods of clicker and no clicker) as compared to control sessions and IV (intravenous) injection of ACTH (16 mg/kg). The values represent average of six monkeys with minimum of one separate observation in each. Note reduction of steroid level in the experimental situation after termination of the stress (*from* Mason et al., 1957).

Joseph V. Brady

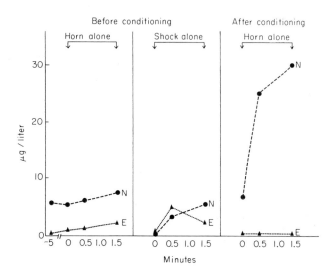

Fig. 6. Plasma norepinephrine (N) and epinephrine (E) responses before and after emotional conditioning in monkey M-9. Exposure to the horn or the shock alone prior to the conditioned pairing of the two produced only mild elevations in catecholamine levels. Following a series of conditioning trials, however, during which horn-sounding for 3 min was terminated contiguously with shock, presentation of the horn alone markedly increased norepinephrine levels without eliciting any epinephrine response (*from* Mason *et al.*, 1966, pp. 227–248. In R. Levine (Ed.) "Endocrines and the Central Nervous System." Copyright, 1966, Williams and Wilkins, Baltimore, Maryland; reprinted by permission).

tioned emotional response model have recently been obtained with a series of monkeys catheterized for cardiovascular measurements (Brady, Kelly, & Plumlee, 1969). Heart rate, and both systolic and diastolic blood pressure were recorded continuously during experimental sessions involving both lever pressing alone and exposure to the conditioned emotion procedure. During a control session prior to emotional behavior conditioning, lever-pressing performance, heart rate, and blood pressure were all stable (Figure 8). By contrast, Figure 9 shows the suppression of performance during clicker stimulation, accompanied by a drop in heart rate and blood pressure.

Significantly, however, continued pairing of clicker and shock superimposed upon the lever-pressing performance produced abrupt reversals in the direction of these autonomic changes. Cardiac acceleration and blood-pressure elevation appeared and persisted in response to the clicker during the later stages of emotional conditioning. Figure 10 shows the sequence of changes in the form of the autonomic responses for an animal in the course of 50 such emotional conditioning trials.

When the conditioned emotional response was extinguished by repeated presentations of clicker alone without shock during daily lever-pressing sessions, with such animals following extended exposure to recurrent emotional conditioning of this type, a further divergence between autonomic and behavioral responses was observed. Figure 11 illustrates this characteristic difference in extinction rates for the cardiovascular and instrumental components of the conditioned emotional response. Although lever-pressing performance in

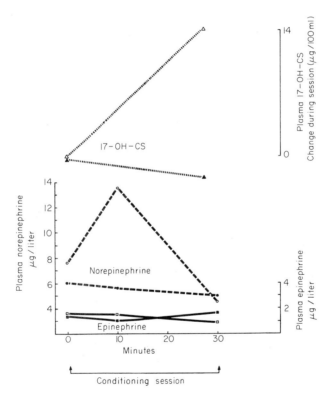

Fig. 7. Mean plasma 17-OH-CS, norepinephrine, and epinephrine levels during conditioned "anxiety" sessions; average values of six monkeys. "Anxiety" sessions indicated by △, ◯, and ☐, normal sessions by ▲, ●, and ■. The blood samples were obtained during 30-min control and experimental sessions. Note the rise in both 17-OH-CS and norepinephrine, in contrast to the negligible change in the levels of epinephrine (*from* Mason *et al.*, 1961c).

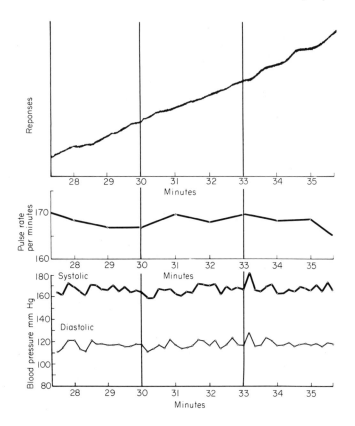

Fig. 8. Lever-pressing performance, heart rate, and blood-pressure values during control session prior to emotional conditioning in monkey 6. These values were obtained during approximately nine minutes of a one-hour control session. The stable lever-pressing performance was accompanied by equally stable heart rate and blood-pressure values throughout the session (*from* Brady, 1967).

the presence of the clicker recovers rapidly, the rapid pulse and pressor response persist for a longer period. Finally, as shown in Figure 12, reconditioning of the emotional response with this same animal rapidly produces behavioral suppression, accompanied immediately by the tachycardic and pressor responses. Significantly, the initial cardiac decelerative response characteristic of the early trials during the original emotional conditioning fails to appear during reconditioning with any of the animals.

THE CONDITIONED AVOIDANCE MODEL

The experimental approaches, thus far described, to the psychophysiological analysis of emotion have emphasized the *suppressive* effects upon behavior of exposure to such conditioning situations. Under certain conditions, however, the arrangements of environmental contingencies involving avoidance of such aversive events can be seen to generate marked increases in the frequency of specific behaviors in response to emotional stress. The conditioned-avoidance model which has provided the basis for extensive experimental analysis in this area has been described in previous reports on the

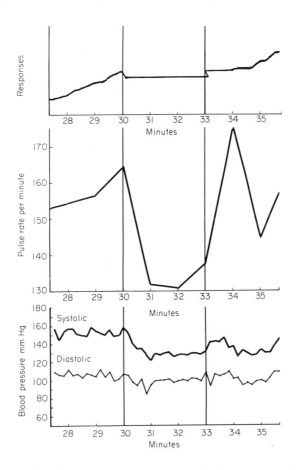

Fig. 9. Changes in lever pressing, heart rate, and blood pressure during conditioned "anxiety" session after emotional conditioning in monkey 6. These results were obtained during an early experimental session following a series of only five conditioning trials involving 3-min presentations of a clicking noise terminated contiguously with foot shock superimposed upon the lever-pressing performance. The complete suppression of lever pressing during clicker presentation is accompanied by a dramatic drop in heart rate accompanied by a somewhat less vigorous blood-pressure decrease (*from* Brady, 1967).

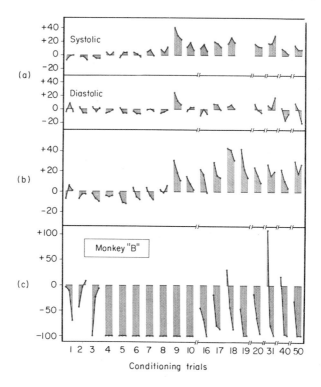

Fig. 10. Minute-by-minute changes in (a) blood pressure (mmHg), (b) heart rate (beats per min), and (c) lever-pressing response rate (percent change) for an animal (monkey "B") on successive 3-min clicker-shock trials during acquisition of the conditioned emotional response. Blood pressure, heart rate, and lever-pressing rate for successive conditioning trials are shown as changes during the 3-min clicker period as compared to baseline values (the 0 point on each graph) representing averages for each measure of the 3-min interval immediately preceding the clicker. The blood-pressure and heart-rate values are shown as absolute changes in millimeters of mercury and beats per minute, respectively. The lever-pressing values are shown as percent changes in response rate during the clicker as compared to the preclicker baseline.

In this animal, development of complete behavioral suppression by Trial 4 is accompanied by the decelerative change in heart rate which appears repeatedly in response to the clicker through Trial 7. Again, only minimal changes in blood pressure could be discerned during these early pairings of clicker and shock. And on Trial 9, the cardiac accelerative response emerged precipitously in response to the clicker, persisting in the form of substantial elevations in both blood pressure and heart rate on succeeding acquisition trials (*from* Brady *et al.*, 1969. Annals of The New York Academy of Sciences, Vol. 159, Art. 3, J. D. Brady, D. Kelly, and L. Plumlee, pp. 959–975. © The New York Academy of Sciences, 1969; reprinted by permission.).

psychophysiology of emotional behavior (Sidman, 1953; Mason *et al.*, 1957; Sidman *et al.*, 1962; Brady, 1965, 1967). Briefly, the basic procedure involves programming shocks to the feet of the monkey in the primate chair every 20 sec unless the animal presses the lever within that interval to postpone the shock another 20 sec. This avoidance requirement generates stable and durable lever-pressing performance, as illustrated in Figure 13. The procedure has been shown to be consistently associated with twofold to fourfold rises in corticosteroid levels for virtually all animals during 2-hour experimental sessions, as shown in Figure 14, even in the absence of any shock (Mason *et al.*, 1957; Brady, 1966, pp. 609–633). It has also been possible to demonstrate quantitative relations between the rate of avoid-

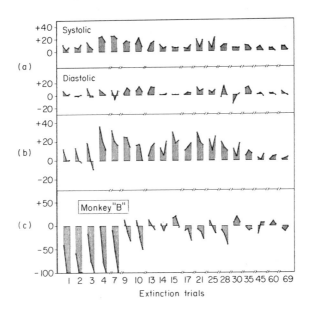

Fig. 11. Extinction of conditioned emotional response. Minute-by-minute changes in (a) blood pressure (mmHg), (b) heart rate (beats per min) and (c) lever-pressing rate (percent change) are shown for same animal (monkey "B") as in Figure 10, on successive 3-min presentations of the clicker alone *without* shock. The zero points represent control values calculated from the 3-min interval immediately preceding the clicker.

Although virtually complete recovery of the lever-pressing rate in the presence of the clicker can be seen to have occurred within 10 such extinction trials, both heart-rate and blood-pressure elevations in response to the clicker alone persisted well beyond the 40th extinction trial (*modified from* Brady *et al.*, 1969. Annals of The New York Academy of Sciences, Vol. 159, Art. 3, J. D. Brady, D. Kelly, and L. Plumlee, pp. 959–975. © The New York Academy of Sciences, 1969; reprinted by permission.).

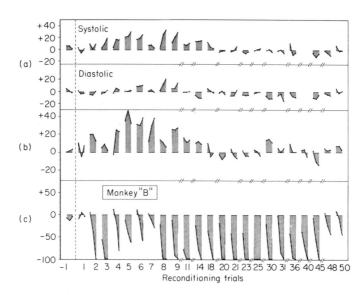

Fig. 12. Reacquisition of the conditioned emotional response. This record is from the same animal (monkey "B") as in Figures 10 and 11. Changes in (a) blood pressure (mmHg), (b) heart rate (beats per min), and (c) lever-pressing response rate (percent change) are shown on the last extinction trial (far-left section), and on successive 3-min clicker-shock trials. The zero points represent control values calculated from the 3-min interval immediately preceding the clicker (*from* Brady *et al.*, 1969. Annals of The New York Academy of Sciences, Vol. 159, Art. 3, J. D. Brady, D. Kelly, and L. Plumlee, pp. 959-975. © The New York Academy of Sciences, 1969; reprinted by permission.).

ance-responding in the monkey and the level of pituitary-adrenal cortical activity independently of the shock frequency (Sidman *et al.*, 1962). Marked differences in the hormone response have been observed, however, when the avoidance procedure includes a discriminable exteroceptive warning signal presented prior to administration of the shock. Figure 15 compares the 17-OH-CS levels in the monkey measured during "regular" and "discriminated" avoidance sessions and shows the consistently reduced corticosteroid response associated with programming such a warning signal. Conversely, superimposing so-called "free" or unavoidable shocks upon a well-established avoidance baseline without a warning signal has been observed to produce marked elevations in 17-OH-CS. Figure 16 shows that the presentation of such "free shocks" more than doubles the corticosteroid response as compared to the regular nondiscriminated avoidance procedure.

Concurrent biochemical measurements of plasma corticosteroid and catecholamine levels have also been made in the course of several avoidance experiments with the monkey. The results confirm the previously described (see Figure 7) emotional stress pattern of 17-OH-CS and norepinephrine elevations, showing no significant alteration in epinephrine levels. Two experimental manipulations involving the avoidance procedure, however, have been observed to produce significant variations in this hormone pattern. In one series of experiments, after removal of the response lever from the restraining chair, there occurred a modest epinephrine elevation with no change in norepinephrine accompanying presentation of the avoidance signal (Figure 17). The results obtained with a second se-

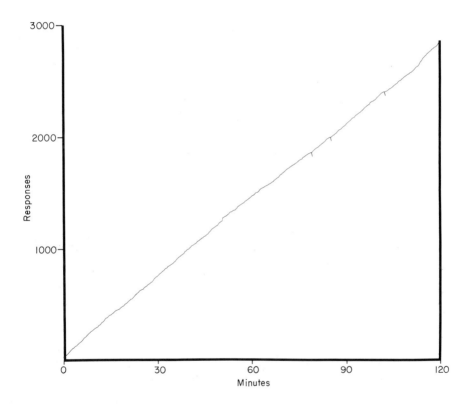

Fig. 13. Cumulative record of avoidance lever pressing in a monkey, showing high, stable rate of approximately 1500 responses per hour. The three small vertical marks on the cumulative record indicate the occurrence of shocks when 20 sec elapsed between lever responses (*from* Mason *et al.*, 1957).

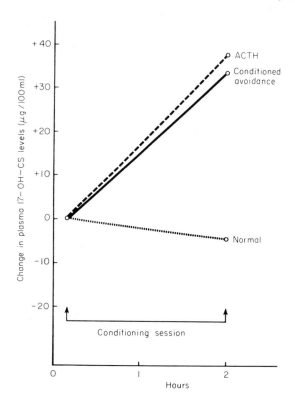

Fig. 14. Changes in plasma 17–OH–CS during 2-hour avoidance performance. The heavy dotted line labeled "ACTH" shows the rate of steroid rise over a 2-hour period following only one I.V. injection of 16 mg/kg ACTH. The heavy solid line labeled "conditioned avoidance" compares the rate of steroid elevation during a 2-hour exposure to the shock avoidance contingency with the ACTH response and the "normal" levels for a similar 2-hour control period represented by the smaller dotted line in the lower portion of the figure (*from* Brady, 1966. In W. Honig (Ed.), "Operant Behavior areas of Research and Application." Copyright, 1966, Appleton-Century-Crofts, New York; reprinted by permission.).

ries of experiments involving such variations in catecholamine levels are illustrated in Figure 18 which shows the effects of "free shock" administration to a monkey at different stages in the course of avoidance training.

In experiments involving more complex sequences of emotional stress patterns in the monkey, it has been possible to observe differential changes in catecholamine levels under specified conditions. Figure 19 summarizes the results obtained in an experiment during which the withdrawal of a blood sample 10 min prior to the start of a session produced marked elevations in both epinephrine and norepinephrine. A similar experiment, illustrated in Figure 20, involved a combination of randomly programmed segments of "time out" (S^A), the shock avoidance procedure described above, and a conditioned "punishment" or "conflict" situation. The latter provided for the production of shock by each lever response emitted in the presence of a specific auditory stimulus. Extremely large epinephrine and norepinephrine responses were again observed during the initial "time out" component prior to the unpredictable onset of a specifically conditioned emotional stress signal. Interestingly, both epinephrine and norepinephrine levels can be seen to decline again

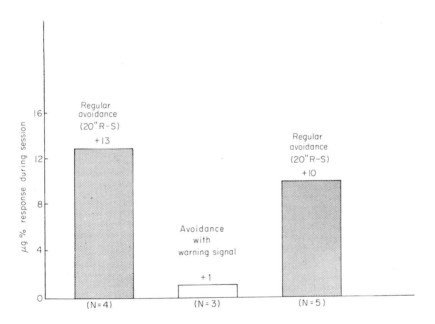

Fig. 15. Plasma 17-OH-CS responses during nondiscriminated ("regular") and discriminated ("warning signal") avoidance sessions. A warning signal was presented 5 sec before the shock whenever 15 sec had elapsed since the previous response. The three histograms are based on sequential observations in monkey M-488; note the reduction in corticosteroid response when a warning signal is given, and the reappearance of the steroid response (see histogram on right) during a subsequent regular avoidance session.

N, number of observations; $R-S$, response-shock interval (*from* Mason *et al.*, 1966, pp. 227-248. In R. Levine (Ed.) "Endocrines and the Central Nervous System." Copyright, 1966, Williams and Wilkins, Baltimore, Maryland; reprinted by permission.).

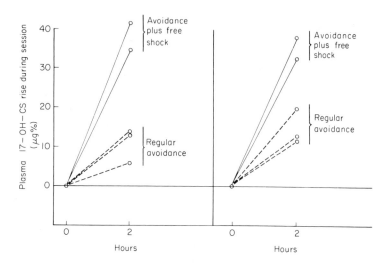

Fig. 16. Plasma 17-OH-CS responses during "regular" nondiscriminated avoidance and during avoidance with "free shocks." Presentation of "free shocks" during 2-hour avoidance sessions markedly increases the corticosteroid response. The consistency of the response from animal to animal is illustrated here by monkeys M-738 and M-734 (*from* Mason *et al.*, 1966, pp. 227–248. In R. Levine (Ed.) "Endocrines and the Central Nervous System." Copyright, 1966, Williams and Wilkins, Baltimore, Maryland; reprinted by permission.).

after presentation of the first specific signal even though in this case it required participation in a shock avoidance task.

Extended exposure to continuous 72-hour avoidance sessions has recently provided the setting for an analysis of a broader spectrum of hormonal changes in relationship to emotional behavior in the rhesus monkey (Mason *et al.*, 1961a, 1961b). The pattern of corticosteroid and pepsinogen changes observed before, during, and after such a continuous 72-hour avoidance experiment is shown in Figure 21. Although plasma 17-OH-CS levels showed the expected substantial elevation throughout the 72-hour avoidance session, plasma pepsinogen levels were consistently depressed below baseline values during this same period. The postavoidance recovery period, however, was seen to have been characterized by a marked and prolonged elevation of pepsinogen levels which endured for several days beyond the 48-hour postavoidance interval required for recovery of the preavoidance corticosteroid baseline. The consequences of repeated exposure to such continuous 72-hour avoidance requirements over extended periods, up to and, in some cases, exceeding one year, upon patterns of thyroid, gonadal, and adrenal hormone secretion have most recently been the focus of studies with a series of five chair-restrained rhesus monkeys. Two of the five monkeys participated in the 72-hour avoidance experiment on six separate occasions over a 6-month period with an interval of approximately 4 weeks intervening between each exposure. The remaining three animals performed on a schedule which repeatedly programmed 72-hour avoidance cycles followed by 96-hour nonavoidance or "rest" cycles (3 days "on" and 4 days "off") for periods up to and exceeding one year.

The two animals exposed to repeated 72-hour avoidance at monthly intervals for 6 months showed a progressively increasing lever-pressing response rate with each of the six successive 72-hour avoidance sessions, as illustrated in Figure 22. During the initial 72-hour avoidance experiment with these two animals, response rates

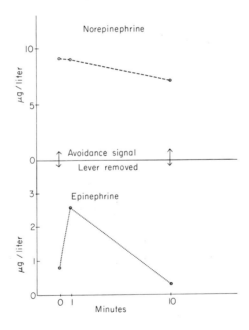

Fig. 17. Plasma epinephrine and norepinephrine levels following removal of the lever during an avoidance session with a well-trained monkey (M-45). Note epinephrine elevation without an associated alteration in norepinephrine. Significantly, the effect occurred within 1 min of the signal presentation and could not be observed following 10 min of continued exposure (*from* Mason *et al.*, 1966, pp. 227–248. In R. Levine (Ed.) "Endocrines and the Central Nervous System." Copyright, 1966, Williams and Wilkins, Baltimore, Maryland; reprinted by permission.).

Joseph V. Brady

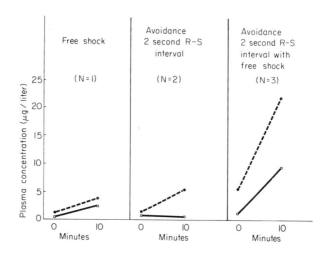

Fig. 18. Plasma epinephrine (—) and norepinephrine (---) responses to "free shock" alone, "regular" nondiscriminated avoidance, and avoidance with "free shock," in monkey M-579. The mild norepinephrine and epinephrine elevations shown at the left side of the figure were obtained during an early conditioning session involving more than 100 "free shocks" before the monkey had acquired the avoidance behavior. The middle section of the figure shows the modest rise in norepinephrine levels with no change in epinephrine which accompanied later experimental sessions involving performance of the well-learned avoidance response. Finally, the right side of the figure shows the results of a series of experiments in which "free" or unavoidable shocks were programmed at the rate of one per minute (approximately the shock frequency occurring during a typical avoidance session) with this same monkey. Significantly, dramatic elevations in both epinephrine and norepinephrine can be seen to have accompanied this procedural change, even though the animal received no more shock than during previous regular avoidance sessions.

N, number of observations for the respective experimental situations; $R–S$, response-shock interval (*from* Mason *et al.*, 1966, pp. 227–248. In R. Levine (Ed.) "Endocrines and the Central Nervous System." Copyright, 1966, Williams and Wilkins, Baltimore, Maryland; reprinted by permission.).

averaged 16 and 18 per min, respectively. Response-rate values for these same monkeys during the sixth 72-hour avoidance experiment averaged 28 and 27 per min, respectively. In contrast, shock frequencies over this same period showed a sharp decline within the first two 72-hour avoidance sessions and remained at a stable low level (not exceeding two shocks per hour for either animal) for the remaining four 72-hour avoidance cycles. Hormone changes related to the repeated 72-hour avoidance cycles showed consistent and replicable patterns over the 6-month experimental period for both animals. During the initial experimental sessions, as shown in Figure 22, both

monkeys showed approximately threefold elevations in 17–OH–CS
levels during 72-hour avoidance and returned to near baseline levels
about 6 days afterwards. The remaining four monthly experiments
were characterized by substantial, though diminished steroid responses (approximately twofold elevations in 17–OH–CS levels)
during avoidance, with essentially the same 6-day period required
for recovery of basal levels. Significant changes related to the extended avoidance performance were also observed in catecholamine,
gonadal, and thyroid hormone levels, with recovery cycles extending
in some instances (thyroid) for 3 weeks following the 72-hour avoidance period.

The three remaining monkeys which performed on the 3 day "on,"
4 days "off" avoidance schedule showed an initial increase in lever-

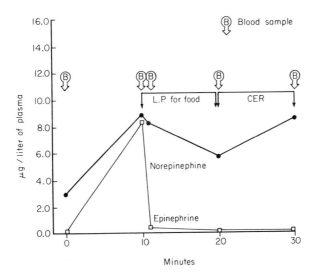

Fig. 19.   Plasma epinephrine and norepinephrine responses to ambiguous blood-
withdrawal signal in monkey M-32. In the course of previous conditioning trials, several different combinations of lever pressing for food alone, clicker–shock pairing
alone, and both lever pressing and clicker–shock pairing concurrently (the conditioned emotional response) had been randomly programmed in such a way that the
blood-withdrawal signal could not be predictably associated with any specific component of the sequence. Under these somewhat ambiguous circumstances both epinephrine and norepinephrine levels rose significantly during the 10 min preceding the
programmed session although epinephrine levels fell precipitously immediately after
presentation of the first specific lever-pressing signal.

L.P., lever pressing; CER, conditioned emotional response (*from* Mason *et al.*,
1961c).

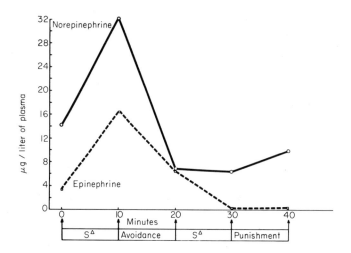

Fig. 20. Plasma epinephrine and norepinephrine responses to randomly programmed components of a multiple-schedule conditioning procedure, consisting of 10 min segments of "time out" (S^Δ), a shock avoidance procedure, and a conditioned punishment or conflict situation. Data based on monkey M-144. Note the marked epinephrine and norepinephrine responses during the initial 10 min "time out" component prior to the onset of the conditioned emotional stress signal (*from* Mason *et al.,* 1961c).

pressing response rates for approximately the first 10 avoidance sessions similar to that seen with the two animals described above. By approximately the 29th weekly session with these animals, however, lever-pressing response rates during the 72-hour avoidance period had decreased to a value well below that observed during the initial avoidance sessions, and the performance tended to stabilize at this new low level for the ensuing weeks of the experiment. In contrast, shock frequencies for all animals quickly approximated a stable low level within the first two or three exposures to the avoidance schedule and seldom exceeded a rate of 2 shocks per hour for the remainder of the experiment.

The typical pattern, exemplified by monkey M-157, is illustrated in Figure 23. The initial 72-hour avoidance sessions were characterized by progressive increases in lever-pressing and elevations in 17-OH-CS levels. In the succeeding weeks, 17-OH-CS levels gradually declined but rose again by the 30th week.

The general pattern obtained with M-157 has been replicated with only minor variations in the two additional animals completing 56 and 46 weeks, respectively, on this same experimental program. The change in responsivity of the pituitary–adrenal system to the avoidance stress with continued exposure to this procedure over extended time periods is perhaps the most consistent and striking observation in all three monkeys. This is somewhat at variance with the repeated finding in many previous acute studies of a close positive relationship between steroid elevations and avoidance performance. These recent findings, however, indicate that continued exposure to this repeated performance requirement on the time schedule programmed in this experiment, produces an apparent dissociation between the avoidance performance and the 17–OH–CS response. Al-

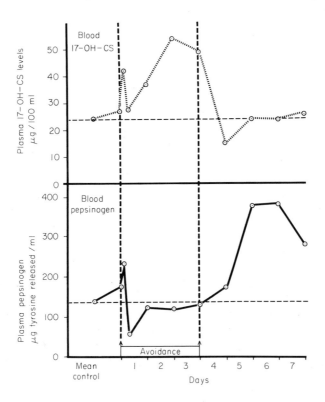

Fig. 21. Mean blood levels of 17–OH–CS and pepsinogen during 72-hour continuous avoidance sessions. (Plasma pepsinogen level is expressed in terms of μg tyrosine released per ml.) The level of 17–OH–CS was elevated while that of pepsinogen was decreased. Note the reversal in their respective levels during the postavoidance recovery period (*from* Mason *et al.*, 1961a, *Science* 133, 1596–1598. Copyright 1961 by the American Association for the Advancement of Science.).

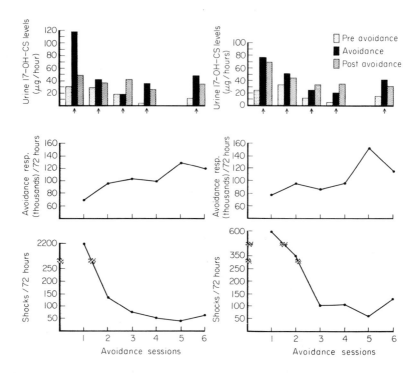

Fig. 22. Steroid levels, avoidance response rates, and shock frequencies for monkeys M-736 and M-77, respectively, during six monthly 72-hour avoidance sessions. The vertical arrows in the upper third of the figure direct attention to the respective avoidance histograms, in contrast to the pre- and postavoidance values. See text for discussion (*from* Brady, 1965).

though a definitive analysis of such relationship is not possible on the basis of these data alone, a critical role of the temporal parameters (work-rest cycles) is clearly indicated. Certainly, related findings on the course of recovery for a broad range of hormone measures presently being pursued provide additional support for this focus upon temporal factors in the psychophysiological analysis of emotion.

SUMMARY AND CONCLUSIONS

The results of these experiments establish firm relationships between a broad range of autonomic-endocrine system activity and behavioral interactions involving various aspects of emotion. The initial findings emphasizing changes in absolute levels of selected hor-

mones can be viewed as reflecting relatively undifferentiated consequences of arousal states associated with such emotion-inducing
situations. The definite temporal course of visceral and steroid
changes under such conditions and the quantitative nature of the relationship between degree of behavioral involvement and level of
physiological response has been well documented. In addition, the

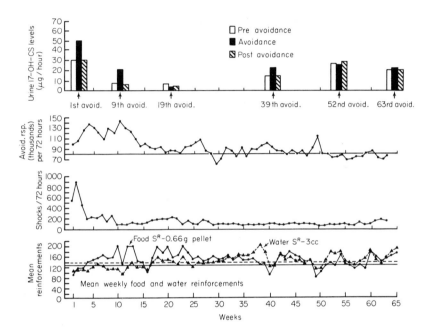

Fig. 23.   Steroid levels, avoidance response rates, shock frequencies, and food and
water intake levels for monkey M-157 throughout 65 weekly 72-hour avoidance sessions. There was an average response rate of 23 resp/min during the initial 72-hour
avoidance session, 32 resp/min during the 10th avoidance session, 19 resp/min during
the 20th avoidance session, and 16 resp/min, 20 resp/min, and 19 resp/min during the
30th, 40th, and 50th weekly avoidance sessions, respectively. The initial 72-hour
avoidance sessions characterized by progressive increases in lever-pressing rate were
invariably accompanied by elevations in the 17-OH-CS levels. By the 20th weekly
avoidance-rest cycle, however, steroid levels had dropped below initial basal values,
and no elevation in response to the 72-hour avoidance performance could be observed. By the 30th weekly session, 17-OH-CS levels had returned to their preexperi-
mental basal values but continued exposure to the 3-day "on," 4-day "off" schedule
failed to produce any further steroid elevation in response to the 72-hour avoidance
requirement up through the 65th experimental session. Note also that, following initial adjustments during the early sessions of the program, shock frequencies remained
at a stable low level and normal food and water intake was maintained essentially
unchanged throughout the extended course of the experiment (*from* Brady, 1965).

critical role of an organism's behavioral history in determining the
nature and extent of autonomic-endocrine response to emotional situations has been convincingly demonstrated.

Clearly, however, the most meaningful dimension for hormone
and visceral analysis in relationship to more chronic emotional interactions would appear to be the broader patterning or balance of se-
cretory and visceral change in many interdependent autonomic and
endocrine systems which in concert regulate metabolic events. The
extensive and prolonged participation of these fundamental systems
in behavioral interactions suggests a relationship between such
physiological activity and the more durable consequences of emotion
involving generalized mood states and affective dispositions. Indeed,
the differentiation of such autonomic-endocrine response patterns in
relationship to the historical and situational aspects of behavioral
events may well provide a first approximate step in the direction of
identifying distinguishable intraorganismic consequences associated
with both episodic and persistent emotional interactions.

REFERENCES

Ader, R., & Friedman, S. B. Psychological factors and susceptibility to disease in animals. *Medical aspects of stress in the military climate.* Washington, D. C.: Government Printing Office, 1965.
Ader, R., & Plaut, S. M. Effects of prenatal maternal handling and differential housing
  on offsprings' emotionality, plasma corticosterone levels, and susceptibility to gastric erosions. *Psychosomatic Medicine,* 1968, **30**, 277-286.
Berlanger, D., & Feldman, S. Effects of water deprivation upon heart rate and instrumental activity in the rat. *Journal of Comparative and Physiological Psychology,*
  1962, **55**, 220-225.
Brady, J. V. Further comments on the gastrointestinal system and avoidance behavior.
  Psychological Report, 1963, **12**, 742.
Brady, J. V. Experimental studies of psychophysiological responses to stressful situa-
  tions. *Symposium on the Medical Aspects of Stress in the Military Climate, 1965,*
  pp. 271-289. Washington, D. C.: Government Printing Office, 1965.
Brady, J. V. Operant methodology and the production of altered physiological states.
  In W. Honig (Ed.), *Operant behavior areas of research and application.* New York:
  Appleton, 1966.
Brady, J. V. Emotion and the sensitivity of the psychoendocrine systems. In D. Glass
  (Ed.), *Neurophysiology and emotion. Proceedings of a Conference on Biology and
  Behavior, 1967,* pp. 70-95. New York: The Rockfeller University Press and Russell
  Sage Foundation, 1967.
Brady, J. V., Kelly, D., & Plumlee, L. Autonomic and behavioral responses of the
  rhesus monkey to emotional conditioning. *Annals of the New York Academy of Sci-
  ences,* 1969, **159**, 959-975.

Brady, J. V., & Polish, E. Performance changes during prolonged avoidance. *Psychological Reports*, 1960, **7**, 554.

Brady, J. V., Porter, R. W., Conrad, D. G., & Mason, J. W. Avoidance behavior and the development of gastroduodenal ulcers. *Journal of the Experimental Analysis of Behavior*, 1958, **1**, 69-72.

Brush, F. R., & Levine, S. Adrenocortical activity and avoidance learning as a function of time after fear conditioning. *Physiology and Behavior*, 1966, **1**, 309-311.

Cannon, W. B. *Bodily changes in pain, hunger, fear, and rage.* New York: Appleton, 1915.

Clark, R., & Polish, E. Avoidance conditioning and alcohol consumption in rhesus monkeys. *Science*, 1960, **132**, 223-224.

Conger, J. J., Sawrey, W. L., & Turrell, E. S. The role of social experience in the production of gastric ulcers in hooded rats placed in a conflict situation. *Journal of Comparative and Physiological Psychology*, 1958, **51**, 214-220.

DeToledo, L., & Black, A. H. Heart rate: Changes during conditioned suppression in rats. *Science*, 1966, **152**, 1404-1406.

Eldridge, L. Respiration rate change and its relation to avoidance behavior. Unpublished doctoral dissertation, Columbia University, 1954.

Estes, W. K., & Skinner, B. F. Some quantitative properties of anxiety. *Journal of Experimental Psychology*, 1941, **29**, 390-400.

Gantt, W. H. *Experimental basis of neurotic behavior.* New York: Harper (Hoeber), 1944.

Gantt, W. H. Cardiovascular component of the conditional reflex to pain, food and other stimuli. *Physiological Review*, 1960, **40**, 266-291.

Hahn, W. W., Stern, J. A., & McDonald, D. G. Effects of water deprivation and bar-pressing activity on heart rate of the male albino rat. *Journal of Comparative and Physiological Psychology*, 1962, **55**, 786-790.

Harwood, C. T., & Mason, J. W. A systematic evaluation of the Nelson-Samuels plasma 17-hydroxycorticosteroid method. *Journal of Clinical Endocrinology*, 1956, **16**, 790-800.

Hearst, E., Beer, B., Sheatz, G., & Galambos, R. Some electrophysiological correlates of conditioning in the monkey. *Electroencephalography and Clinical Neurophysiology*, 1960, **12**, 137-152.

Hunt, H. F., & Brady, J. V. Some effects of electro-convulsive shock on a conditioned emotional response ("anxiety"). *Journal of Comparative and Physiological Psychology*, 1951, **44**, 88-98.

John, E. R., & Killam, K. F. Electrophysiological correlates of avoidance conditioning in the cat. *Journal of Pharmacology and Experimental Therapeutics*, 1959, **125**, 252-274.

Lacey, J. I. The evaluation of autonomic responses: Toward a general solution. *Annals of the New York Academy of Sciences*, 1956, **67**, 123-164.

Levine, S., & Treiman, D. M. Differential plasma corticosterone response to stress in four inbred strains of mice. *Endocrinology*, 1964, **75**, 142-144.

Liddel, H. S. *Emotional hazard in animals and man.* Springfield, Ill.: Thomas, 1956.

Mahl, G. F. Effect of chronic fear on gastric secretion of HCL in dogs. *Psychosomatic Medicine*, 1949, **11**, 30.

Mahl, G. F. Relationship between acute and chronic fear and the gastric acidity and blood sugar levels in macaca mulatta monkeys. *Psychosomatic Medicine*, 1952, **14**, 182-210.

Malmo, R. B. Experimental studies of mental patients under stress. In M. L. Reymert (Ed.), *Feelings and emotions.* New York: McGraw-Hill, 1950.

Malmo, R. B. Slowing of heart rate after septal self-stimulation in rats. *Science,* 1961, 133, 1129.

Mason, J. W. Restraining chair for the experimental study of primates. *Journal of Applied Physiology,* 1958, 12, 130-133.

Mason, J. W., & Brady, J. V. Plasma 17-hydroxycorticosteroid changes related to reserpine effects on emotional behavior. *Science,* 1956, 124, 983-984.

Mason, J. W., Brady, J. V., Polish, E., Bauer, J. A., Robinson, J. A., Rose, R. M., & Taylor, E. D. Patterns of corticosteroid and pepsinogen change related to emotional stress in the monkey. *Science,* 1961, 133, 1596-1598. (a)

Mason, J. W., Brady, J. V., Robinson, J. A., Taylor, E. D., Tolson, W. W., & Mougey, E. H. Patterns of thyroid, gonadal and adrenal hormone secretion related to psychological stress in the monkey. *Psychosomatic Medicine,* 1961, 23, 446. (b)

Mason, J. W., Brady, J. V., & Sidman, M. Plasma 17-hydroxycorticosteroid levels and conditioned behavior in the rhesus monkey. *Endocrinology,* 1957, 60, 741-752.

Mason, J. W., Brady, J. V., & Tolson, W. W. Behavioral adaptations and endocrine activity. In R. Levine (Ed.), *Endocrines and the central nervous system.* Vol. 43. Baltimore: Williams & Wilkins, 1966.

Mason, J. W., Mangan, G., Brady, J. V., Conrad, D., & Rioch, D. McK. Concurrent plasma epinephrine, norepinephrine and 17-hydroxycorticosteroid levels during conditioned emotional disturbances in monkeys. *Psychosomatic Medicine,* 1961, 23, 344-353. (c)

Pavlov, I. P. Uber die normalen blutdruckschwandungen beim hunde. *Archiv fuer die Gesamte Physiologie des Menschen und der Tiere,* 1879, 20, 215.

Perez-Cruet, J., Black, W. C., & Brady, J. V. Heart rate: Differential effects of hypothalamic and septal self-stimulation. *Science,* 1963, 140, 1235-1236.

Perez-Cruet, J., Tolliver, G., Dunn, G., Marvin, S., & Brady, J. V. Concurrent measurement of heart rate and instrumental avoidance behavior in the rhesus monkey. *Journal of the Experimental Analysis of Behavior,* 1963, 6, 61-64.

Polish, E., Brady, J. V., Mason, J. W., Thach, J. S., & Niemeck, W. Gastric contents and the occurrence of duodenal lesions in the rhesus monkey during avoidance behavior. *Gastroenterology,* 1962, 43, 193-201.

Porter, R. W., Brady, J. V., Conrad, D., Mason, J. W., Galambos, R., & Rioch, D. McK. Some experimental observations on gastrointestinal lesions in behaviorally conditioned monkeys. *Psychosomatic Medicine,* 1958, 20, 379-394.

Porter, R. W., Conrad, D. G., & Brady, J. V. Some neural and behavioral correlates of electrical self-stimulation of the limbic system. *Journal of the Experimental Analysis of Behavior,* 1959, 2, 43-55.

Rasmussen, A. J., Marsh, J. T., & Brill, N. Q. Increased susceptibility to Herpes Simplex in mice subjected to avoidance-learning stress or restraint. *Proceedings of the Society for Experimental Biology and Medicine,* 1957, 96, 183-189.

Ross, G. S., Hodos, W., & Brady, J. V. Electroencephalographic correlates of temporally spaced responding and avoidance behavior. *Journal of the Experimental Analysis of Behavior,* 1962, 5, 467-472.

Sawrey, W. L. Conditioned responses of fear in relationship to ulceration. *Journal of Comparative and Physiological Psychology,* 1961, 54, 347-348.

Sawrey, W. L., Conger, J. J., & Turrell, E. S. An experimental investigation of the role of psychological factors in the production of gastric ulcers in rats. *Journal of Comparative and Physiological Psychology,* 1956, 49, 457-461.

Sawrey, W. J., and Weisz, J. D. An experimental method of producing gastric ulcers. *Journal of Comparative and Physiological Psychology,* 1956, **49,** 269-270.

Shapiro, A. P., & Horn, P. W. Blood pressure, plasma pepsinogen, and behavior in cats subjected to experimental production of anxiety. *Journal of Nervous and Mental Disease,* 1955, **122,** 222-231.

Sidman, M. Avoidance conditioning with brief shock and no exteroceptive warning signal. *Science,* 1953, **118,** 157-158.

Sidman, M., Mason, J. W., Brady, J. V., & Thach, J. Quantitative relations between avoidance behavior and pituitary-adrenal cortical activity. *Journal of the Experimental Analysis of Behavior,* 1962, **5,** 353-362.

Stebbins, W. C., & Smith, O. A. Cardiovascular concomitants of the conditioned emotional response in the monkey. *Science.* 1964, **144,** 881-883.

Weisz, J. D. The etiology of experimental gastric ulceration. *Psychosomatic Medicine,* 1957, **19,** 61-73.

Wenzel, B. M. Changes in heart rate associated with responses based on positive and negative reinforcement. *Journal of Comparative and Physiological Psychology,* 1961, **42,** 638-644.

Williams, D. R., & Teitelbaum, P. Control of drinking behavior by means of an operant conditioning technique. *Science.* 1956, **124,** 1294-1296.

4

NEUROPHYSIOLOGICAL CORRELATES

7

THE LIMBIC BRAIN IN RELATION TO THE PSYCHOSES

Paul D. MacLean

Rather than adhere strictly to my assigned topic of the relation of the limbic system to emotion, I thought it would be opportune to take a side trip to one of the frontier regions of the brain to explore some volcanic terrain. The purpose in going there is to sound out the possibility that rumblings in the hippocampal portion of the limbic brain may cause certain types of upheaval in the endogenous and toxic psychoses. In particular we shall want to explore the possibility that eruptions in this part of the brain may give rise to (a) disturbances of emotion and mood, (b) feelings of depersonalization, (c) distortions of perception, and (d) paranoid symptoms.

The timeliness of this expedition will be apparent when we stop by the way to examine some of the chemical properties of the limbic brain in the light of speculations about disorders of catechol and serotonin metabolism in the genesis of the psychoses. The timeliness is further brought home by the alarming, popular use of psychedelic drugs and the realization that these hallucinogenic agents may precipitate psychoses. These drugs, among their other possible actions, interfere with the metabolism of the cerebral amines, and single doses of lysergic acid diethylamide (LSD) have been said to precipitate recurring psychotic symptoms in individuals showing no evidence of a prepsychotic personality.

MAN'S CEREBRAL INHERITANCE

Our starting point will be two hundred million years ago in the Age of Reptiles. Perhaps the most revealing thing about the study of man's brain is that he has inherited the structure and organization of three basic cerebral types which for purposes of discussion may be referred to as *reptilian, old mammalian,* and *new mammalian* (MacLean, 1962, 1964). Despite great differences in structure and chemistry, all three brains must intermesh and function together. The hierarchy of the three brains is schematically shown in Figure 1. Man's brain of oldest heritage is basically reptilian. It forms the matrix of the upper brainstem and comprises much of the reticular system, midbrain, and basal ganglia. The reptilian brain is characterized by greatly enlarged striatal structures which resemble the *corpus striatum* of mammals.

But in contrast to mammals there is only an incipient cortex. A

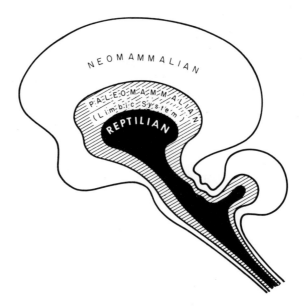

Fig. 1. Scheme of hierarchic organization of the three basic brain types which, in the evolution of the mammalian brain, become part of man's inheritance. They are referred to here as the reptilian, paleomammalian, and neomammalian brains. Man's counterpart of the old mammalian comprises the so-called limbic system (MacLean, 1952) or limbic brain, which has been found to play an important role in emotional behavior (*from* MacLean. Journal of Nervous and Mental Disease, © 1967, The William and Wilkins Co., Baltimore, Maryland, 21202, U.S.A.; reprinted by permission.).

well-developed cortex is a typically mammalian feature. The evolving old mammalian brain is distinctive because of marked expansion and a differentiation of the primitive cortex, which, as we will explain in a moment, is synonymous with the limbic cortex. Finally, there appears late in evolution a more highly differentiated type of cortex called neocortex which is the hallmark of higher mammals and which culminates in man to become the brain of reading, writing, and arithmetic.

In the popular language of today, the reptilian and the old and new mammalian brains might be regarded as biological computers, each with its own subjective, gnostic, time-measuring, memory, motor, and other functions.[1] On the basis of behavioral observations of ethologists, there are indications that the reptilian brain "programs" stereotyped behaviors according to instructions based on ancestral learning and ancestral memories. In other words, it seems to play a role in such instinctually determined functions as establishing territory, finding shelter, hunting, homing, mating, breeding, imprinting, forming social hierarchies, selecting leaders, and the like. It seems to be a brain that is in love with precedent. It would be interesting to know to what extent the reptilian counterpart of man's brain determines his obeisance to precedent in ceremonial rituals, legal actions, political persuasions, and religious convictions. In his essay on the pleasure principle, Freud (1922) mentions over and over again man's "compulsion to repeat." Obeisance to precedent is the first step to obsessive compulsive behavior, and this is well illustrated by the turtle's always returning to the same place year after year to lay its eggs. Indeed, in many of its actions it was as though the reptilian brain was neurosis-bound by an "ancestral superego." At all events it appears to have inadequate machinery for learning to cope with new situations.

The evolutionary development in lower mammals of a respectable cortex might be regarded as Nature's attempt to provide the reptilian brain with a "thinking cap" and emancipate it from stereotyped behavior. In all mammals most of the primitive cortex is found in a large convolution which Broca (1878) called the limbic lobe because it surrounds the brainstem. (Limbic means "forming a border around.") From the standpoint of behavioral implications it is significant that this lobe, as shown in Figure 2, is found as a common denominator in the brains of all mammals. The evolutionary stability of this old brain contrasts with the mushrooming of the neocortex

[1]The wording of this and the following paragraph is taken from my Salmon Lectures (MacLean, 1966b).

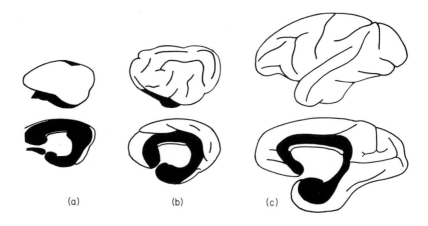

Fig. 2. As illustrated by these drawings showing the relative sizes of the rabbit (a), cat (b), and monkey (c) brains, the limbic lobe (represented in black) is found as a common denominator in the brains of all mammals. For each species, the upper drawing represents the lateral view, and the lower drawing the medial view. The enveloping cortex shown in white represents the neocortex which mushrooms late in phylogeny (*from* MacLean, 1954a, pp. 101-125).

which culminates in man and gives him the unique power of a written and spoken language.

Because of its close relationship to the olfactory apparatus, the old mammalian brain was formerly believed to subserve purely olfactory functions and was accordingly referred to in many texts as the rhinencephalon. Papez's famous paper of 1937 struck a mortal blow to this line of thinking. Since then, extensive investigation has shown that, in addition to olfactory functions, this brain plays an important role in viscerosomatic activity and in elaborating emotions that guide behavior with respect to the two basic life principles of self-preservation and the preservation of the species (for reviews see MacLean, 1949, 1958). In 1952 I suggested the term "limbic system" as a suitable designation for the limbic cortex and structures of the brainstem with which it has primary connections (MacLean, 1952).

It should be emphasized that the limbic cortex has similar features in all mammals and is structurally primitive compared with the neocortex. From this it might be inferred that it continues to function at an animalistic level in man as in animals. Also, in marked contrast to the neocortex, it has strong connections with the hypothalamus which plays a basic role in integrating emotional expression and viscerosomatic behavior.

SUMMARY OF LIMBIC ANATOMY AND FUNCTIONS

Our expedition to the volcanic terrain of the psychoses will be more meaningful if we pause briefly to summarize some of the anatomy and functions of the limbic brain. This is most easily done by reference to an anatomical diagram of pathways linking three main subdivisions of the limbic system. Figure 3 focuses on three branching pathways connecting the ring of limbic cortex with the hypothalamus and other parts of the brainstem. The two upper branches of the medial forebrain bundle meet with descending fibers from the olfactory apparatus and feed into the lower and upper halves of the ring through the amygdala and the septum at the points marked 1 and 2. The third large pathway, branching lower down

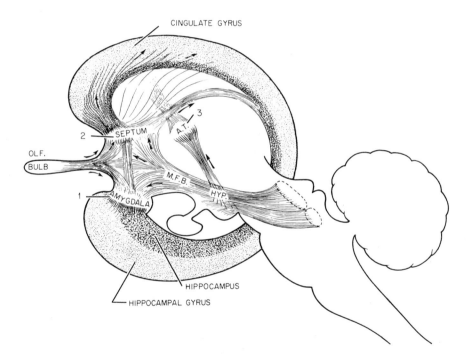

Fig. 3. Diagram of pathways connecting three main subdivisions of the limbic system. The ring of limbic cortex is shown in light and dark stipple. The two subdivisions connected with the amygdala and septum, respectively, are intimately related to the olfactory apparatus. The pathway linking the third subdivision largely bypasses the olfactory apparatus. See text for implications. A.T., anterior thalamic nuclei; M.F.B., medial forebrain bundle; HYP., hypothalamus (*modified from* MacLean, 1957).

from the hypothalamus, largely bypasses the olfactory apparatus. It leads to the anterior and medial thalamus and from there to the large cingulate gyrus in the upper half of the ring.

Clinical and experimental findings suggest that the lower part of the ring fed by the amygdala is primarily concerned with feelings, emotions, and behavior that insure self-preservation. Its circuits are kept busy with the selfish demands of feeding, fighting, and self-protection.

In contrast, structures in the upper part of the ring connected with the septal pathway appear to be involved in expressive and feeling states that are conducive to sociability, procreation, and the preservation of the species. In male cats, for example, stimulation in parts of this circuit results in pleasure and grooming and sexual reactions seen in courtship behavior. We have found in the monkey that the medial septal preoptic region is a nodal point for penile erection (for review see MacLean, 1962).

The intimate organization of these two subdivisions involved in oral and genital functions is presumably attributable to the olfactory sense, which, dating far back in evolution, plays an important role in both feeding and mating. The persistence of this antique relationship in mammals makes it understandable that excitation in one region readily spills over into the other so that sexual excitation may result in reflex mouthing, biting, and vice versa.

It is relevant to sadomasochistic behavior that pathways for oral and genital functions funnel into that same part of the hypothalamus that Hess (1943) and others have found to be central for angry and other forms of agonistic behavior. As fighting is frequently a preliminary to mating as well as feeding, the findings suggest that Nature uses the same neural mechanisms for combat in both situations (cf. MacLean, 1964).

We will now direct our attention to the third pathway, shown in Figure 3, which bypasses the olfactory apparatus. This pathway which is virtually nonexistent in reptiles becomes progressively larger in the evolution of primates and reaches its greatest size in man. There is some evidence that this reflects a shifting of emphasis from olfactory to visual influences in sociosexual behavior (MacLean, 1962, 1968b, pp. 24–34). Significantly, in this respect, stimulation within parts of this circuit, as in the septal circuit, elicits sexual responses in monkeys.

Finally, we will pause to note that this third subdivision of the limbic system establishes connections with the prefrontal cortex, an evolutionary new formation of the brain that culminates in man. Clinical analysis of cases with frontal lesions suggests that the prefrontal cortex is instrumental in providing the combination of insight and foresight that is required for promoting both our own welfare and the welfare of others.

In terms of mass, the third subdivision of the limbic system is much larger than the first subdivision which serves to insure survival of the individual. As witness the high survival rate of the opossum and the rabbit right in the middle of our highly populated suburban areas, it requires relatively little brain to insure self-preservation. On the contrary, it involves an enormous expansion of the brain to achieve the highly cultivated society of man. It is possible that the principle of reciprocal innervation applies to subdivisions of the brain respectively concerned with self-preservation and the preservation of the species. If so, it would suggest that it would be therapeutically helpful to encourage patients to develop an altruistic concern and feeling of responsibility for others. With a shift of neural traffic from the first to the third subdivision, one might expect a reciprocal inhibition of neural mechanisms involved in selfish concerns and fears for oneself.

That the limbic brain is a functionally, as well as an anatomically, integrated system is convincingly demonstrated by mapping the propagation of hippocampal seizure discharges. If one of these discharges is elicited by electrical stimulation of the hippocampus it has the tendency to spread throughout and be confined to the limbic system. The impulses of the discharging neurons might be imagined as stampeding bulls which do not jump the fence and leave the corral of the limbic system (cf. MacLean, 1958). Nothing brings home so dramatically the functional dichotomy, or schizophysiology as it has been called (MacLean, 1954b, 1958), of the limbic and neocortical systems. As regards this dichotomy of function it is significant that patients with smoldering limbic epilepsy may manifest the various symptoms of schizophrenia.

NEUROCHEMICAL DISTINCTIONS

Before moving on into the psychotic area, however, we should interrupt our metaphorical expedition to look at a number of chemical differences which, like the anatomical and physiological distinctions already mentioned, serve to distinguish the old mammalian from the reptilian and new mammalian brains. The Vogts (1953) in documenting the topistic theory, cited several conditions suggestive of a distinctive chemistry of different parts of the hippocampus. Additional studies have served to emphasize distinctive chemical properties of the hippocampal formation. It has been found, for example, that dithizone, a chelating agent (i.e., a heavy-metal binder) for zinc, strongly stains the mossy fiber system (McLardy, 1962; Euler, 1962), giving a deep red color to the region of CA4 and CA3 of the hippocampus (Maske, 1955; Fleischhauer & Horstmann, 1957). The chemical, 3-acetylpyridine, an antimetabolite of the antipellagra vitamin niacin, may selectively destroy the neurons of this same region (Coggeshall & MacLean, 1958; Niklowitz, Bak, & Hassler, 1964). Radioautographic studies have shown an unusually high uptake of methionine in the hippocampal formation and other limbic areas (Flanigan, Gabrieli, & MacLean, 1957). There are indications that testosterone is bound to cells of the hippocampal formation, suggesting that these neurons may serve as receptors for gonadal hormones (Altman & Gopal, 1965). And then as regards the amines, serotonin has been found in relatively high concentration in the gray matter of the hippocampus (Paasonen, MacLean, & Giarman, 1957), while radioautographic (Csillik & Erulkar, 1964; Reivich & Glowinski, 1967) and fluorescent (Fuxe, 1965) studies have detected a notable concentration of noradrenalin in the radiate layer of the hippocampus. These findings are of special interest in view of evidence that tranquilizing and psychotropic drugs known to affect the metabolism of serotonin and the catechols appear to have some predilection of action on hippocampal function as revealed by changes in the EEG (electroencephalogram) (e.g., Killam, Killam, & Thomason, 1957; MacLean, Flanigan, Flynn, Kim, & Stevens, 1955). Finally, studies employing the Koelle stain have indicated that the main afferent pathways to the hippocampus are "cholinergic" in type (Shute & Lewis, 1961). The apparent presence of cholinergic and adrenergic fibers in the limbic system suggests a certain parallel with the peripheral autonomic nervous system.

These considerations recall that the three major classes of psychotomimetic drugs are (a) substituted indole alkylamines, (b) substituted phenylalkylamines, and (c) agents interfering with cholinergic mechanisms (cf. Cohen, 1967). In LSD, dimethyltryptamine, bufotenine, psilocybin and harmine, one sees the indole nucleus of serotonin. In mescaline, one sees the phenyl nucleus of the catechols such as noradrenaline. Denckla (1968) has made the interesting observation that for every tranquilizer there is a compound with a similar structure that has an hallucinogenic action.

PSYCHOTIC MANIFESTATIONS OF LIMBIC DYSFUNCTION IN MAN

Case histories of psychomotor epilepsy provide crucial evidence that the limbic cortex is implicated in the generation of emotional states, as well as symptoms of a psychotic nature. Irritative lesions in or near the limbic cortex in the lower part of the ring (cf. Figure 3) give rise to epileptic discharges accompanied by emotional feelings that under ordinary conditions are important for survival. Among these are feelings of terror, fear, foreboding, familiarity, strangeness, unreality, wanting to be alone, sadness, and feelings of a paranoid nature.

Discharges in or near the basal limbic cortex may also result in feelings of depersonalization—comparable to what Hughlings Jackson (1899) called "mental diplopia"—in which the individual feels as if he is viewing himself and what is going on from a distance, a symptom so common in individuals taking psychedelic drugs.

There may also be distortions of perception, again reminding one of the endogenous and toxic psychoses. Knowledge about the correlation of the site of the lesion and the symptomotology has been advanced particularly by Penfield and Jasper (1954) in their operative studies. They have observed that similar symptoms may occur either with the epileptic discharge or with local electrical stimulation. Objects may appear large or small, near or far; sounds may seem loud or faint; one's tongue, lips and extremities may seem swollen to large proportions. Time may appear to speed up or slow down, and so forth. Individuals suffering from "return trips" after LSD commonly experience such distortions of perception.

The interseizure symptomotology of some patients with limbic epilepsy may be indistinguishable from that of paranoid schizophrenia. One such patient, for example, was continually obsessed by the feeling that God was punishing her for overeating. While she was expressing such thoughts, the basal electroencephalogram showed random spiking at the site of the tympanic electrode underneath the temporal lobe (personal observation). Malamud (1966) has emphasized the high incidence of medial temporal sclerosis in cases of psychomotor epilepsy and has stated that sclerosis of the hippocampus is a common denominator of this condition. On the basis of clinical and experimental findings it is probable that in limbic epilepsy the hippocampus is nearly always involved in the seizure discharge, with the discharge either arising within it or spreading to it secondarily from other structures.

RELEVANT EXPERIMENTAL FINDINGS

Before describing some experimental observations relevant to neural mechanisms underlying psychotic symptoms let me emphasize that I am not implying that schizophrenia or other types of psychosis represent a form of epilepsy. Rather, I am placing emphasis on the study of psychomotor epilepsy as a means of learning what parts of the brain may be responsible for some of the symptomotology seen in the psychoses. Of all the clinical entities there is perhaps none that has a greater potentiality for shedding light on mechanisms underlying psychic functions in man than psychomotor or limbic epilepsy.

It is obvious that in dealing with such questions as depersonalization, one must depend solely on subjective reports of patients, but there are some psychotic manifestations concerning which animal experimentation is helpful in elucidating the underlying neural mechanisms.

DISTURBANCES OF EMOTION AND MOOD

Some experimental observations are pertinent to the question of disturbances of emotion and mood in the psychoses. Sometimes in the wake of afterdischarges induced by stimulation in the amygdaloid-hippocampal region, a cat may be in an agitated state for several minutes, meowing, running around the room and trying to climb the walls (MacLean, 1959, p. 47). In contrast, following afterdischarges induced by stimulating the caudal hippocampus there may be enhanced grooming, pleasure, and sexual reactions that may persist for several minutes (MacLean, 1957). After stimulations of limbic nuclei that induce penile erection and hippocampal afterdischarges, aggressive monkeys may become placid and tame, and these apparent changes in mood sometimes seem to linger for several hours (MacLean & Ploog, 1962). The septum is one of the main sources of connections to the hippocampus. Olds and Milner (1954) discovered that rats would repeatedly press a bar to obtain electrical stimulation of the septum. At meetings in 1952 Heath and his collaborators had reported that patients receiving electrical stimulation of the septum experienced pleasurable feelings and persisting changes in mood (1954, p. vii).

ALTERATIONS OF PERCEPTION

As classical anatomy provides no evidence of inputs to the limbic cortex from the auditory, somatic, and visual systems, it has always been puzzling that with epileptic discharges arising in or near the limbic cortex of the insula, hippocampal gyrus, and hippocampal formation, patients may experience alterations of perception and hallucinations involving any one of the sensory systems. Malamud (1966), for example, recently reported a case of a 26-year-old man with a small ganglioma in the uncus-amygdaloid-hippocampal region who variously experienced ictal gustatory, olfactory, auditory, visual, and somatic delusions or hallucinations without loss of consciousness. As not uncommon, this patient subsequently developed mental symptoms diagnostic of a schizophrenic reaction.

In a paper on the "visceral brain" in 1949, I presented a diagram suggesting that all the sensory systems feed into the hippocampal formation. At that time it was known that the olfactory apparatus was indirectly connected with the hippocampal formation, but there was no experimental evidence of representation of the other senses. For several years we have been concerned with the question of visual connections (see summary by MacLean, 1966a, pp. 443-453). Recently we have demonstrated by microelectrode recording in awake, sitting monkeys that individual nerve cells in the posterior parahippocampal cortex are activated by photic stimulation (MacLean, Yokota, & Kinnard, 1968). Figure 4 shows records of units in this region responding throughout a period of illumination of the eye. In an anatomical study on squirrel monkeys, it was found that after lesions in the ventrolateral part of the lateral geniculate body (the main visual subcortical nucleus), a continuous band of degeneration extends into the core of the hippocampal gyrus; some fibers enter the cortex here and in neighboring areas (MacLean & Creswell, 1970). The lower part of this degenerating band shown in Figure 5 corresponds to the temporal loop in man. It has always been a mystery why the optic loop makes this long temporal detour, but it now appears, on the basis of the anatomic and microelectrode studies, that it travels this roundabout course in order to distribute fibers to the posterior limbic cortex. The inferior pulvinar, which is regarded as a visual association nucleus, also contributes fibers via a band lying just lateral to the optic radiation.

It deserves emphasis that in the phyletic development of primates, the convolutions neighboring the hippocampus have undergone great expansion. Indeed, the fusiform gyrus which is folded against the hippocampal gyrus represents a new convolution in the primate brain. The cortical expansion in this region may explain the great increase in the number of fornix fibers found in man (Daitz & Powell, 1954). There are some indications from the observations of Penfield and others that this region of the brain may be implicated in

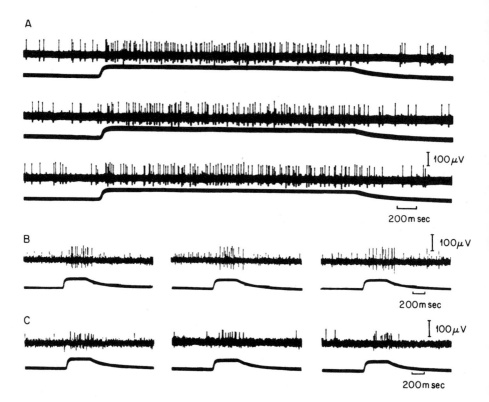

Fig. 4. This and Figure 5 pertain to questions of visual input to the limbic cortex. A, B, and C illustrate a series of on-responses to photic stimulation recorded from units in the posterior hippocampal gyrus of three different squirrel monkeys. Duration of light stimulation is shown in accompanying records by the response of a photocell. In A, the eye was illuminated for 2.5 sec; in B and C the stimulus duration was 0.4 sec (*from* MacLean *et al.*, 1968).

Fig. 5. Histological section on left shows continuous band of degeneration extending from lesion in ventrolateral part of lateral geniculate body into the core of the hippocampal gyrus (arrow). With greater magnification some degenerating fibers can be traced into the posterior hippocampal gyrus, as well as into contiguous areas of the fusiform and lingual cortex. The lower part of the degenerating band corresponds to Meyer's "temporal loop" in man. The control unoperated side from the same histological section is shown on the right with the key structures labeled. CGL, lateral geniculate body; GH, hippocampal gyrus; H, hippocampus; C, caudate nucleus (*from* MacLean, P. D., The limbic and visual cortex in phylogeny: Further insights from anatomic and microelectrode studies, pp. 443–453. In Hassler, R., Stephan, H. *Evolution of the Forebrain*, Georg Thieme Verlag, Stuttgart, 1966a.).

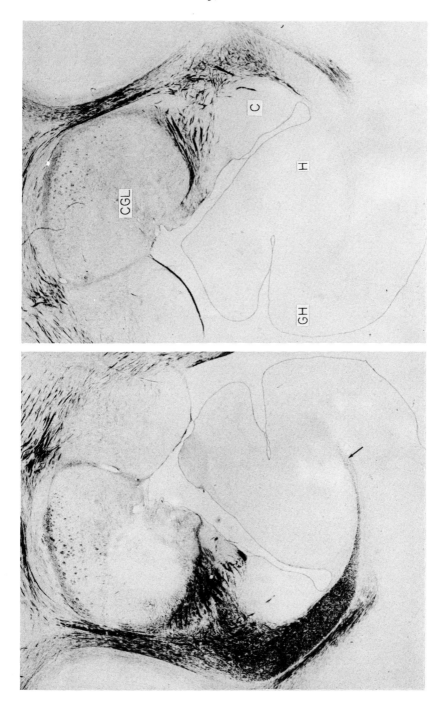

dreaming (Penfield & Jasper, 1954). Schizophrenia has often been likened to a waking dream.

From the standpoint of paranoid symptoms it is possibly significant that some cells in the limbic retrosplenial cortex are photically activated only by the contralateral eye, suggesting that the impulses originate in the primitive temporal monocular crescent (MacLean, Yokota & Kinnard, 1968). As we well know from personal experience, objects entering this part of our peripheral field commonly cause emotional startle and alarm. I remember a young man who at the beginning of a limbic seizure had the feeling of fear that someone was standing behind him. If he turned to see who it was, the feeling of fear became intensified. During interseizure periods, as already noted, patients may have persistent paranoid feelings.

The parahippocampal cortex transmits impulses to the hippocampus which in turn projects to the hypothalamus and other structures of the brainstem involved in emotional, endocrine, and somatovisceral functions. Through such connections there is one possible mechanism by which the brain transforms the cold light with which we see into the warm light with which we feel.

We are currently exploring the limbic cortex of the claustral insula for evidence of inputs from the somatic and auditory systems. Auditory and somatic stimulation evoke responses of a significant number of units in this area (Reeves, Sudakov, & MacLean, 1968). No unit has responded to more than one modality. Two main types of auditory units are found, one of which responds with latencies as short as 10 msec. Somatic units are activated by pressure alone or by pressure and light touch. The receptive fields are usually large and bilateral. As the claustral insula has connections with the hippocampal formation, the findings suggest a pathway by which impulses of auditory and somatic origin may reach the hypothalamus and influence vegetative and emotional functions.

Klüver (1951, pp. 147-181) has emphasized that the visual cortex surpasses all other sensory structures in guaranteeing the constancy of the external environment. It would therefore seem reasonable to look elsewhere than the primary visual cortex for the neural disturbance underlying visual hallucinations and delusions. The same would seem to apply to the other primary sensory areas of the neocortex. On the basis of the experimental material just reviewed, it is possible that distortions of perceptions could arise from dysfunction within the limbic structures themselves, or they might also result from the effects of limbic perturbations on either the primary sensory areas or the so-called association areas. Such perturbations might be transmitted through cortical association fibers or the diffuse thalamic projection system.

A smoldering volcano does not amount to much in the daily lives of a people living under its shadow. It is only when it erupts that it throws them into panic. Similarly, a structure such as the hippocampus may have no disruptive effect on the individual unless it is thrown into perturbation by injury, toxic agents, or stressful situations. Because of its peculiar blood supply (Nilges, 1944) and its location in the cranium, the hippocampus has long been recognized to be especially vulnerable to mechanical injury, vascular insufficiency, and infection. As mentioned earlier, the hippocampus has its own peculiar chemistry. What was not emphasized is that it is probably the most unstable structure of the brain and has the lowest seizure threshold (see Green, 1964). Experimentally it is striking to observe the tendency of the hippocampal formation to show prolonged spiking activity after intense afferent bombardment (MacLean & Ploog, 1962). This abnormality is presumably due to the peculiarity of its chemistry and synapses. It is conceivable that in constitutionally disposed individuals, day-to-day bombardment of this primitive cortex by impulses initiated by stressful situations could lead to a functional disturbance resulting in persistent paranoid or other abnormal feeling states with attendant delusional thinking (MacLean, 1966a, pp. 443–453, 1968a, pp. 97–106).

Granted that there is no immediate prospect of answering questions of this kind, the celebration of the opening of the Psychiatric Research Center at the Spring Grove gives promise of gaining substantial knowledge about disordered mechanisms underlying the psychoses.

SUMMARY

In its evolution the brain of man retains the organization of three basic types of brains, here designated in ascending order as reptilian, old mammalian, and new mammalian. This presentation focuses on the primate counterpart of the old mammalian brain (alias limbic system or limbic brain) which is of special psychiatric interest because of clinical and experimental evidence of its important role in emotional behavior. A common denominator of all mammals, it stands in an intermediate position between the reptilian brain with instinctual functions and the rapidly evolving new brain which in man acquires the capacity for symbolic language. The three brains differ in their structure, organization, and chemistry. Electrophysiological findings indicate a functional dichotomy ("schizophysiology") of the limbic and new brains.

The limbic brain comprises three main subdivisions, two of which are closely related to the olfactory apparatus and are respectively involved in oral and sexual functions insuring self-preservation and the preservation of the species. The third subdivision develops somewhat independently of the olfactory apparatus and reaches its maximum size in man. There is evidence that this condition reflects a shifting of emphasis from olfactory to visual influences in sociosexual behavior.

Case histories of psychomotor epilepsy illustrate that neural perturbations of the limbic brain may result in symptoms observed in the endogenous and toxic psychoses, including (a) disturbances of emotion and mood, (b) feelings of depersonalization, (c) distortions of perception, and (d) paranoid states. Some relevant experimental findings on animals are described, along with a discussion of their implications.

REFERENCES

Altman, J., & Gopal, D. D. Autoradiographic and histological evidence of postnatal hippocampal neurogenesis in rats. *Journal of Comparative Neurology,* 1965, **124,** 319-336.

Broca, P. Anatomie comparée des circonvolutions cérébrales. Le grand lobe limbique et la scissure limbique dans la série des mamifères. *Revue d' Anthropologie,* 1878, **1,** 385-498.

Coggeshall, R. E., & MacLean, P. D. Hippocampal lesions following administration of 3-acetylpyridine. *Proceedings of the Society for Experimental Biology and Medicine,* 1958, **98,** 687-689.

Cohen, S. Psychotomimetic agents. *Annual Review of Pharmacology,* 1967. **7,** 301-318.

Csillik, B., & Erulkar, S. D. Labile stores of monamines in the central nervous system: A histochemical study. *Journal of Pharmacology and Experimental Therapeutics,* 1964, **146,** 186-193.

Daitz, H. M., & Powell, T. P. S. Studies of the connexions of the fornix system. *Journal of Neurology, Neurosurgery and Psychiatry,* 1954, **17,** 75-82.

Denckla, D. Personal communication, 1968.

Euler, C., Von On the significance of the high zinc content in the hippocampal formation. *Physiologie de l'hippocampe, Montpellier, 1961,* pp. 135-145. Paris: Du Centre National de la Recherche Scientifique, 1962.

Flanigan, S., Gabrieli, E. R., & MacLean, P. D. Cerebral changes revealed by radioautography with S^{35}-labeled l-methionine. *AMA Archives of Neurology and Psychiatry,* 1957, **77,** 588-594.

Fleischhauer, K., & Horstmann, E. Intravitale Dithizonfarbung homologer Felder der Ammonsformation von Säugern. *Zeitschrift fuer Zellforschung und Mikroskopische Anatomie,* 1957, **46,** 598-609.

Freud, S. *Beyond the pleasure principle*. Translated by C. J. M. Hubback. London and Vienna: The International Psycho-Analytical Press, 1922.

Fuxe, K. Evidence for the existence of monoamine neurons in the central nervous system. IV. Distribution of monoamine nerve terminals in the central nervous system. *Acta Physiologica Scandinavica*, 1965, 64, 37-84.

Green, J. D. The hippocampus. *Physiological Review*, 1964, 44, 561-608.

Heath, R. G. *Studies in Schizophrenia*. A multidisciplinary approach to mind-brain relationships. Cambridge: Harvard University Press, 1954.

Hess, W. R., & Brugger, M. Das subkortikale Zentrum der affektiven Abwehrreaktion. *Helvetica Physiologica et Pharmacologica* Acta, 1943, 1, 33-52.

Jackson, J. H., & Stewart, P. Epileptic attacks with a warning of a crude sensation of smell and with the intellectual aura (dreamy state) in a patient who had symptoms pointing to gross organic disease of the right temporo-sphenoidal lobe. *Brain*, 1899, 22, 534-549.

Killam, E. H., Killam, K. F., & Thomason, S. The effects of psychotherapeutic compounds on central afferent and limbic pathways. *Annals of the New York Academy of Sciences*, 1957, 66, 784-805.

Klüver, H. Functional differences between the occipital and temporal lobes with special reference to the inter-relations of behavior and extracerebral mechanisms. In L. A. Jeffress (Ed.), *Cerebral mechanisms in behavior*. New York: Wiley, 1951.

MacLean, P. D. Psychosomatic disease and the "visceral brain." Recent developments bearing on the Papez theory of emotion. *Psychosomatic Medicine*, 1949, 11, 338-353.

MacLean, P. D. Some psychiatric implications of physiological studies on frontotemporal portion of limbic system (visceral brain). *Electroencephalography and Clinical Neurophysiology*, 1952, 4, 407-418.

MacLean, P. D. Studies on limbic system ("Visceral Brain") and their bearing on psychosomatic problems. In: E. Wittkower and R. Cleghorn (Eds.), *Recent developments in psychosomatic medicine*. London: Pitman, 1954. (a)

MacLean, P. D. The limbic system and its hippocampal formation. Studies in animals and their possible application to man. *Journal of Neurosurgery*, 1954, 11, 29-44. (b)

MacLean, P. D. Chemical and electrical stimulation of hippocampus in unrestrained animals. Part II. Behavioral findings. *AMA Archives of Neurology and Psychiatry*, 1957, 78, 128-142.

MacLean, P. D. Contrasting functions of limbic and neocortical systems of the brain and their relevance to psychophysiological aspects of medicine. *American Journal of Medicine*, 1958, 25, 611-626.

MacLean, P. D. The limbic system with respect to two basic life principles. *Conference on the Central Nervous System and Behavior*, 2nd, Transactions, pp. 31-118. New York: Josiah Macy, Jr. Foundation, 1959.

MacLean, P. D. New findings relevant to the evolution of psychosexual functions of the brain. *Journal of Nervous and Mental Disease*, 1962, 135, 289-301.

MacLean, P. D. Man and his animal brains. *Modern Medicine (Chicago)*, 1964, 32, 95-106.

MacLean, P. D. The limbic and visual cortex in phylogeny: Further insights from anatomic and microelectrode studies. In R. Hassler and H. Stephan (Eds.), *Evolution of the forebrain*, Stuttgart: Thieme, 1966. (a)

MacLean, P. D. Brain and vision in the evolution of emotional and sexual behavior. *Thomas William Salmon lectures*. New York: New York Academy of Medicine, Dec. 7, 1966. (b)

MacLean, P. D. The brain in relation to empathy and medical education. *Journal of Nervous and Mental Disease*, 1967, **144**, 374-382.

MacLean, P. D. The limbic system in relation to sexual and visual functions: Findings since 1958. In E. Gellhorn (Ed.), *Biological foundations of emotion*, Glenview: Scott, Foresman, 1968. (a)

MacLean, P. D. Alternative neural pathways to violence. In L. Ng (Ed.), *Alternatives to violence*. New York: Time-Life Books, 1968. (b)

MacLean, P. D., & Creswell, G. Anatomical connections of the visual system with limbic cortex of monkey. *Journal of Comparative Neurology*, 1970, **138**, 265-278.

MacLean, P. D., Flanigan, S., Flynn, J. P., Kim, C., & Stevens, J. R. Hippocampal function: tentative correlations of conditioning, EEG, drug, and radioautographic studies. *Yale Journal of Biology and Medicine*, 1955/56, **28**, 380-395.

MacLean, P. D., and Ploog, D. W. Cerebral representation of penile erection. *Journal of Neurophysiology*, 1962, **25**, 29-55.

MacLean, P. D., Yokota, T., & Kinnard, M. A. Photically sustained on-responses of units in posterior hippocampal gyrus of awake monkey. *Journal of Neurophysiology*, 1968, **31**, 870-883.

Malamud, N. The epileptogenic focus in temporal lobe epilepsy from a pathological standpoint. *Archives of Neurology (Chicago)*, 1966, **14**, 190-195.

Maske, H. Über den topochemischen Nachweis von Zink im Ammonshorn verschiedener Säugetiere. *Naturwissenschaften*, 1955, **42**, 424.

McLardy, T. Zinc enzymes and the hippocampal mossy fibre system. *Nature (London)*, 1962, **194**, 300-302.

Niklowitz, W., Bak, I. J., & Hassler, R. Electron microscopical observations of pyramidal cells in the hippocampus after 3-acetylpyridine treatment. *International Kongress für Histo- and Cytochemie, Proceedings, 2nd, Frankfurt/Main, 1964*, pp. 172-173. Berlin: Springer, 1964.

Nilges, R. G. The arteries of the mammalian cornu ammonis. *Journal of Comparative Neurology*, 1944, **80**, 177-190.

Olds, J., & Milner, P. Positive reinforcement produced by electrical stimulation of septal areas and other regions of the rat brain. *Journal of Comparative and Physiological Psychology*, 1954, **47**, 419-427.

Paasonen, M. K., MacLean, P. D., & Giarman, N. J. 5-Hydroxytryptamine (serotonin, enteramine) content of structures of the limbic system. *Journal of Neurochemistry*, 1957, **1**, 326-333.

Papez, J. W. A proposed mechanism of emotion. *Archives of Neurology and Psychiatry*, 1937, **38**, 725-743.

Penfield, W., & Jasper, H. *Epilepsy and the functional anatomy of the human brain*. Boston: Little, Brown, 1954.

Reeves, A. G., Sudakov, K., & MacLean, P. D. Exploratory unit analysis of exteroceptive inputs to the insular cortex in awake, sitting, squirrel monkeys. *Federation Proceedings, Federation of American Societies for Experimental Biology*, 1968, **27**, 388.

Reivich, M., & Glowinski, J. An autoradiographic study of the distribution of C^{14}-norepinephrine in the brain of the rat. *Brain*, 1967, **90**, 633-646.

Shute, C. C. D., & Lewis, P. R. The use of cholinesterase techniques combined with operative procedures to follow nervous pathways in the brain. *Bibliotheca Anatomica*, 1961, **2**, 34-49.

Vogt, C., & Vogt, O. Gestaltung der topistischen Hirnforschung und ihre Förderung durch den Hirnbau und seine Anomalien. *Journal für Hirnforschung*, 1953, **1**, 1-46.

8

THE ROLE OF NONSPECIFIC RETICULO-THALAMO-CORTICAL SYSTEMS IN EMOTION

Donald B. Lindsley

INTRODUCTION: NEURAL MECHANISMS IN EMOTION AND MOTIVATION

Some years ago in a chapter on Emotion in the *Handbook of Experimental Psychology* (Lindsley, 1951), I introduced a neural "activation theory" of emotion as a possible basis for explaining the arousal and excitement aspects of emotion and affective states. A few years later (Lindsley, 1957), I attempted to extend this concept to account for the drive or activating aspects of motivation. Malmo (1959) supplied an excellent critical review of activation as a neuropsychological dimension.

The activation theory of emotion, as presented in 1951, rested upon the following facts. (1) The electroencephalogram (EEG) in emotion is characterized by a desynchronization or activation pattern (Lindsley, 1950). Blocking of the alpha rhythm with startle was first reported by Berger, the founder of the EEG, in 1933. (2) The blocking or activation pattern of the EEG can be induced in animals by electrical stimulation of the brainstem reticular formation or by stimulation of various sense modalities (Moruzzi & Magoun, 1949). (3) Interruption of the ascending reticular activating system by lesion

of the rostral midbrain tegmentum or by destruction of the basal diencephalon abolishes activation of the EEG and restores synchrony;
spindle bursts and slow waves occur simultaneously in the EEG and
midline thalamic nuclei (Lindsley, Bowden, & Magoun, 1949). (4) In
chronic cat preparations with lesions of the midbrain tegmentum the
behavioral state is the opposite of emotional excitement or arousal,
namely, one of apathy, somnolence, hypokinesis, indeed usually a
comatose state (Lindsley, Schreiner, Knowles, & Magoun, 1950). (5)
The mechanism of the basal diencephalon and lower brainstem reticular formation responsible for the objective features of emotional
expression, posture and behavior, including autonomic outflow and
the regulation of somatomotor activities, overlaps the EEG activating
mechanism which arouses the cortex (Ranson & Magoun, 1939;
Sprague, Schreiner, Lindsley, & Magoun, 1948; Schreiner, Lindsley,
& Magoun, 1949).

By 1957 it was possible to add several additional points in support
of the general thesis that the descending and ascending reticular systems, together with thalamo-cortical and limbic system interactions,
play a significant role not only in the mechanisms underlying emo-
tional-motivational behavior, but also in relation to alerting, attention, vigilance, and the regulation and control of sensory input (Lindsley, 1957).

For example, it was demonstrated that the reticular formation can
be activated not only through collaterals from specific sensory afferents, but also through connections with the cerebral cortex (French,
Hernández-Peón, & Livingston, 1955). This made it possible to
conceive of internal states such as thoughts, worries, and apprehensions generating arousal activity in the reticular formation. Accordingly, through descending pathways, there can be modification of
visceral and somatosensory activity, and through ascending pathways
affecting cortical excitability and inhibitory control there can be
arousal, alerting, attention, and enhanced or suppressed perceptual
effects. All of these features have the potentiality of affecting emotional and motivational behavior.

Also, it has been demonstrated that through corticifugal and reticular stimulation it is possible to modify afferent influx at any synaptic
level from the most peripheral or first synapse (Hagbarth & Kerr,
1954; Kerr & Hagbarth, 1955; Granit, 1955; Hernández-Peón, 1955;
and others) to the most central thalamic or cortical synapses
(Hernández-Peón, Scherrer, & Velasco, 1956; Bremer & Stoupel,
1959; Dumont & Dell, 1960). Although such centrifugal or negative
feedback control of sensory influx is usually inhibitory, it has also

been shown that reticular stimulation is capable of enhancing evoked potentials in thalamic relays and cortex (Bremer & Stoupel, 1959; Dumont & Dell, 1960) and in facilitating temporal resolution of evoked responses to paired flashes in the visual cortex (Lindsley, 1958). Fuster (1958) showed that reticular stimulation in monkeys speeded up their reaction time in a visual discrimination situation, and Lansing, Schwartz, and Lindsley (1959) showed that a preparatory signal decreased reaction time in human subjects coordinate with the desynchronization or alpha blocking time.

That the reticular formation of the lower brainstem is not alone in achieving all of these effects was emphasized by Murphy and Gellhorn (1945a, 1945b) whose studies of diencephalic–cortical interactions were discussed in terms of their significance for emotion. It is well known of course that the upward extensions of the ascending reticular activating system (ARAS) invade the hypothalamus and the so-called nonspecific or unspecific midline thalamic nuclei, sometimes referred to as the diffuse thalamic projection system (DTPS) (Jasper & Ajmone-Marsan, 1952; Lindsley, 1960). Thalamocortical integrating mechanisms were dealt with extensively by Jasper and Ajmone-Marsan (1952) and in subsequent studies by Jasper and collaborators. They argued that the reticular formation of midbrain and diencephalon was clearly related to the control of electrical rhythms of the cortex and therefore to levels of consciousness, alertness, and attention. They emphasized too that the lateral and medial nuclear masses of the thalamus increase markedly during phylogeny and that strong connections with the basal ganglia, cerebellum and motor cortex tend to indicate that the thalamus is in a position to play an integrative role, involving both sensory and motor functions. In addition they comment, as was done above, about the overlap and interconnections of these reticulo–thalamo–cortical systems with those subserving visceral and autonomic functions, including the limbic system.

The limbic system and its importance in emotion is dealt with in this volume by MacLean (Chapter 7) but mention of it here should be made because of its overlap and interconnections with the midbrain, hypothalamic, and thalamic reticular systems and their interactions with the cortex, especially from an electrophysiological viewpoint. Green and Arduini (1954) studied the 5-to-7-per-sec theta wave activity in the hippocampus of rabbits and found that it bore a reciprocal relationship to the alpha rhythm of the cortex, i.e., when a stimulus caused desynchronization and blocking of the alpha rhythm it caused a synchronized theta rhythm in the hippocampus and, vice versa, there tended to be desynchronization in the hippocampus when the alpha rhythm and synchrony was restored to the cortex. They proposed three hypotheses concerning the role of the hippocampus in relation to the cortex: (1) the hippocampus facilitates or induces changes in the cortex, (2) the hippocampus exerts a restraining or controlling influence on cortical activity, and (3) the hippocampus is affected by the same afferent modalities as the cerebral cortex, but subserves an entirely different function. They concluded that the arousal response in the hippocampus (rhythmic synchronized waves) has many features in common with EEG arousal in the cortex (desynchronization), and therefore also with behavioral arousal and alerting.

Green and Arduini (1954) point out that hippocampal and cortical responses, although opposite in type, have much in common; they are induced by all modalities of sensory stimulation, they are generalized in their respective areas and persist after cessation of stimulation, they both accommodate or "habituate" to repetition of a given stimulus and are reinstated by slight changes in the mode or type of stimulation. Both of these arousal response mechanisms, activated on the afferent side through the reticular system (ARAS) have similar sensitivity, persistence and adaptivity and both play a role in the initiation and maintenance of emotional–motivational activity. The hippocampus has strong two-way connections with the reticular formation, hypothalamus, thalamus, and cortex, so it is not surprising that these arousal interactions occur and that the limbic and reticular systems both play a significant role in emotional, motivational, and learning behavior.

Delgado, Roberts, and Miller (1954) found that stimulation in tectal, lateral thalamic, and hippocampal regions produced fearlike reactions which have all the drive properties of true emotion and could be used to establish conditioned responses, to motivate trial and error learning of an instrumental response or to condition avoidance responses to food. Roberts, Steinberg, and Means (1967) have found differentiating regions in the hypothalamus and preoptic regions of the opossum where stimulation will produce a variety of emotionally based and motivating behaviors, including mating, attack, defense, eating, escape, and grooming. They find close anatomical correspondence with similar mechanisms in higher species suggesting considerable phylogenetic continuity. Interestingly enough, responses elicited which were relevant to goals could not be elicited without the goal objects present, which suggests that the mechanisms involved were facilitative of, but did not initiate, the responses.

Kaada (1967) has reviewed a number of studies, including those from his own laboratory, which have sought to localize brain mechanisms related to aggressive behavior. He indicates that there are many problems with respect to the refinement of methods for evaluating emotional behavior as well as a complex diffuseness of the systems or structures involved. Kaada includes under agonistic or aggressively expressive emotional behavior in the cat defense, attack and flight; he finds evidence, however, that these three types of behavior have somewhat widespread (in terms of different brain structures), but separated, though partially overlapping representations (especially in the same structure) in the brain. There seems to be general agreement that the hypothalamus is a central structure in the organization and elaboration of such emotional behavior, but that much of the control and regulation of it is dependent upon other structures such as neocortex and forebrain mechanisms, limbic system structures (particularly amygdala and hippocampus), and lower brainstem, especially the reticular and central gray substances.

Defense and flight reactions in the cat have been elicited in medially located structures extending from the forebrain, through the hypothalamus, to the central gray substance of the midbrain (Hunsperger, 1956, 1965; Romaniuk, 1965); in the forebrain and rostral hypothalamus, defense reactions appear to be located more ventrally and flight reactions more dorsally. Stalking and attack reactions, according to Wasman and Flynn (1962), can be elicited with low intensity stimulation in the lateral hypothalamus. Ursin and Kaada (1960), by stimulation methods, have found differentiable areas of the amygdaloid region for defense and flight, but these reactions are dependent upon intact defense and flight zones of midline hypothalamus and midbrain central gray substance (Fernandez de Molina & Hunsperger, 1959.

Neocortical ablations which spare limbic structures and bilateral lesions of the amygdalae in most species studied tend to produce tameness and placidity, although there are some indications that contrasting reactions are sometimes produced. Sham rage reactions have generally been found to be produced by removing supposedly inhibitory rostral structures and leaving only the caudal hypothalamus, but the tameness and placidity mentioned above would seem to be the result of reducing excitatory or facilitatory influx into defense, flight, attack, or rage-like centers. However, as is the case in most mechanisms, both excitatory and inhibitory systems are required to maintain balance, and there is evidence that stimulation in different regions of the amygdala is capable of suppressing or facilitating attack initiated by stimulation of the attack zone in the hypothalamus (Egger & Flynn, 1963).

Carli, Malliani, and Zanchetti (1963), in investigating the descending paths mediating rage in thalamic cats, found extensive and diffuse connections in the midbrain (reticular and central gray) with pathways involving the medial forebrain bundle and dorsal longitudinal fasciculus of Schütz. According to Nauta (1964), both have widespread connections throughout the hypothalamus, but particularly with midline ventral hypothalamus structures and perhaps with the forebrain via the inferior thalamic peduncle. An illuminating and comprehensive study by Millhouse (1967, 1969), using rapid Golgi technique, of the medial forebrain bundle (MFB) and its pre- and postsynaptic endings and the extensive intermingling with it of so-called path neurons attests to widespread and diffuse interconnectedness of this system throughout the diencephalon, including structures of the basal forebrain, limbic system, mediobasal neuroendocrine areas, midline diffuse thalamic projection nuclei, and midbrain reticular formation and periaqueductal gray substance, as well as probably lower brain stem and spinal autonomic outflows. Although there are undoubtedly ascending and descending through-way paths in the medial forebrain bundle of the lateral hypothalamus, the extensive interconnections of path neurons with collaterals of the MFB and the fact that their axons bifurcate and send long extensions both rostrally and caudally suggests that it has extensive integrating possibilities.

With this kind of diffuse interconnection of various portions of the diencephalon with rostral forebrain and neocortical structures and limbic system structures such as septum, hippocampus, and amygdala it is easy to understand why emotional and motivational aspects of behavior are so complex and why it is so difficult to separate systems or isolate patterns of behavior. In view of this apparent and potential complexity it is all the more remarkable that some neural systems have been partially segregated experimentally to the extent that stimulation or lesions have provided differentiable patterns of behavior, autonomic activity, or electrophysiological change in cortex, hippocampus, and elsewhere. The self-stimulation experiments initiated by Olds and Milner (1954) and extended by Olds (1962) and others have emphasized the drive properties, both positive and negative, of stimulation throughout much of this general field of intermingled neural systems. Although here, as in other experimental studies, there has been much overlapping of responsive and unresponsive areas, the highly motivating or rewarding areas of self-stimulation seem to lie generally along the diffuse course of the medial forebrain bundle and the extensions of its path neurons.

Whereas the integration and organization of autonomic, neuroendocrine, and somatomotor patterns of behavior seem to be generally centered in the diencephalon and basal ganglia, there would seem to be little doubt that further processing of these outflows takes place in the lower brainstem, particularly in the reticular formation and its numerous associated nuclei. Also it seems that insofar as sensory and other input to these organizing systems are concerned, especially in matters of arousal, alertness, and attention, it is necessary to consider the "energizing" aspects of the ascending reticular formation. As mentioned earlier, electrophysiological and behavioral evidence (Moruzzi & Magoun, 1949; Lindsley, Bowden, & Magoun, 1949; Lindsley *et al.*, 1950; and others) of this was manifested electrocortically (activation or desynchronization) and behaviorally (arousal and alertness). Although many subsequent studies have added important new information, sometimes seemingly contradictory in nature, it nevertheless seems to remain true that the general principle, concerning the role of the reticular formation as a sleep-wakefulness controlling arousal mechanism, has remained intact. Sleep and arousal may be initiated by certain kinds of electrical stimulation in certain midline thalamic and basal forebrain structures, and likewise in pontine structures below the originally designated mesencephalic tegmentum, but these findings add new dimensions and complexity to the general picture. They do not, apparently, destroy or invalidate the original principle of arousal and activation by means of the ascending reticular activating system, whose rostral extensions through hypothalamus and thalamus play upon an exceedingly complex network of interconnections which, as was mentioned above, include basal forebrain, neocortex, limbic, and other structures.

The foregoing discussion of possible neural mechanisms involved in emotional and motivational behavior is by no means comprehensive, nor was it intended to be. Samplings from the literature have been cited mainly to indicate how complex the neural structures and mechanisms which underlie emotion, drive, and motivation are, but also to give some indication of the relative success in isolating or segregating systems of neural interaction electrophysiologically and behaviorally. This has also been done by other procedures which have not been described. Thus through the use of various techniques and procedures available there seems to be hope of reaching a better understanding of the neural mechanisms underlying emotional and other types of behavior.

Our approach in the laboratory has been to try to identify, and to some extent isolate, a "system" which can be tentatively defined in terms of something it does or something it mediates, whether that be a natural type of function or one of artificial nature imposed upon it, such as by electrical stimulation, lesion, or reversible cryogenic blockade. I would now like to direct attention to a reticulo-thalamo–orbitocortical system, believed to be concerned with the control and regulation of electrocortical rhythms, particularly their synchronized state, and by assumption therefore, with states of arousal, awareness, alertness, vigilance, and attention (Velasco & Lindsley, 1965; Skinner & Lindsley, 1967, 1968; Velasco, Skinner, Asaro, & Lindsley, 1968; Velasco & Lindsley, in press; Velasco, Weinberger & Lindsley, in press). I will also review some of the results of our studies of human average evoked potentials in relation to attention and vigilance and to selective attentiveness (Haider, Spong, & Lindsley, 1964; Spong, Haider and Lindsley, 1965; Spong, 1966). Whereas the above "system" approach concerns itself with the role of so-called nonspecific thalamic midline nuclei, which are a part of the nonspecific ascending reticular activating system, and the role such a system plays in regulating electrocortical rhythms, it also attempts to show the effect of blockade of this system on behavior of the animal and upon specific sensory evoked potentials. Another "system" approach has been to study and differentiate the specific and nonspecific visual sensory systems as these evolve in the developing kitten brain (Rose and Lindsley, 1965, 1968). In still another "system" approach an attempt has been made to study and assess the role of the phylogenetically burgeoning lateral association nuclear group, especially the pulvinar, which has been found to be a polysensory center (Huang, 1968; Kreindler, Crighel, & Marinchescu, 1968; Huang & Lindsley, in preparation).

Before turning to the results of some of these so-called system approaches, particularly the reticulo-thalamo-cortical system, I should like to review briefly, and illustrate, some of the effects I referred to at the outset which bear upon the role of the reticular formation in both its descending and ascending aspects. Mention has already been made that these aspects relate to emotional behavior through their role in the control of somatomotor and autonomic outflow and through their central integrating effects upon mechanisms concerned with arousal, orienting behavior, alerting, attention, preception, emotion and affect, as well as the associated electrical changes in cortex and hippocampus. The foregoing discussion has touched upon the complexity of neuroanatomical interconnections within the diencephalon which somehow tie together functionally the reticular formation, hypothalamus, thalamus, forebrain, neocortex, and hippocampal structures. Although these functional relations are by no means completely clear, there are some helpful clues emerging.

THE RETICULAR FORMATION: DESCENDING AND ASCENDING ASPECTS

Figure 1 illustrates on a diagram of the cat brain a general schematic outline of the bipartite (facilitatory and inhibitory) nature of the descending influences of the reticular formation upon spinal motor outflow, and perhaps upon autonomic outflow as well. Magoun and collaborators (Bach & Magoun, 1947; Magoun & Rhines, 1948;

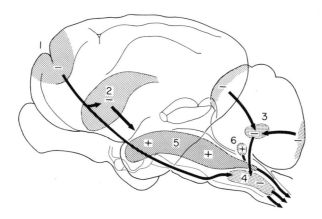

Fig. 1. Reconstruction of cat's brain showing the suppressor and facilitatory systems concerned in spasticity. Suppressor pathways are 1: cortico-bulbo-reticular, 2: caudato-spinal, 3: cerebello-reticular and 4: reticulo-spinal. Facilitatory pathways are 5: reticulo-spinal and 6: vestibulo-spinal (*from* Lindsley, Schreiner and Magoun, 1949).

Lindsley, Schreiner, & Magoun, 1949) demonstrated that the rostral portion of the reticular formation and associated nuclei of the lower brainstem (the cross-hatched region labeled 5 and marked with a plus sign) when stimulated directly causes facilitation or enhancement of spinal reflexes as well as of cortically induced movement. Both this region of the reticulo-spinal system (labeled 5) and the vestibulo-spinal system (labeled 6) have facilitatory influences, but the former appears to be more *phasic* in nature and the latter *tonic*, or postural, in its effects. By contrast, stimulation of the caudal reticular formation (labeled 4 with minus sign) has an inhibitory effect on spinal motor outflow and reduces spasticity and hyperreflexia. Stimulation at points 1, pericruciate region of cortex, 2, caudate nucleus, or 3, cerebellum (anterior lobe and fastigial nuclei) reinforces the suppressor or inhibitory role of the caudal reticular formation of the lower brainstem. Lesions of any of these regions, on the other hand, result in an appreciable increment in spasticity and hyperreflexia due to the dominance of the facilitatory portion of the reticular formation over that of the inhibitory portion. Thus it is seen that an appropriate balance between facilitation and inhibition can be maintained by such a mechanism, with the normal state in a waking animal being one favoring facilitation of spinal reflexes and of pyramidal and extrapyramidal systems of motor outflow which maintain posture and provide a state of readiness to respond. On the other hand, in relaxation, drowsiness or sleep, there is a progressive tendency for the inhibitory system to dominate with resulting absence or sluggishness of reflexes, and general muscular relaxation and loss of postural control. One can envisage how emotionally exciting events which lead to action and tension are apparently due to a dominance of the facilitatory system, except perhaps in the case of "freezing" behavior resulting from fright, which in some manner (possibly through an overload or overstimulation of the phasic portion of the facilitatory system), enables the tonic or vestibulo-spinal portion of the system to dominate and cause the freezing posture. No doubt the many and diversified forms of body posture and facial expression observed in various emotional behaviors could be accounted for by "built in" reflex interactions of such a bipartite lower brainstem reticular system and its descending influences combined with "voluntary" or learned reactions. Obviously, the pyramidal and extrapyramidal systems, including the basal ganglia, would be involved as well as the lower brainstem reticular formation, but it is through this region of the brainstem that all such influences must funnel, and the possibilities for interactive regulation and control are great (see Lindsley, 1952a).

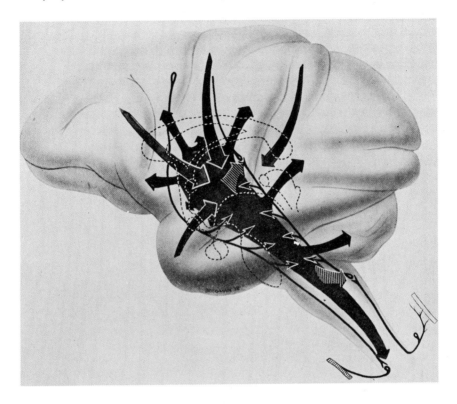

Fig. 2. Schematic representation of descending and ascending influences of the reticular formation imposed on a montage of the monkey brain. See text for explanation. (*from* Worden and Livingston, 1961.).

Let us turn now to the role of the ascending reticular activating system (ARAS) and its connection with emotional and other aspects of behavior, since it relates more directly to the main purpose of this presentation.

Figure 2 represents an attempt to bring together in schematic form some of the principal roles of the reticular formation, both descending and ascending. This schema has been imposed upon a montage of the monkey brain. There is shown a dark central core extending from the medullary regions of the lower brainstem up through the region of the pons, midbrain, and diencephalon. This symbolizes the reticular formation of the lower brainstem. The downward pointing arrow at the caudal end of this central core represents the dual facilitatory and inhibitory descending influences of the reticular formation imposed on spinal motor outflow to body muscles, or to autonomic effector mechanisms. The upward and outward pointing arrows at the rostral end of the dark central core represent the ascending reticular activating system (ARAS) imposing its effects upon neocortex diffusely and upon forebrain, hippocampal, septal, hypothalamic, and thalamic nuclei. Stimulation of the midbrain reticular formation (Moruzzi & Magoun, 1949) causes activation or desynchronization of electrocortical activity diffusely and induces hippocampal theta rhythm (Green & Arduini, 1954). These effects are presumed to occur through thalamic and extrathalamic extensions of the ARAS, the former via the diffuse thalamic projection system (DTPS), particularly nonspecific midline thalamic nuclei, and the latter effects are probably via the medial forebrain bundle (MFB) or pathways closely paralleling the MFB. Because of widespread interconnection of MFB with other systems in the diencephalon, it undoubtedly plays an important role in activation not only within the diencephalon but in the hippocampus and other central structures as well. However, as noted above, electrocortical activation results in desynchronization of slow wave activity whereas synchronized slow waves or theta rhythm is the counterpart in the hippocampus.

The arrows originating in various cortical regions which are directed into the central core of the reticular formation represent the corticifugal pathways by means of which it is possible to stimulate the cortex and record evoked potentials in the reticular formation (French, *et al.*, 1955). Such pathways are presumed to mediate the effects of cortical activity such as might be engendered by thinking, worry, apprehension, and the like, activities which tend to reexcite the reticular activating system and in turn tend to make wakefulness and arousal persist, perhaps to the detriment of one trying to get to sleep or avoid such troublesome worries and apprehensions.

The solid black line with multiple arrows directed into the central reticular core represents a typical classical afferent pathway from receptor sources internally (proprioceptive) or externally (visual, auditory, tactual), which, via lateral afferent pathways or other avenues, proceeds through its synaptic relays to a final thalamic relay nucleus and then projects to its primary cortical receiving station. The collaterals (symbolized by arrows) from such afferent sources enter the reticular formation and constitute the principal sensory inputs to it. The cross-hatched arrows represent centrifugal or feedback control of sensory influx which, as was mentioned earlier, has been shown to act at any synaptic relay along the afferent pathways. Stimulation of the reticular formation (and presumably a sudden surge of sensory input via the collaterals) gives rise to an inhibitory or negative feedback control, although in some instances the effect results in an enhancement of some components of the response at or beyond the synaptic level involved, in which case the effect would be facilitatory.

Thus, in summary, Figure 2 illustrates descending influences of the reticular formation upon spinal motor outflows; ascending influences which produce electrocortical desynchronization and hippocampal synchronization with behavioral arousal, attention, etc.; corticifugal excitation of the reticular formation as well as the classical sensory influx via collaterals; and reticular feedback controls.

From a correlative viewpoint, considering the EEG and behavior, what may be said about the activation or arousal mechanism? How does it operate? What sort of mechanism is involved? Some years ago (Lindsley, 1952b) I prepared a sort of behavioral continuum (see Table I) ranging from death, coma, sleep, light sleep, drowsiness, relaxed wakefulness, alert attentiveness to excited emotion. In death the electrical activity of the EEG subsides and is permanently lost and in coma there is sometimes a temporary absence of electrical activity, a seemingly isoelectric state of the cortex, but usually large, very slow, synchronized waves similar to those seen in deep sleep.

Considering the normal range of sleep–waking behavior, there are the large, slow waves of deep sleep, the mixture of slow waves and spindle bursts of light sleep, and mixtures of low amplitude slow waves and alpha waves of reduced amplitude and frequency during drowsiness. There are several moderately well-defined patterns of the EEG which characterize the several stages or depths of sleep. Generally these can be described as on a kind of continuum from large slow synchronized waves of deep sleep to less slow and large waves as sleep lightens. The beginning or onset of sleep, in which a person may remain for a time, is characterized by lower amplitude, higher frequency slow waves, usually better organized and more regular in waveform than those of deeper sleep. In this initial stage of sleep, where consciousness is lost and the subject is unaware of what is going on around him, the slow waves are interrupted periodically by quite well-defined spindle-shaped bursts comprised of 14-per-sec waves. These spindle bursts are a phasic feature in that they occur, often quite regularly, every few seconds and are superimposed on a more pervasive background of slow waves. They also occur mainly in this first stage of true sleep.

In recent years a new and interesting EEG pattern has been described, which also appears to be a phasic aspect of sleep in that it occurs periodically during the course of a night's sleep, interrupting the more pervasive flow of slow waves during deep sleep. This pattern is characteristic of a phase of sleep referred to as "paradoxical" or REM (rapid eye movement) sleep. The term paradoxical was applied originally because during the relatively brief episodes of paradoxical or REM sleep the EEG was characterized by low amplitude fast activity, or the waking type of EEG, although the subject seemed to be in a profoundly deep sleep with very relaxed body muscles and was more difficult than usual to arouse. Furthermore, it was observed that quick or rapid eye jerks or movements often occurred; when a person was awakened he was usually able to report having been dreaming in contrast to awakening from the pervasive slow waves of deep sleep forming the background of the night's sleep against which these phasic paradoxical episodes occurred several times or more during the night.

Looked at as a whole, it might be said that apart from the two phasic types of activity mentioned above, namely, the 14-per-sec spindle bursts in the first stage of sleep and the low amplitude fast activity of paradoxical or REM sleep which occurs periodically in deeper stages of sleep, there is an EEG continuum which matches roughly the behavioral or psychological state of the human from deep sleep to normal waking relaxation and on to higher levels of mental or emotional activation or excitement. The patterns of the EEG activity comprising this continuum would vary on a frequency dimension, ranging from the very low frequency waves of deep sleep to the higher frequency slow waves of light sleep or drowsiness. These stages of sleep would be followed by the still higher frequency waves of relaxed wakefulness in the absence of stimulation, namely, the alpha waves of about 10 per sec. Beyond this point in the waking portion of the overall sleep–waking continuum, the alpha waves tend to be blocked, broken up, desynchronized, or displaced by still faster waves of perhaps 15 to 50 per sec, during periods of stimulation, excitement, anxiety, and the like. But one cannot speak only of a frequency continuum for there tends to be a progressive reduction in amplitude from the large slow waves of deep sleep to the alpha waves of the relaxed waking state and to the low amplitude fast waves of the emotionally aroused or excited individual. There also appears to be an increase in the regularity of the wave form of the waves at least from the slow waves of deep sleep to the alpha waves of relaxed wakefulness.

On the assumption that the larger and slower the waveform the greater the degree of synchrony of the activity of the underlying

TABLE I

PSYCHOLOGICAL STATES AND THEIR EEG, CONSCIOUS, AND BEHAVIORAL CORRELATES[a]

Behavioral continuum	Electroencephalogram	State of awareness	Behavioral efficiency
Strong, excited emotion (fear, rage anxiety)	Desynchronized: low to moderate amplitude; fast, mixed frequencies.	Restricted awareness; divided attention; diffuse, hazy; "confusion."	Poor: lack of control, freezing-up, disorganized.
Alert attentiveness	Partially synchronized: mainly fast, low amplitude waves.	Selective attention, but may vary or shift, "concentration" anticipation. "set."	Good: efficient selective, quick, reactions; organized for serial responses.
Relaxed wakefulness	Synchronized: optimal alpha rhythm.	Attention wanders, not forced; favors free association.	Good: routine reactions and creative thought.
Drowsiness	Reduced alpha and occasional low amplitude slow waves.	Borderline, partial awareness, imagery reverie; "dream-like states."	Poor: uncoordinated, sporadic, lacking sequential timing.
Light sleep	Spindle bursts and slow waves (larger); loss of alpha.	Markedly reduced consciousness; loss of consciousness; dream state.	Absent
Deep sleep	Large and very slow waves; synchrony but on slow time-base; random, irregular pattern.	Complete loss of awareness; no memory for stimulation or for dreams.	Absent
Coma	Isoelectric to irregular large slow waves.	Complete loss of consciousness, little or no response to stimulation; amnesia.	Absent
Death	Isoelectric: gradual and permanent disappearance of all electrical activity.	Complete loss of awareness as death ensues.	Absent

[a]From Lindsley, 1952b, 443–456.

neural elements contributing these electrical potentials, one could say that the highest degrees of synchrony involving the greatest masses of neural tissue are those of the slow waves of deep sleep, whereas the rhythmic synchrony of the lower amplitude alpha waves of relaxed wakefulness, with differentiable form and pattern over different regions of the head, probably is derived from more localized sources of cortical generators. It is uncertain whether the low amplitude fast activity, or the relative absence of alpha activity, during a so-called activated or aroused state is due to still further differentiation of generator sources or to a combination of this plus increased discharge of neurons with summated multiple spike potentials manifesting themselves. In any event it has been customary to speak of slow waves and alpha waves as synchronized states, and of activation, alpha blockade and so forth as desynchronized states.

Elsewhere (Lindsley, 1950, 1951), human EEG patterns have been illustrated which show that in a normal relaxed subject sitting in a dark room there are more or less continuous rhythmic alpha waves of about 10 per sec, but that when an unexpected weak flash of light or a low intensity auditory signal was presented the alpha rhythm was blocked and the tracing became relatively flat. At the same time a galvanic skin response (GSR) was recorded and there was a slight change in heart rate. Whereas the alpha rhythm was blocked or desynchronized in about two-tenths of a second, the GSR had a latency of at least one second. Also illustrated were the EEGs from a normal subject taken about five minutes apart; initially when the subject was "apprehensive" about the procedure and a little later when he had been reassured and put at ease. The first of these EEGs during "apprehension" showed very little alpha activity and of low amplitude, whereas the second showed strong, persistent alpha activity. In other words, during worry about the experiment and while tense with apprehension the EEG was essentially one of activation and desynchronization, whereas with reassurances and relaxation it became one of synchronized, rhythmic, persistent quality. Still another EEG recorded in a person known to have been in a state of chronic stress and anxiety showed a marked suppression of alpha rhythm. These examples, in the human, tend to confirm the belief that the spontaneous EEG, which is thought to arise from cortical generators (probably dendrites of cortical neurons, but not necessarily discharging neurons), is synchronized and regulated by influences originating in midline nonspecific thalamic nuclei, part of the so-called diffuse thalamic projection system (DTPS). It was in connection with stimulation of these midline thalamic nuclei at low frequencies (7 per sec) that Morison and Dempsey (1942) and Dempsey and Morison (1942a, 1942b) first described the classical recruiting response recorded at the cortical surface as a wave-complex of increasing amplitude and synchrony as the repetitive stimulus continued. Further reference to recruiting responses of this type will be made later, in connection with blockade of the thalamo-orbitocortical system, but suffice it to say at this point that the midline thalamic nuclei which play a role in electrocortical synchronization and regulation of EEG rhythms as mentioned above receive projections from the ascending reticular activating system. Consequently stimulation of the reticular formation (or of the midline thalamic nuclei directly) with electric shocks of 100 to 300 per sec causes desynchronization and blocking of the electrocortical spontaneous rhythms regulated from these nonspecific thalamic centers.

Figure 3 illustrates behavioral and EEG arousal in a sleeping monkey. At the left recordings from the cingulate gyrus and the reticular formation, show synchronized slow wave activity while the monkey is in a sleeping posture with eyes closed; at the right the electrical recordings show low amplitude fast activity, described as

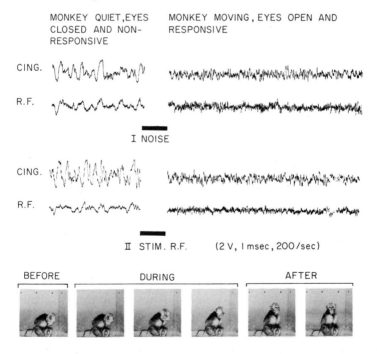

Fig. 3.   Electrophysiological and behavioral arousal in a monkey. See text for explanation. CING., cingulate gyrus; R.F., reticular formation; STIM. R.F., electrical stimulation of reticular formation. (*modified from* Segundo, *et al.*, 1955).

activation or desynchronization, when the monkey is awakened and behaviorally aroused by a sensory stimulus (noise) or by electrical stimulation through electrodes implanted in the reticular formation. At the bottom of the figure is shown the behavioral state before, during, and after stimulation of the reticular formation with the behavior of the monkey shifting from a sleeping to a waking or an aroused and alert state. It should be noted that the electrical recordings show the same type of change from the slow waves and synchrony of sleep to the activated or desynchronized patterns of wakefulness whether the arousing stimulus was a natural sensory one such as noise or direct electrical stimulation of the mesencephalic reticular formation. Segundo, Arana, and French (1955) showed that concurrent behavioral awakening and EEG desynchronization occurred in the monkey whether the arousing stimulus was natural (noise) or artificial (electrical stimulation of reticular formation or cortex). In the case of cortical stimulation it was inferred that the effect was via the reticular formation. Not all cortical sites elicited arousal and differential thresholds were observed. The lowest thresholds were found in the hippocampus, cingulate gyrus, and orbital cortex, regions known to be closely connected with the reticular formation and its projections centralward as mentioned above. The lowest thresholds for arousal were found in the mesencephalic reticular formation. Whereas threshold stimulation in this region produced behavioral arousal from drowsiness or sleep, slightly stronger stimulation produced alerting responses, and still stronger stimulation tended to produce reactions of defense or flight. In a quiet waking animal stimulation of the same sites that produced arousal from sleep caused the animal to raise its head, look around, and become alert as if preparing for possible danger or threat.

Animals with lesions of the midbrain tegmentum or basal diencephalon, thus blocking the ascending reticular activating system (ARAS), were akinetic, somnolent animals unresponsive to sensory arousal stimuli with continuous slow wave and spindle burst activity characteristic of sleep in their electroencephalograms (Lindsley, *et al.*, 1950; French & Magoun, 1952). Similarly, animals under deep ether or pentobarbital anesthesia were unresponsive to sensory stimulation and responses in the reticular formation to such stimuli disappear. However, evoked responses to sciatic nerve stimulation and auditory stimulation may be recorded in the classical afferent pathways of the medial and lateral lemniscii and also in the somatosensory and auditory cortex if the anesthetic state is not too profound (French, Verzeano & Magoun, 1953; French & King, 1955). Thus in the specific sensory system, that is, the primary or classical afferent pathways, the responses to sensory stimulation may be unimpaired when blockade of the ARAS is made by lesion or anesthesia, but the behavior of the animal is one of limpness and anesthetic coma and the electrocortical ongoing activity is one of slow waves and synchrony or marked suppression; responses in the reticular formation are abolished or markedly reduced. This indicates that the nonspecific sensory system, that is the ARAS, is essential to arousal and wakefulness and, as well, to alerting, attention, and discrimination response to the stimuli. In human subjects with damage to the reticular formation of the lower brainstem through disease or injury, there is not only a comatose state but an unawareness and lack of responsiveness to sensory stimulation (French, 1952).

Figure 4 shows the effect of anesthesia upon evoked responses in specific and nonspecific sensory systems. In locally anesthetized, curarized cats and monkeys, electrical recordings were made in the reticular formation and in the medial lemniscus when brief, single

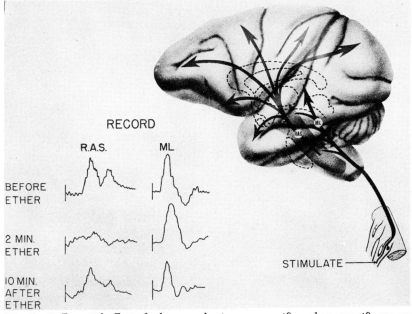

Fig. 4. Differential effect of ether anesthesia upon specific and nonspecific sensory systems. Recording sites are shown on diagram at right ML, classical sensory pathway, medial lemniscus, and RAS, nonspecific reticular activating system. Note that responses to peripheral nerve stimulation during ether are abolished in reticular formation but are relatively unaffected in medial lemniscus (*from* French, J. D. and King, E. E., *Surgery* **38**, 228-238 (1955)).

shocks were administered to the central cut-end of a branch of the sciatic nerve (French, *et al.*, 1953; French & King, 1955). As shown in Figure 4 the response in medial lemniscus (ML) to a single sciatic shock had a short latency and a definite form and pattern all of which were retained before, during and after ether anesthesia. By contrast, the response in the reticular formation was of longer latency before and after ether anesthesia, but was abolished during two minutes of ether. It is apparent that the impulses in the specific or classical sensory pathways were getting through, whereas those in the diffuse, nonspecific sensory system were not. Although specific sensory messages are apparently getting through to the cortex under ether and pentobarbital anesthesia, we know that an anesthetized human is unable to discriminate stimuli or respond to them and likewise an animal trained to make sensory discriminations is unable to do so when anesthetized. Since evoked responses in the ARAS or nonspecific, diffuse, sensory system are lost during the anesthetic state when awareness and ability to discriminate sensory stimuli are also lost, it appears that specific and nonspecific sensory systems must work together to elaborate and decode the messages. Thus an intact and functional ARAS is required for conscious awareness, for wakefulness, for alertness and attention, for discrimination and perception, and indeed for learning. Undoubtedly underlying these processes are the energizing aspects of drive, motivation, and emotion and their regulation and control which must also depend heavily upon this diffuse, nonspecific arousal mechanism.

How do the specific and nonspecific sensory systems work together, as it seems they must? Does the latter serve as a "priming" system for the elaboration of messages or impulses arriving at central stations over the former or specific pathways? Do nonspecific, diffuse, influences via ARAS somehow provide, by appropriate timing and excitability changes or regulation, for short-term memory storage or persistence of messages which must become related to or associated with more permanently stored messages and events in order to be perceived? We do not have answers to these questions, nor do we know how the apparent gradations of arousal, alerting, attention, and so forth are regulated or serve the purpose of rapid scanning, switching, and the like which must take place in a dynamically functioning organism. The diffuse and widespread influence of the ARAS upon the diencephalon, limbic system, and neocortex and reciprocal interactions of these structures and the forebrain upon the lower brainstem reticular formation, discussed at the outset, attest to a complex integrative role. The polysynaptic, multineuronal nature of the reticular formation and its ascending pathways via extrathalamic and thalamic routes, including its interrelationships with ventromedial hypothalamic, dorsomedial thalamic nuclei, and with the medial forebrain bundle and other more laterally placed hypothalamic and thalamic structures, suggest a slower more pervasive effect of ARAS stimulation. This seems to be borne out whether one is recording the evoked responses in the ARAS and contrasting them with those in the specific or classical sensory pathways involving few synapses, or whether one is observing the effects of reticular stimulation upon the ongoing electrocortical background activity of neocortex and hippocampus where reciprocal states of desynchrony and synchrony are observed in response to sensory stimulation. Latency to desynchronization or to synchronization from the onset of a sensory stimulus or electrical stimulation of the reticular formation seems to require 0.1 to 0.3 sec. Elicitation of cortical evoked responses to direct stimulation of the ARAS or via sensory channels and ARAS seems to require about twice as long as those elicited by discharges over direct classical, sensory specific pathways.

Figure 5 illustrates the differences in latencies of evoked potentials via the specific and nonspecific sensory systems, more specifically the classical auditory and somatosensory pathways as contrasted with the ARAS and its diffuse, multineuronal, pathways and their response to auditory and sciatic nerve stimulation. In most instances, at comparable ascending levels, the latency of response to the same stimulus, whether auditory or sciatic, is about double in the diffuse, nonspecific pathways. Delays of the order of 10 to 20 millisec or more in the initiation of nonspecific, diffuse cortical responses over that of locally generated and delimited primary responses seemingly could have a reinforcing effect locally, or a priming effect upon more remote areas not involved in the primary receiving area responses. That is, persistence or pervasiveness of the effect of locally arriving messages could be one role, and elaboration or spread of effect to other more remote areas could be another. The shorter latency delays of ARAS elicited responses would seem to be more in accord with the effects in local receiving areas, whereas the longer latencies to desynchronization of the more widespread ongoing electrocortical activity would be consistent with the time required to initiate action or effect changes in more remote association areas.

How do such influences, both local and the more widespread ones, via the ARAS reach the cortex? What role does the midline thalamic system play in this transmission and in the regulation of electrocortical activity and synchronization? Morison and Dempsey (1942) and

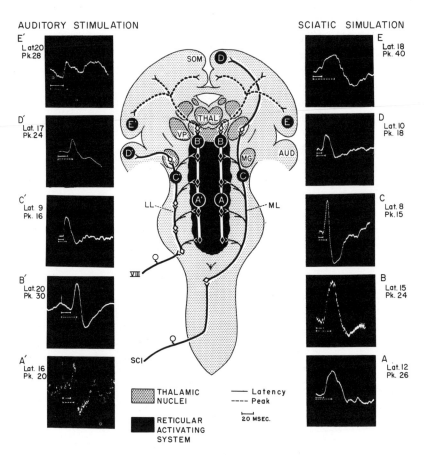

Fig. 5. Latencies of auditory and sciatic nerve stimulation along classical specific sensory pathways to cortex and via the nonspecific ascending reticular activating system from reticular formation to cortex. Auditory and sciatic elicited potentials in lateral specific sensory pathways C' and C, respectively, and in cortical receiving areas D' and D are of considerably shorter latency than those in nonspecific sensory pathways A', A (reticular formation), B', B (medial thalamus) and E', E (association cortex). Both peak, Pk., and onset latency, Lat., are given. SCI, sciatic nerve; VIII, eighth cranial (auditory) nerve; LL, lateral lemniscus; ML, medial lemniscus; MG, medial geniculate; VP, nucleus ventralis posterior; THAL, thalamus; SOM, somatic cortex; AUD, auditory cortex (*from* French, *et al.*, 1953).

Dempsey and Morison (1942a, 1942b) had observed that stimulation of certain midline and intralaminar nuclei in the cat would produce recruiting responses at a frequency of stimulation (7-8 per sec) comparable to that of the ongoing rhythms of the cortex and proposed a regulatory interaction. Lindsley, Bowden, and Magoun (1949), after lesions of the midbrain tegmentum, found persistent and periodic electrocortical spindle bursts with similar simultaneous bursts in midline thalamic and intralaminar nuclei. Lesions of intralaminar thalamus abolished the cortical spindles. Here were two reliably produced effects: recruiting responses, and spindle bursts, each having synchronous, wave-like components and characteristic temporal features not unlike those of the spontaneous background activity. The effects were dependent upon reticulo–thalamocortical interactions. Extensive midline thalamic lesions (intralaminar and/or more rostral midline nuclei) blocked these effects in the cortex. What region of the cortex might be crucial to them?

EFFECT OF BLOCKADE OF RETICULO-THALAMO-ORBITOFRONTAL CORTEX SYSTEM

Systematic ablations of the cortex were made in an effort to abolish recruiting responses and spindle bursts (Velasco and Lindsley, 1965; Velasco, *et al.*, 1968). Cortical ablations in cats were made in three steps; first, ablations of primary, specific, sensory areas including visual, auditory, and somatosensory; second, ablations of association cortex (suprasylvian and cingulate gyri) and motor cortex; finally, ablations of orbital cortex. Only the last type of lesion was effective in blocking recruiting responses and spindle bursts, and such a lesion of the orbital cortex alone, with all other cortex intact, was similarly effective. Figure 6 shows the blocking of spindle bursts (A) and recruiting responses (B) by orbitofrontal cortex ablation. Therefore, the orbitofrontal cortex, it was concluded, plays a crucial role in the regulation of thalamocortical synchronizing and integrating functions. These functions are believed to be associated with a nonspecific reticulo-thalamo-cortical system governing internal inhibition which manifests itself in inattention, drowsiness, and sleep. Synchronized slow waves and spindle bursts are characteristic of sleep, and even the synchronized, rhythmic, alpha waves of normal relaxed waking states are associated with inattentiveness, whereas desynchronization or blocking of the alpha rhythm is associated with alertness and attention.

Thus it became apparent that an important link in the thalamo-cortical synchronizing system responsible for spindle bursts and recruiting responses was the orbito-frontal cortex, and that this region was linked with the midline thalamus. In animals with intact reticular formation, and therefore no spindle bursts except in natural sleep, recruiting responses with widespread but differential areal representation were blocked by high frequency stimulation of the

A   B

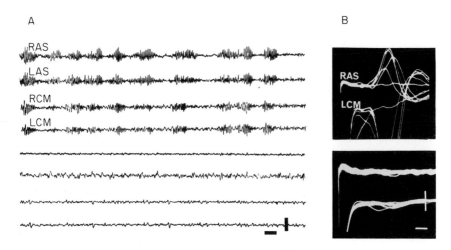

Fig. 6. Abolition of spindle bursts and recruiting responses in cortex and thalamus of cat following orbitofrontal cortical ablation. A (top): periodic, spontaneous spindle bursts in cortex and thalamus simultaneously following blocking lesion of midbrain tegmentum; (bottom) all spindle bursts absent following lesion of orbital cortex. B (top): recruiting responses elicited in cortex (RAS) and thalamus (LCM) by low-frequency stimulation of nuclei of midline thalamus; (bottom) absence of recruiting responses following orbital cortex lesion. Recording sites: right and left anterior sigmoid gyri (RAS and LAS) of cortex; right and left nucleus centrum medianum (RCM and LCM). Calibrations: A, 1 second, 400 μV.; B, 20 msec., 200 μV (*from* Velasco, M. and Lindsley, D. B., *Science*, 149, 1375-1377, (17 September 1965). Copyright 1965 by the American Association for the Advancement of Science.).

reticular formation. Such reticular activation interferes with the incrementation process of recruiting responses and also with the waxing and waning amplitude modulation of such responses (Velasco, *et al.*, in press).

To further probe the nature of this reticulo-thalamo-cortical system along midline thalamic pathways, lesions were made anterior to the recruiting stimulation sites in nucleus centralis lateralis or other regions of the midline nuclear complex. In particular, lesions of the nucleus ventralis anterior (VA), especially involving the midline region, were made and found to abolish recruiting responses and spindle bursts. Next, electrolytic lesions were made in the bundle of fibers constituting the inferior thalamic peduncle (ITP), in the forebrain region, which is assumed to be a connecting link between midline thalamus and orbito-frontal cortex. Lesions of ITP were effective in blocking recruiting and spindle bursts. Finally, a cryogenic probe, capable of being cooled at its tip to 10°C. without damaging the tissue cooled, was inserted in the region of ITP. When cooled it blocked recruiting responses and spindle bursts and when warmed again to normal temperature there was a reversible effect with return of recruiting responses and spindle bursts (Skinner & Lindsley, 1967; for method of cooling see Skinner & Lindsley, 1968). When the cooling probe was 2–3 mm lateralward and in the region of the internal capsule, recruiting responses were not blocked but augmenting responses elicited by stimulation in nucleus ventralis lateralis were reduced or blocked. These augmenting effects, characteristic of recruiting-type stimulation in the region of specific thalamic relay nuclei, are transmitted via the internal capsule in contrast to the recruiting responses initiated in midline nonspecific thalamic nuclei which are blocked by lesions or cooling of the ITP.

Figure 7 shows the blocking effects of cooling on spindle bursts and recruiting responses when the ITP on one side was blocked by cryogenic lesion and on the other side by cooling of ITP with a cryogenic probe. Augmenting responses were not affected since cooling in the region of ITP did not involve the internal capsule. Figure 7A,

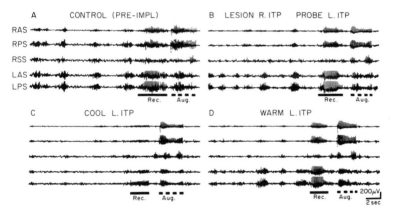

Fig. 7. Effect of lesion and reversible cryogenic blockade of inferior thalamic peduncle (ITP) on spindle bursts, recruiting responses and augmenting responses recorded from right and left cortical sites in cat. A, control, (PRE–IMPL), prior to implantation of cryoprobe but following blocking lesion of mesencephalic tegmentum causing periodic and simultaneous spindle bursts diffusely in cortex; recruiting (Rec.) and augmenting (Aug.) responses elicited by low-frequency stimulation of left centralis medialis and right ventralis lateralis nuclei, respectively; B, following lesion of right ITP and uncooled cryoprobe in left ITP, spindle bursts abolished on right and present on left, recruiting and augmenting responses unaffected; C, cooling of left ITP blocks remaining spindle bursts and reduces recruiting responses but does not affect augmenting responses; D, following warming of left ITP to normal level the spindle bursts and recruiting responses return. Recording sites on cortex: right and left anterior sigmoid gyri (RAS and LAS), right suprasylvian gyrus (RSS), right and left posterior sigmoid gyri (RPS and LPS). Recruiting site: left nucleus centralis medialis; augmenting site: right nucleus ventralis lateralis (*from* Skinner, J. E. and Lindsley, D. B., *Brain Research* 6, 95–118 (1967)).

prior to implantation of the cryoprobe in the left ITP, shows the regularly recurring spindle bursts on both right and left sides of the cortex following bilateral lesion of the midbrain tegmentum, recruiting responses elicited by stimulation of a nucleus in the nonspecific midline nuclear complex (left nucleus centralis medialis) and augmenting responses elicited by stimulation of the right nucleus ventralis lateralis. Prior to record B, a cryogenic lesion of the right ITP was made and the cryoprobe was implanted in the region of the left ITP, but not yet cooled. Lesion of the right ITP markedly reduced the spindle bursts on the right side, but did not affect those on the left side, nor did the presence of the uncooled cryoprobe in the region of the left ITP. Neither recruiting responses (elicited by stimulation of the left nucleus centralis medialis) nor augmenting responses (elicited from right nucleus ventralis lateralis) were affected since in the case of the former the ITP lesion was on the opposite side, and in the case of the latter the lesion was in the right ITP and did not involve the right internal capsule. Although unilaterally initiated in the thalamus, both recruiting and augmenting effects tend to spread to the contralateral side, though they are larger on the side of stimulation. In record C, the tip of the cryoprobe in the intact left ITP was cooled and resulted in the blocking of the spindle bursts over the left cortical recording sites (spindle bursts on the right were already absent due to cryogenic lesion of the right ITP), and marked reduction or blocking of the recruiting responses on the right, but no effect on the augmenting responses mediated by the internal capsule rather than ITP. Record D shows the reversible effect of warming the cryoprobe to normal temperature; both spindle bursts and recruiting responses return to precooling level. Thus we see that the inferior thalamic peduncle (ITP) is a crucial forebrain link in the reticulo–thalamo–orbitocortical system mediating electrocortical synchronization and regulation and presumably internal inhibition associated with synchronization and progressively slower and larger waves and spindle bursts such as occur in sleep.

In addition to the above effects of ITP blockade by lesion or cooling upon recruiting responses and spindle bursts, cooling of ITP in acute cat preparations under gallamine triethiodide and local anesthesia enhanced the amplitude of evoked potentials (both primary and secondary components) elicited in the visual cortex by photic stimulation or by electrical stimulation of the optic tract. It was as if a partial inhibitory "blanket" affecting widespread cortical areas was removed thus allowing enhancement of the evoked responses.

In chronic cat preparations with cryoprobes bilaterally implanted in the region of ITP, bar-pressing for a milk reward was avidly performed in hungry animals trained for this purpose when ITP was not cooled, but stopped when cooling was maintained at 10°C. and reinstated when the region of ITP was brought back to normal temperature. Thus a trained behavioral act (bar-pressing) readily performed under normal conditions of arousal and motivation was interrupted by cryogenic blockade of the reticulo-thalamo-orbitocortical system. The cat simply turned away from the bar-pressing lever as if disinterested or inattentive to an instrumental task which previously satisfied a motivated drive state. Rattling the lever would often cause the cat to return and make a few presses and then stop pressing again. Thus it could and did press for food reward when the lever was brought to its attention, but it seemed that it could not maintain attention to the task while ITP was blocked by cooling. However, the cat resumed bar-pressing as soon as ITP returned to normal temperature. Thus the drive state was not lost by cooling and behavioral responses were reversibly resumed when the blocking effect of cooling was removed.

Figure 8E shows three effects of cooling ITP in a chronic cat preparation with bilateral cryoprobes in the region of ITP. In the top tracing, evoked responses, elicited by optic tract stimulation and recorded from visual cortex, are shown in the precool and cooled state, and illustrate the enhancement of the amplitude of the evoked response during blockade of the ITP during cooling. In the middle tracing recruiting responses, initiated by 8-per-second stimulation in nucleus centralis medialis, are seen prior to cooling, but are blocked in the cooled state. In the bottom tracing, showing a cumulative record of bar-pressing for milk reward, the approximately 45 degree slope of the curve indicates a steady bar-pressing rate during the precooling phase, but a complete cessation of pressing during cooling. Figure 8C shows that precooling and cooling phases in a control cat with cryoprobe near, but not in, ITP give essentially the same evoked visual cortex responses, similar recruiting responses and steady bar-pressing responses, although the rate of pressing was lower in the cooling phase. The solid triangle midway in the cooling phase of bar-pressing indicates an attempt to distract the cat from bar-pressing by introducing a distracting stimulus. It caused only momentary cessation of pressing and the bar-pressing was resumed at the previous rate. Thus, in this instance, distracting the cat's attention from the bar-pressing task did not prevent it from resuming immediately once its curiosity had been satisfied or the distracting stimulus was removed.

In the foregoing results dealing with lesions of the orbitofrontal

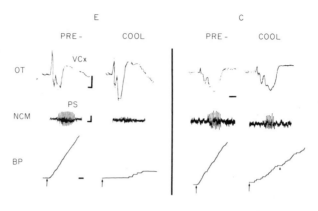

THREE EFFECTS OF COOLING ITP TO + 10°C

Fig. 8. Effects of cryogenic blockade of inferior thalamic peduncle (ITP) upon (1) visual cortex (VCX) evoked responses elicited by optic tract (OT) stimulation; (2) posterior sigmoid gyrus (PS) recruiting responses elicited by stimulation of nucleus centralis medialis (NCM); and (3) rate of cumulative bar-presses (*BP*) for food reward. Experimental condition (E) with ITP cooled shows enhanced evoked potentials of visual cortex, blocked recruiting responses and stoppage of bar-pressing. Control condition (C) in another cat with cryoprobes near, but not in, region of ITP shows little effect of cooling of the three types of response. Cooling to 10° C. Calibrations: time 0.5 sec for recruiting, 5 msec for visual response, 1 min. for bar-pressing; all amplitude marks 100 μV. OT potentials represent the mean of 30 responses computer-averaged; 3 such averages superimposed (*from* Skinner, J. E. and Lindsley, D. B., *Brain Research* 6, 95-118 (1967)).

cortex or with interruption or cryogenic blockade of the pathways mediating the reticulo–thalamo–orbitocortical effects (blockade of electrocortical synchronizing and regulating influences as manifested by spindle bursts and recruiting responses) we have seen evidence of a "system" which seems to regulate and govern to some extent not only the ongoing electrocortical activity with respect to its synchronization and modulation, but also influencing evoked potentials in the cortex. There is indication that both early and late components of the evoked response may be enhanced when the synchronizing, slow wave, inhibitory system is blocked. Such a mechanism of regulation of evoked responses by suppression or enhancement might, if differentially effective on sensory input, serve as a basis for explanation of the selective effect of focusing attention upon one sensory mode or another. In fact there is evidence from human average evoked potentials recorded from the surface of the scalp to suggest that such differential effects can be produced by attention. There is also some evidence that the background level of electrocortical activity, particularly that associated with activation or arousal level (desynchronization), may influence the extent to which average evoked potentials are enhanced by attention or vigilance. Brief mention will now be made of some of these effects observed in humans.

EXPERIMENTS ON VIGILANCE, ATTENTION, AND SELECTIVE ATTENTIVENESS

Several investigators in varied types of experiments, involving different sense modalities, have found that some of the components of average evoked potentials, particularly the later ones, manifest an increased amplitude when attention to the task involving the stimuli (e.g., discrimination of a particular stimulus from others, such as detecting weaker or dimmer stimuli imbedded in a series of stronger or brighter stimuli) is stressed in the instructions to the subject (Garcia-Austt, 1963; Garcia-Austt, Bogacz, & Vanzulli, 1964; Haider, Spong, & Lindsley, 1964; Davis, 1964; Chapman & Bragdon, 1964; Spong, Haider, & Lindsley, 1965; Satterfield, 1965; and others). A few investigators have found, on the contrary, that attention may reduce the amplitude of certain evoked potential components or produce no reliable change (Van Hof, Van Hof-Van Duin, Van der Mark, & Rietveld, 1962; Satterfield & Cheatum, 1964; Callaway, Jones & Layne, 1965). In some studies the tension or stress involved in the task seems to raise the level of activity of the arousal or activation mechanism generally and be responsible for some of the enhancement of average evoked potentials observed. Thus it becomes apparent that more than one mechanism may be involved in the enhancement of the various components of the evoked potential; some may involve predominantly inhibitory and some predominantly excitatory processes, but the ARAS and DTPS as these may be represented in the reticulo-thalamo–orbitocortical system seem likely to play a significant role.

Figure 9 illustrates the effect of attention and prolonged vigilance upon averaged visually evoked potentials in humans. This experiment by Haider, *et al.* (1964) required that a subject lie quietly and comfortably upon a cot looking into a radar-like viewing hood at an opal glass diffusing plate upon which moderately bright, brief, photoflashes were imposed at the rate of one every 3 sec. The subject's task was merely to remain alert and observe these passively, but for 10 dimmer flashes interspersed among the 100 bright flashes presented in a five minute period he was to press a key as quickly as possible. This discrimination detection task was to keep the subject

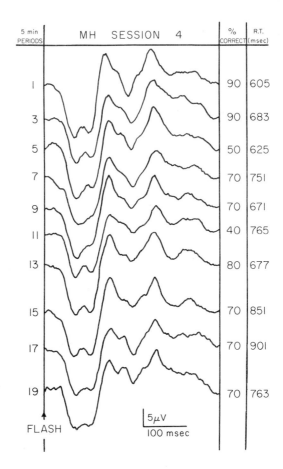

Fig. 9. Computer-averaged evoked potentials for 100 nonsignal visual stimuli presented during successive 5-minute periods of a 1½-hour visual vigilance task, together with the percentages of randomly interspersed dim visual stimuli detected during the same time periods. Recordings: occipital to vertex reference; negativity upwards. Subject MH (*from* Haider, M., *et al.*, *Science* **145**, 180–182 (10 July 1964). Copyright 1964 by the American Association for the Advancement of Science.).

alert and provide a measure of the percentage of dim flashes detected in each five-minute period during a session about 1½ hours long. It was assumed that vigilance (and attentiveness) would wax and wane during this prolonged session, and it did. Figure 9 shows, in the percent-correct column, that the number of dim signals detected and responded to in this particular 1½-hour session varied from 90% at the start to 70% at the end of the session. Generally there was an overall reduction in detection of dim signals over the 20 five-minute periods constituting the 1½-hour vigilance session. Average reaction times to the dim signals detected and responded to increased as the percent of correct detections diminished. It was inferred that with a low percentage of detections the subject's attentiveness or vigilance had diminished since the subject could readily discriminate between the bright and dim lights when alert and attentive.

Each tracing shown represents the average evoked response (algebraic sum of 100 responses) to the 100 bright flashes. It will be noted that when the percent of correct detections fell to 40% during the 11th five-minute period that the amplitude of the average evoked response for that period was markedly diminished from that of the first or third five-minute period where the dim signals were responded to 90% of the time. Thus, in most instances where attention or vigilance remained high during a given 5-minute period, the amplitude of the average evoked response was enhanced and where attention waned it was diminished. Percent of correct detections of dim signals in each five minute period over the 1½-hour session diminished and, more or less parallel with this change, there was a progressive reduction in the amplitude of the average evoked potentials. The correlation between these two functions for 3 subjects each studied during 5 sessions was +0.75. The correlation between percentage correct and the latency of the average evoked potentials measured to some characteristic peak was −0.75. Thus we see that when attention is well maintained the evoked responses to stimuli during that particular 5-minute period of time (or over a longer time) are enhanced in amplitude and, contrastingly, when inattentiveness prevailed and signals went undetected and not responded to, or were detected and responded to with a long reaction time, the amplitude was reduced. When the average evoked responses to 49 dim signals correctly detected were compared to the average evoked responses to 49 dim signals which were missed, the former showed high amplitude average evoked responses whereas the latter showed markedly diminished amplitude even though the eyes, monitored by television camera, were open and the dim signal flashes were the same throughout. To remain alert and attentive through a long vigilance period such as this suggests that the reticulo-thalamo-cortical activating system must be fairly steadily functional, reinforced presumably by the instructions to remain alert and attentive and respond as quickly as possible to the dim flashes. It is believed that the activating system, which presumably increases the level of excitability of the visual cortex to the flashes (since the size of the summed elec-

trical responses was greater during attentiveness), does so by regulating the degree of asynchrony of the background electrical activity.
Attentiveness does wax and wane; so does the degree of synchrony
or asynchrony of the background electrical activity. The degree of
synchrony as manifested in alpha-like waves or other slower waves is
a function of the degree of arousal or wakefulness, and the degree of
asynchrony is presumably related to the degree of alertness, attentiveness, and vigilance. Slow waves of synchronous nature abound
during drowsiness and sleep and are believed to represent a state of
internal inhibition; suppressed alpha waves and low amplitude fast
waves representing activation and asynchrony seem to be associated
with enhanced excitability of cortical units and reduced internal inhibition. Under conditions which go beyond alertness and an attentive set to remain vigilant, such as during emotional excitement, fear,
anger, worry, or apprenhension, the emotional or affective component may be responsible for the EEG desynchronization. It would be
interesting to know whether average evoked potentials recorded
under these conditions would be enhanced as they are under an attentive set. It is generally recognized with respect to performance
that a certain amount of tension or stress (activation or arousal) enhances performance but that, when the tension and anxiety are too
great, performance suffers. Thus it would appear that, within limits,
attentive activation mechanisms and affective or emotional activation
mechanisms may be reinforcing of each other, but that when the
degree of activity of the emotional activation mechanism reaches certain limits there may be interferences and conflicts between the
functioning of the two mechanisms. Thus there is reason to explore
further the possible interactions and relationships which exist between "systems" such as the reticulo–thalamo–orbitocortical system
dealt with above and the reticulo–diencephalic–limbic system discussed at the outset of this paper. As was emphasized, there is a great
deal of overlap of these neural systems, and probably certain interactive limits within which they can function cooperatively or antago-
nistically.

We have seen that states of attentiveness and vigilance seem to
increase the amplitude of average evoked potentials to bright visual
stimuli passively received (i.e., requiring no key-pressing response)
though requiring discrimination from interspersed dimmer visual
flashes. Similarly, the dim flashes detected and responded to by a
key-press gave average evoked potentials of higher amplitude than
those of dim flashes not detected by the subject. Since the subject's
eyes were open and directed toward the stimulus source, it is as-

sumed that he "saw" the undetected dim flashes but was not sufficiently attentive to discriminate them from the brighter flashes among which they were intermingled. In this experiment the enhancement of average evoked potentials with attentiveness involved visual stimuli only; the next experiment to be discussed involves two sense modes.

Figure 10 illustrates results in an experiment by Spong *et al.*, (1965) in which it was demonstrated that there was enhancement of average evoked potentials to the stimuli in a given sense mode to which the subject was asked to attend selectively in contrast to stimuli in another sense mode which he was asked to ignore. Briefly, the subject received flashes and clicks alternately every second (e.g., flash-click-flash-click, etc.). As in the experiment previously reported there were dim flashes and weak clicks imbedded in the regular series of flashes and clicks to which the subject was asked to respond by pressing a key in order that he would remain alert and attentive to the task. The subject was instructed either to attend to the flashes and ignore the clicks, or vice versa; the first situation was called the visual task, the second the auditory task. Average evoked responses to flashes and clicks were recorded over visual and auditory areas, respectively. Figure 10 shows the responses recorded over visual (occipital) and auditory (temporal) areas for two subjects under the two task conditions. The top pair of traces for each subject shows the flash responses recorded over the occipital area when the subject had the visual task (pay attention to flashes and ignore clicks) and when he was given the auditory task (pay attention to clicks and ignore flashes). It will be noted for each subject that the amplitude of the average evoked potentials for the visual stimuli was greater when the subject was attending to flashes and ignoring clicks, than when attending to clicks and ignoring flashes. Similarly, in the bottom pair of tracings for each subject, the average evoked responses to clicks recorded over the temporal area were larger when the subject was instructed to attend to clicks and ignore flashes than when he attended to flashes and ignored clicks.

This experiment was repeated by Näätänen (1967), working in my laboratory, with identical results, but he found that by making the alternating presentation of flashes and clicks irregular (i.e., with differing durations between two consecutive stimuli) that enhancement of evoked responses did not occur in the case of the sense mode to which the subject was asked to attend. One may fairly raise the question, however, whether it is possible to maintain attention selectively to a task where the stimuli occur repetitively but quite irregularly.

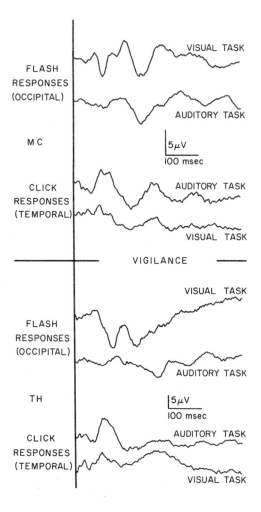

Fig. 10. Computer-averaged cortical evoked potentials from two subjects (MC and TH) in response to flash and click stimuli in a selective attention experiment, under a vigilance task, either attending to flashes and pressing a key to interspersed dim flashes or attending to clicks and pressing key to weak clicks. Flashes alternated with clicks throughout; clicks were ignored during visual attention task and vice versa. Each trace represents the average for 300 stimuli. Analysis time 500 msec. Recordings: right occipital and temporal areas, reference to left ear; negativity upward (*from* Spong, P., *et al.*, *Science* **148**, 395–397 (16 April 1970). Copyright 1970 by the American Association for the Advancement of Science.).

Attention seems to be facilitated by one's ability to organize his responses (and his attention) according to a rhythmic or periodic schedule. Otherwise there is constant need for adjustment which may interfere with the maintenance of a selectively attentive set.

It seems likely that, in addition to a diffusely organized reticulo-thalamo-cortical system for arousal and alerting, as well as for the activation of emotional and motivational states, it is necessary to involve some kind of interaction between nonspecific general arousal systems and specific sensory systems in the case of selective attentiveness, whether it involves a single sense mode or different sense modes. Such switching of influence from one mode to another, or to different attentive features within a given mode, would seem to be most efficiently accomplished at the thalamic level where there is close association between nonspecific and specific systems.

DIFFERENTIATION OF SPECIFIC AND NONSPECIFIC SENSORY SYSTEMS

The last "system" approach to be taken up here relates to an understanding of some of these mechanisms of nonspecific and specific nature and may be illustrated from the results of some experiments by Rose and Lindsley (1965; 1968). Visually evoked responses were recorded (see Figure 11) in the same kitten at different times from 4 to 42 days of age. At an early age (4 days) a single photoflash stimulus to the right eye caused a single, long-latency (about 200 msec) nega-

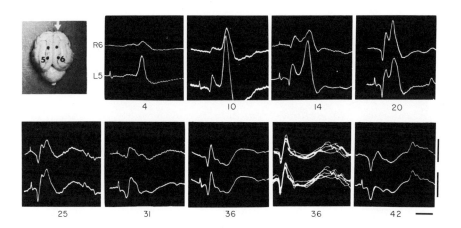

Fig. 11. A series of recordings of visually evoked cortical responses in the same kitten from 4 to 42 days of age. Tracings were obtained under light pentobarbital anesthesia. Arrow before brain photo indicates eye stimulated. Initial upward deflection indicates light flash. Note single negative wave over contralateral cortex at 4 days; but a short latency positive-negative complex and the longer latency negative wave from 10 to 20 days; finally coalescence of latter with former. Calibrations: 100 msec; 100 μV. Negativity upward (*from* Rose and Lindsley, 1968).

tive wave in the contralateral visual cortex. By 10 days of age this response had grown in amplitude and shortened in latency; at the same age a shorter latency positive-negative wave complex appeared. By 20 days of age the short latency positive-negative response and the longer latency negative wave were present over both contralateral and ipsilateral visual cortices, but the original long-latency negative wave had begun to overlap the negative phase of the positive-negative short latency wave complex. By 31 days of age this coalescence was about complete and the negative wave seemed to encompass both forms of these developing responses. By 36 days the response pattern was very much as it is observed in an adult cat and was quite consistently repeated as the several overlapping responses to repeated stimuli show. It was hypothesized that when there were the two kinds of responses which could be distinguished (from about 10 to 20 days), the shorter latency positive-negative complex was the result of impulses arriving at the visual cortex over the classical visual pathway via lateral geniculate nucleus and that the longer latency negative wave which first became manifest at 4 or 5 days was the result of impulses arriving over the branch of the optic tract which sends fibers via the brachium of the superior colliculus to the midbrain tectal region. There are several possibilities by means of which impulses reaching the tectum could find their way into the nonspecific sensory system, including the reticular formation and the several so-called nonspecific nuclei of the thalamus, including midline nuclei and/or posterolateral association nuclei, especially the pulvinar.

On the basis of this hypothesis with respect to the specific and nonspecific origins of these short and longer latency responses seen separately in the 10-to-20-day kitten, lesions were made in the superior colliculus and pretectal region which abolished the long latency negative wave but left the positive-negative short latency response complex unaffected. When a lesion was made in the dorsal nucleus of the lateral geniculate body the short latency positive-negative response disappeared but the long latency negative response remained. Thus the hypothesis was confirmed to the extent that these developing visually evoked responses appear to involve different routes from the eye to the cortex; one follows the classical specific sensory visual pathway, while the other follows a route consistent with activation of the ARAS or DTPS nonspecific and diffusely effective systems. It should be mentioned that the positive-negative short latency specific response could be recorded only over the visual cortex, whereas the long latency negative nonspecific responses could be recorded over nonvisual areas of the cortex as well and in this sense it was contrastingly nonspecific.

Thus we have seen that at certain early developmental stages specific and nonspecific sensory systems can be distinguished; as the kitten matures certain portions of these previously separated responses overlap and eventually coalesce into one characteristic evoked response. However, there is reason to believe that these specific and nonspecific mechanisms continue to exist and function with respect to sensory input via two routes, and because of the activating and arousal nature of the ARAS, and the diffusing, modulating and regulating nature of the DTPS system which has been shown to control electrocortical background activity, it seems likely that some of the manifestations of arousal, alerting, and attention may occur due to interactions of these specific and nonspecific systems.

Another route of nonspecific nature which we have explored by mapping responses in the pulvinar and other lateral association nuclei to visual, auditory, and somatosensory stimuli, may well be of significance (Huang, 1968). We have found it to be a polysensory system, responding to each of these sense modes, though with some suggestion of differentiation regionally. Experiments, by Huang and Lindsley, as yet unpublished, have sought to define the route by which these polysensory convergence centers receive their input and in what manner they influence cortical evoked responses. Since the pulvinar is known to project to a region bordering the visual, auditory, and somatosensory cortex it would seem to be in a unique position to influence sensory input and the integration of it. Certainly, traced phylogenetically, it is observed that the pulvinar and associated nuclei increase markedly in size as encephalization and elaborative functions increase to the level of man.

SUMMARY

Underlying emotion, which expresses itself through various cortical, visceral, and somatomotor channels, are mechanisms of arousal and activation which involve reticulo-thalamo-cortical systems. Thought, worry, and anxiety reflect emotional arousal at the cortical level; weeping, sweating, intestinal, and other visceral activities regulated by the autonomic nervous system reflect cortical, diencephalic, and brain stem arousal; facial expression, muscle tension, and tremors manifest somatomotor arousal. Mechanisms of arousal and activation are especially identified with the reticular formation of the lower brainstem. Upward extensions, including the ascending reticular activating system and its subsystems are closely related to, and interactive with, diencephalic and limbic systems which control emotional expression and emotional–motivational behavior.

The concept of an activation theory of emotion is discussed in the light of early and more recent supporting evidence. Functions of the descending and ascending reticular systems are discussed, including sleep-wakefulness, arousal, alerting, attention, selective attentiveness, and vigilance. The extensive overlap and interaction of the ascending reticular activating system with other central neural structures involved in emotion are believed to be important factors in the control of autonomic activity, emotional behavior, and internal inhibition at the cortical level which is manifested in electrocortical synchrony. Recent experiments are described in which the effect of blockade of the reticulo-thalamo-cortical system is assessed in terms of electrocortical activity, both spontaneous and evoked, and behavior. Specific and nonspecific sensory systems are differentiated experimentally, and their role in perceptual discrimination, attention, and emotion are discussed. Human experiments on vigilance, attention, and selective attentiveness are presented.

ACKNOWLEDGMENTS

Research supported by Office of Naval Research (nonr-4756); National Aeronautics and Space Administration (NASA NGL-05-007-049) and United States Public Health Service (NS 08552-01).

REFERENCES

Bach, L. M. N. and Magoun, H. W. The vestibular nuclei as an excitatory mechanism for the cord. *Journal of Neurophysiology* 1947, **5**, 331–337.

Berger, H. Über das Electrenkephalogramm des Menschen. *Archiv für Psychiatrie und Nervenkrankheiten.* 1933, 99, 555–574.

Bremer, F. and Stoupel, N. Facilitation et inhibition des potentiels évoqués corticaux dans l'éveil cérébral. *Archives Internationales de Physiologie et de Biochimie.* 1959, 67, 240–275.

Callaway, E., Jones, R. T. and Layne, R. S. Evoked responses and segmental set of schizophrenia. *Archives General Psychiatry.* 1965, **12**, 83–89.

Carli, G., Malliani, A. and Zanchetti, A. Midbrain course of descending pathways mediating sham rage behavior. *Experimental Neurology* 1963, **7**, 210–223.

Chapman, R. M. and Bragdon, H. R. Evoked responses to numerical and non-numerical visual stimuli while problem solving. *Nature* 1964, **203**, 1155–1157.

Davis, H. Enhancement of evoked cortical potentials in humans related to a task requiring a decision. *Science* 1964, **145**, 182–183.

Delgado, J. M. R., Roberts, W. W. and Miller, N. E. Learning motivated by electrical stimulation of the brain. *American Journal Physiology* 1954, **179**, 587-593.

Dempsey, E. W. and Morison, R. S. The production of rhythmically recurrent cortical potentials after localized thalamic stimulation. *American Journal Physiology* 1942a, **135**, 293-300.

Dempsey, E. W. and Morison, R. S. The interaction of certain spontaneous and induced cortical potentials. *American Journal Physiology* 1942b, **135**, 301-308.

Dumont, S. and Dell, P. Facilitation réticulaire des mécanismes visuels corticaux. *Electroencephalography and Clinical Neurophysiology* 1960, **12**, 769-796.

Egger, M. D. and Flynn, J. P. Effects of electrical stimulation of the amygdala on hypothalamically elicited attack behavior in cats. *Journal of Neurophysiology* 1963, **26**, 705-720.

Fernandez de Molina, A. and Hunsperger, R. W. Central representation of affective reactions in forebrain and brain stem: electrical stimulation of amygdala, stria terminalis, and adjacent structures. *Journal of Physiology* 1959, **145**, 251-265.

French, J. D. Brain lesions associated with prolonged unconsciousness. *Archives of Neurology and Psychiatry, Chicago.* 1952, **68**, 727-740.

French, J. D., Hernández-Peón, R. and Livingston, R. B. Projections from cortex to cephalic brain stem (reticular formation) in monkey. *Journal of Neurophysiology* 1955, **18**, 44-55.

French, J. D. and King, E. E. Mechanisms involved in the anesthetic state. *Surgery* 1955, **38**, 228-238.

French, J. D. and Magoun, H. W. Effects of chronic lesions in central cephalic brain stem of monkeys. *Archives of Neurology and Psychiatry, Chicago.* 1952, **68**, 591-604.

French, J. D., Verzeano, M. and Magoun, H. W. An extralemniscal sensory system in the brain. *Archives of Neurology and Psychiatry, Chicago.* 1953, **69**, 505-518.

Fuster, J. M. Effects of stimulation of brain stem on tachistoscopic perception. *Science* 1958, **127**, 150.

Garcia-Austt, E. Influences of the states of awareness upon sensory evoked potentials. *Electroencephalography & Clinical Neurophysiology* 1963, **Suppl. 24**, 76-89.

Garcia-Austt, E., Bogacz, J. and Vanzulli, A. Effects of attention and inattention upon visual evoked response. *Electroencephalography & Clinical Neurophysiology* 1964, **17**, 136-143.

Granit, R. Centrifugal and antidromic effects on ganglion cells of retina. *Journal of Neurophysiology* 1955, **18**, 388-411.

Green, J. D. and Arduini, A. Hippocampal electrical activity in arousal. *Journal of Neurophysiology* 1954, **17**, 533-557.

Hagbarth, K. E. and Kerr, D. I. B. Central influences on spinal afferent conduction. *Journal of Neurophysiology* 1954, **17**, 295-307.

Haider, M., Spong, P. and Lindsley, D. B. Attention, vigilance and cortical evoked-potentials in humans. *Science* 1964, **145**, 180-182.

Hernández-Peón, R. Central mechanisms controlling conduction along central sensory pathways. *Acta Neurologica Latinoamerica* 1955, **1**, 256-264.

Hernández-Peón, R., Scherrer, R. H. and Velasco, M. Central influences on afferent conduction in the somatic and visual pathways. *Acta Neurologica Latinoamerica* 1956, **2**, 8-22.

Huang, C. Electrophysiological analysis of sensory evoked responses in the posterior thalamic association areas with special reference to the pulvinar. Ph.D. Dissertation, University of California, Los Angeles, 1968.

Hunsperger, R. W. Affektreaktionen auf elektrische Reizung im Hirnstamm der Katze. *Helvetica Physiologica et Pharmacologica Acta* 1956, **14**, 70-92.

Hunsperger, R. W. Neurophysiologische Grundlagen des affektiven Verhaltens. *Bulletin der Schweizerischen Akademie der Medizinischen Wissenschaften* 1965, **21**, 8-22.

Jasper, H. H. and Ajmone-Marsan, C. Thalamocortical integrating mechanisms. *Research Publications Association for Nervous and Mental Diseases* 1952, **30**, 493-512.

Kaada, B. Brain mechanisms related to aggressive behavior. In C. D. Clemente and D. B. Lindsley (Eds.), *Aggression and defense: Neural mechanisms and social patterns.* Los Angeles: University of California Press, 1967. Pp. 95-133.

Kerr, D. I. B. and Hagbarth, K. E. An investigation of centrifugal olfactory fiber system. *Journal of Neurophysiology* 1955, **18**, 362-374.

Kreindler, A., Crighel, E. and Marinchescu, C. Integrative activity of the thalamic pulvinar-lateralis posterior complex and interrelations with the neocortex. *Experimental Neurology* 1968, **22**, 423-435.

Lansing, R. W., Schwartz, E. and Lindsley, D. B. Reaction time and EEG activation under alerted and nonalerted conditions. *Journal of Experimental Psychology* 1959, **58**, 1-7.

Lindsley, D. B. Emotions and the electroencephalogram. In M. L. Reymert (Ed.), *Feelings and emotions: The Mooseheart Symposium.* New York: McGraw-Hill, 1950. Pp. 238-246.

Lindsley, D. B. Emotion. In S. S. Stevens (Ed.), *Handbook of experimental psychology.* New York: Wiley, 1951. Pp. 473-516.

Lindsley, D. B. Brain stem influences on spinal motor activity. *Research Publications. Association for Nervous and Mental Diseases* 1952a, **30**, 174-195.

Lindsley, D. B. Psychological phenomena and the electroencephalogram. *Electroencephalography and Clinical Neurophysiology* 1952b, **4**, 443-456.

Lindsley, D. B. Psychophysiology and motivation. In M. R. Jones (Ed.), *Nebraska Symposium on Motivation.* Lincoln, Nebraska: University of Nebraska Press, 1957. Pp. 44-105.

Lindsley, D. B. The reticular system and perceptual discrimination. In H. H. Jasper *et al.* (Eds.), *Reticular formation of the brain.* Boston: Little, Brown, 1958. Pp. 513-534.

Lindsley, D. B. Attention, consciousness, sleep and wakefulness. In J. Field (Ed.), Handbook of Physiology-Neurophysiology, III. Washington, D. C.: Amer. Physiological Society, 1960. Pp. 1553-1593.

Lindsley, D. B., Bowden, J. W. and Magoun, H. W. Effect upon the EEG of acute injury to the brain stem activating system. *Electroencephalography & Clinical Neurophysiology* 1949, **1**, 475-486.

Lindsley, D. B., Schreiner, L. H., Knowles, W. B. and Magoun, H. W. Behavioral and EEG changes following chronic brain stem lesions in the cat. *Electroencephalography & Clinical Neurophysiology* 1950, **2**, 483-498.

Lindsley, D. B., Schreiner, L. H. and Magoun, H. W. An electromyographic study of spasticity. *Journal of Neurophysiology* 1949, **12**, 197-205.

Magoun, H. W. and Rhines, R. *Spasticity: the stretch reflex and extrapyramidal systems.* Springfield, Ill.: Thomas, 1948.

Malmo, R. B. Activation: a neuropsychological dimension. *Psychological Bulletin* 1959, **66**, 367-386.

Millhouse, O. E. The medial forebrain bundle: A Golgi analysis. Ph.D. dissertation. Univ. of California, Los Angeles, 1967.

Millhouse, O. E. A Golgi study of the descending medial forebrain bundle. *Brain Research* 1969, **15**, 341-363.

Morison, R. S. and Dempsey, E. W. A study of thalamocortical relations. *American Journal of Physiology* 1942, **135**, 280-292.

Moruzzi, G. and Magoun, H. W. Brain stem reticular formation and activation of the EEG. *Electroencephalography & Clinical Neurophysiology* 1949, **1**, 455-473.

Murphy, J. P. and Gellhorn, E. The influence of hypothalamic stimulation on cortically induced movements and on action potentials of the cortex. *Journal of Neurophysiology* 1945a, **8**, 341-364.

Murphy, J. P. and Gellhorn, E. Further investigations on diencephalic-cortical relations and their significance for the problem of emotion. *Journal of Neurophysiology* 1945b, **8**, 431-448.

Näätänen, R. Selective attention and evoked potentials. *Annales Academiae Scientiarum Fennicae*, 1967, **151**, 1-226.

Nauta, W. J. H. Some efferent connections of the prefrontal cortex in the monkey. In J. M. Warren and K. Akert (Eds.), *The frontal granular cortex and behavior.* New York: McGraw-Hill, 1964. p. 397.

Olds, J. and Milner, P. Positive reinforcement produced by electrical stimulation of septal area and other regions of the rat brain. *Journal of Comparative & Physiological Psychology* 1954, **47**, 419-427.

Olds, J. Hypothalamic substrates of reward. *Physiol. Rev.* 1962, **42**, 554-604.

Ranson, S. W. and Magoun, H. W. The hypothalamus. *Ergebnisse der Physiologie* 1939, **41**, 56-163.

Roberts, W. W., Steinberg, M. L. and Means, L. W. Hypothalamic mechanisms for sexual, aggressive and other motivational behaviors in the opossum, Didelphis virginiana. *Journal of Comparative Physiological Psychology* 1967, **64**, 1-15.

Romaniuk, A. Representation of aggression and flight reactions in the hypothalamus of the cat. *Acta Biologiae Expermentalis* 1965, **25**, 177-186.

Rose, G. H. and Lindsley, D. B. Visually evoked electrocortical responses in kittens: Development of specific and nonspecific systems. *Science* 1965, **148**, 1244-1246.

Rose, G. H. and Lindsley, D. B. Development of visually evoked potentials in kittens: specific and nonspecific responses. *Journal of Neurophysiology* 1968, **31**, 607-623.

Satterfield, J. H. Evoked cortical response enhancement and attention in man. A study of responses to auditory and shock stimuli. *Electroencephalography & Clinical Neurophysiology* 1965, **19**, 470-475.

Satterfield, J. H. and Cheatum, D. Evoked cortical potential correlates of attention in human subjects. *Electroencephalography & Clinical Neurophysiology* 1964, **17**, 456.

Schreiner, L. H., Lindsley, D. B. and Magoun, H. W. Role of brain stem facilitatory systems in maintenance of spasticity. *Journal of Neurophysiology* 1949, **12**, 207-216.

Segundo, J. P., Arana, R. and French, J. D. Behavioral arousal by stimulation of the brain in the monkey. *Journal of Neurosurgery* 1955, **12**, 601-613.

Skinner, J. E. and Lindsley, D. B. Electrophysiological and behavioral effects of blockade of the nonspecific thalamo-cortical system. *Brain Research* 1967, **6**, 95-118.

Skinner, J. E. and Lindsley, D. B. Reversible cryogenic blockade of neural function in the brain of unrestrained animals. *Science* 1968, **161**, 595-597.

Spong, P. Cortical evoked potentials and attention in man. Ph.D. dissertation, University of California, Los Angeles, 1966.

Spong, P., Haider, M. and Lindsley, D. B. Selective attentiveness and cortical evoked potentials to visual and auditory stimuli. *Science* 1965, **148**, 395-397.

Sprague, J. M., Schreiner, L. H., Lindsley, D. B. and Magoun, H. W. Reticulospinal influences on stretch reflexes. *Journal of Neurophysiology* 1948, **11**, 501-508.

Ursin, H. and Kaada, B. Subcortical structures mediating the attention response induced by amygdala stimulation. *Experimental Neurology* 1960, **2**, 109-122.

Van Hof, M. W., Van Hof-Van Duin, J., Van der Mark, F. and Rietveld, W. J. The effect of image formation and that of flash counting on the occipitocortical response to light flashes. *Acta physiologica pharmacologica néerlandica* 1962, **11**, 485-493.

Velasco, M. and Lindsley, D. B. Role of orbital cortex in regulation of thalamocortical electrical activity. *Science* 1965, **149**, 1375-1377.

Velasco, M. and Lindsley, D. B. Effect of thalamo-cortical activation on recruiting responses. II. Peripheral and central neural stimulation. *Acta Neurologica Latinoamerica* In press a.

Velasco, M. and Lindsley, D. B. Effect of thalamo-cortical activation on recruiting responses. III. Reticular lesions. *Acta Neurologica Latinoamerica* In press b.

Velasco, M., Skinner, J. E., Asaro, K. D. and Lindsley, D. B. Thalamocortical systems regulating spindle bursts and recruiting responses. I. Effect of cortical ablations. *Electroencephalography & Clinical Neurophysiology* 1968, **25**, 463-470.

Velasco, M., Weinberger, N. W., and Lindsley, D. B. Effect of thalamo-cortical activation on recruiting responses. I. Reticular stimulation. *Acta Neurologica Latinoamerica* In press.

Wasman, M., and Flynn, J. P. Directed attack elicited from hypothalamus. *Archives of Neurology* 1962, **6**, 220-227.

9

MODULATION OF EMOTIONS BY
CEREBRAL RADIO STIMULATION

José M. R. Delgado

INTRODUCTION

It is known that emotions such as a state of grief may be caused by many different stimuli, may be expressed in a variety of ways, and may last minutes or days. In spite of the multiplicity of causes and multiformity of effects, there is a common denominator which in typical cases permits easy identification of emotions by observers and their clear subjective recognition by the individual. During grief, for example, contact with the environment and sensory reactions are diminished, unpleasant feelings are perceived, and interpretation of received messages is distorted with emphasis on their negative aspects; a joke will not sound funny, and a work of art will not be appreciated. We may speak of *emotional tuning* (Gellhorn, 1957) as the bias introduced in sensory reception and in motor expression by the establishment of an emotional state, involving the inhibition of some patterns of response and the facilitation of others which provide the recurrent functional uniformity which characterizes each emotion. Sensory receptors are specialized to discharge in response to certain types of energy such as light for the eye and sound for the ear. At this level, however, the possible emotional significance of the stimuli cannot be distinguished, and the neurophysiology of the receptors is identical for the transmission of insulting, friendly, or neutral words. In a similar way, the mechanical activity and biochemical processes of muscular contraction are alike in emotional and nonemotional responses. Their differences do not reside in the periphery but in their intracerebral organization. At the central level, motor skills and other patterns of activity are stored in the nervous system as ideokinetic formulas which are similar during neutral and during emotional displays. Emotional qualities must depend on a set of specialized structures distinct from the set responsible for performance.

THEORETICAL BASIS FOR THE STUDY OF EMOTIONS

To study emotions I have proposed a working hypothesis derived from the theory of fragmental organization of behavior (Delgado, 1964b), postulating the existence of a constellation of functionally related neuronal groups, located in different parts of the brain, which will introduce a positive or negative bias typical for each emotion. This neuronal activity determines the emotional state which modulates the activity of other neurons related to autonomic, somatic, and behavioral responses. An anatomical and functional differentiation seems to exist between two groups of neural structures, the first related to emotional tuning, and the second to behavioral performance. If this is true, direct stimulation of the brain could induce both effects independently. The fact that "true" and "false" rage can be obtained from different intracerebral points in the same cat is in agreement with this hypothesis. It has also been reported that aggressive gestures lacking negative reinforcing properties may be elicited by stimulation of some points of the reticular formation in the monkey (Delgado, 1967a), and in addition, it is known that different cerebral structures have negative, positive, and neutral reinforcing properties with or without concomitant motor effects.

Experimental investigation of the proposed working hypothesis requires (a) an analysis of the different elements which form part of emotional expression, (b) study of the anatomical representation and physiological mechanisms of each of these elements as separate entities, (c) identification of the neuronal processes for the harmonious integration of these elements as a well organized and purposeful response, and (d) investigation of the cerebral mechanisms of emotional tuning and their correlation with the mechanisms of sensory perception and motor expression. One of the main implications of the theory is that as cerebral mechanisms are different, it should be possible to influence emotional tuning differentially without disturbing other aspects of behavioral responses.

EXPERIMENTAL TESTING

Experimental testing of these ideas encounters one of the main problems shared by most studies of neurophysiological correlates of emotions: the need to collect data and introduce experimental variables without disturbing the phenomenon under consideration. Restraint of the animal, presence of human observers, and isolation from sociological and ecological surroundings represent serious artifacts in the study of emotions and have been a deterrent for research into their neuronal mechanisms. The ideal situation for investigation of how the brain works would be to study completely free subjects forming part of a normal society. Since this is extremely difficult, it has been necessary to compromise by providing the greatest possible normality within the controlled limits of laboratory life. Recent technological developments allow the establishment of two-way communication with the brain of completely unrestrained subjects. This methodology has already been used for research in animals and clinical purposes in man, and it may well broaden present applications of electrical stimulation of the brain.

METHODOLOGY FOR TWO-WAY COMMUNICATION WITH THE BRAIN

IMPLANTED ELECTRODES

The initial step in investigation of the brain in free, behaving subjects is implantation of electrodes in the cerebrum which permits stimulation and recording of brain activity; for details of this technique, see reviews by Delgado, (1964a) and Sheer, (1961). Correlations between neuronal anatomy, physiology, and emotional behavior are poorly understood, and in general it is advisable to implant a large number of contacts in each brain, some within close range of each other and some spread over different areas, in order to study simultaneously the activity in many structures and increase the possibility of identifying neuronal pools involved in specific types of behavior. The use of assemblies of electrodes is practical because with a single penetration of the brain tissue, several contacts are implanted at different depths. Figure 1 shows an electrode assembly of 20 contacts, five in each of four shafts, which is used in our studies. The hook at the lower tip of each shaft is caught by a fine, stainless-steel tubing used to guide stereotaxic introduction. Five of these assemblies (a total of 100 leads) were implanted in each of the chimpanzees shown in Figure 2. This massive introduction of electrodes has been well tolerated and has not produced any observable behavioral deficits.

RADIO STIMULATION

Small animals such as rats tolerate well the presence of wires trailing from their head sockets, and their brains may be explored electrically while they run mazes or press levers, but primates are far more ingenious and destructive, making the use of connecting leads impractical. For these larger animals it is convenient to establish communication by radio using miniaturized stimulators and transmitters which can be worn on a harness or collar. This arrangement has usually been successful for monkeys and chimpanzees, but some of these animals have pulled and broken the connecting leads, and to solve this problem the following two procedures have been developed: (a) the lateral hole of the socket shown in Figure 1 contains an internally threaded metallic tubing 3 mm in diameter which provides a solid anchorage point for instrumentation (after implantation of the sockets into the skull.) Figure 2 shows chimpanzee Carlos at the left with a detachable instrument box mounted on top of the animal's head sockets. (b) The second procedure involved construction of a 48 × 39 × 18 mm teflon box and mounting it permanently, by means of vitallium screws and dental cement, behind the electrode sockets, as shown in Figure 2. This procedure was surgically more complex but it was highly satsifactory because the instruments were protected by the box and could easily be removed or replaced.

Several apparatuses have been described in the literature for brain stimulation by remote control, but as discussed in previous papers (Delgado, 1963, 1964b), very little research has been accomplished with them. This probably reflects the technical difficulties encountered in their use. A problem in most of these instruments was that the intensity of stimulation was controlled by the intensity of the received radio signal, and therefore stimulation could be unpredictably modified by changes in the orientation of antenna, distance of the transmitter, grounding of the subject, reflection of waves by metallic objects, and shielding of transmission by obstacles or other animals.

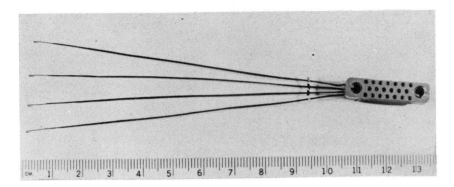

Fig. 1. Multielectrode assembly for brain exploration. Each shaft has five contacts terminating 5 mm from each other. The socket has a total of 20 leads. The hook at the tip of each shaft is caught by a #27 stainless-steel tubing attached to the micromanipulator of the stereotaxic instrument. Several assemblies are implanted in each animal for a wide coverage of cerebral structures. The larger hole at the right of the socket is threaded for anchorage of instrumentation, as shown in Figure 2.

Fig. 2. Each chimpanzee has 100 intracerebral electrodes covering limbic structures and other areas of the brain. The animal on the right has the instrumentation attached on top of the electrode sockets. The animal in the left has a teflon box permanently mounted on the skull, behind the electrode sockets. This box is very convenient for the placement of instrumentation.

These problems can be eliminated by using frequency modulation to control the intensity of stimulation, thus making the instrument insensitive to changes in the amplitude of the received signal. The system developed in our laboratory consists of two parts : (a) A console transmitter originates 100 MHz (megahertz, 1 Hertz is 1 cycle per second) oscillations, depending on a train of pulses from subcarrier oscillators controlled by a manual switch, which represents the total stimulation time. There are three subcarriers which operate in the 100–500 kHz range adjusted by potentiometers in order to determine stimulation intensity independently in each of the three channels of the instrument. Independent controls are also provided to regulate pulse durations between 0.1 and 1.5 msec, and repetition rate between single pulses and 200 Hz. (b) The three-channel receiver-stimulator is mounted on the subject's skull, as shown in Figure 2; it measures $37 \times 30 \times 14$ mm, and weighs 20 g, including its 7 V battery. Its circuitry is solid state and it is encapsulated in epoxy resin to make it waterproof and practically indestructible. The subcarrier frequency is identified from the incoming RF (radio frequency) signal, and is demodulated into an amplitude used to control the current intensity of the output, which is constant current to supersede possible changes in biological impedance. Frequency, pulse duration, intensity, and total duration of stimulation are controlled independently in each of the three channels. With normal intermittent use, battery life is one week, and the operating distance is about 100 ft.

STIMOCEIVER

For two-way communication with the brain, the three-channel stimulator was combined with a three-channel EEG (electroencephalographic) telemetric unit, forming an instrument called a "stimoceiver" (*stim*ulator and EEG re*ceiver*). EEG transmission was accomplished by FM (frequency modulation), using a modification of the circuit described by Meehan (Meehan & Rader, 1965), which consisted of two parts: (a) The EEG transmitter was a miniaturized amplifier with a gain of 100, input impedance of 2 MΩ, frequency response of 2–200 Hz, and it had voltage-controlled oscillators for each channel. The outputs of the three subcarrier oscillators were added as a single FM radio signal which was transmitted in the 216 MHz band. The transmission distance was about 100 ft. With this instrument, the electrical signals from the implanted electrodes were received and amplified in the first stage. The output signal from this stage controlled the frequency of the subcarrier oscillator, the output of which controlled the frequency of the final transmitting stage. (b) The EEG receiver was a console that received, amplified, and demodulated the signals. The composite subcarrier signals were connected to the inputs of three different discriminators in order to separate and demodulate their respective subcarriers and obtain analog information. A 100 μV signal at the input of the EEG amplifier produced 1 V in the output of the discriminator.

LONG-TERM MODULATION OF BRAIN FUNCTIONS

It is known that the brain is in a constant state of activity throughout the entire life of each individual in order to maintain basic cardiovascular, respiratory, and metabolic functions of the organism and to regulate other autonomic functions, glandular secretions, and general emotional tone. In contrast with this functional endurance, the responses evoked by electrical stimulation of the motor cortex fade away in a few seconds and a recovery period of about one minute is usually necessary to regain the initial cortical excitability. Not all the brain, however, has the same lability, and it has been shown (Delgado, 1959) that under continuous stimulation, cerebral structures may be classified in three groups: (a) The cortex has a quick fatigability which is measured in seconds. Considering that spontaneous movements may last for minutes or hours, the effects evoked by cortical stimulation therefore lack an essential physiological characteristic for endurance. (b) The putamen and other structures exhibit a slow fatigability and the responses may be present for up to about one hour. (c) The hypothalamus and other regions can be stimulated indefinitely without fatigue as has been shown, for example, in the monkey by the persistence of pupillary constriction for weeks until electrical excitation is discontinued. In this case, an artificial functional bias was established because the pupil was still able to react to light, but at a different "set point" determined by the intensity of the applied electricity.

There is experimental evidence that some effects induced by brief cerebral stimulation may last for a long time. For example, in cats, excitation of the lateral hypothalamus applied for 0.5 sec every 5 sec for 1 hour daily for several days produced a tenfold increase of food intake which took place during interstimulation periods (Delgado & Anand, 1953). Excitation of the basolateral nucleus of the amygdala, also in cats, produced the contrary effect, and the animals immediately stopped eating, walked slowly away, refused to eat when appetizing food was offered, and rejected the efforts to put food inside their mouths. The inhibition of appetite persisted for minutes or hours after a few seconds of cerebral excitation; in one case, after a single 10-sec stimulation, the cat refused food for 3 days (Fonberg and Delgado, 1961). Along similar lines, Lilly (1958) has described the appearance of a lasting pacifying effect when monkeys were allowed to self-stimulate their cerebral areas with positive reinforcing properties. Usually ferocious monkeys became affectionate toward human observers.

In a recently completed series of still unpublished experiments, it was demonstrated that in rhesus monkeys, nociceptive stimulation of the reticular formation had a powerful and lasting inhibitory effect upon both spontaneous and learned behavior. Each animal in this study was equipped with a radio stimulator and placed in a cage with another monkey. The cage had a lever which delivered food pellets. In this situation, instrumental responses and spontaneous social activities were analyzed before, during, and after radio stimulation of the brain. When a program of one 5-sec stimulation per minute was established, the aggressive responses of the stimulated animal increased greatly, while instrumental lever pressings to obtain food dropped to zero, even if the animal was strongly motivated by previous food deprivation. Reciprocal grooming relations, which were always present during control periods, disappeared as soon as stimulations began. In order to evaluate the efficiency of the stimulations and the duration of the aftereffects, successive experiments were performed, reducing the total duration of reticular stimulation to only 100 msec instead of the original 5 sec. Using 1 mA of intensity, it was demonstrated that application of two to six of these very brief stimulations suppressed all social behavior and all instrumental responses in the stimulated animal for the 30-min duration of the tests. It should be clarified that parameters of stimulation were 100 Hz (thus a total duration of 100 msec represented only 10 pulses), 0.5 msec pulse width, and 1.0 mA intensity. This brief stimulation was still effective in evoking agonistic behavior and, for example, in one monkey programmed reticular stimulation (twice per minute for 30 min during two sessions with a total of 120 stimulations) evoked 93 threatening acts.

The specificity of the lasting inhibitory effects of reticular stimulation was demonstrated in other series of experiments in which radio stimulation of cerebral areas without negative reinforcing properties produced a variety of motor responses with persistence of grooming activities and lever pressing for food at normal rates. In other monkeys equipped with stimoceivers, amygdaloid radio stimulation produced bilateral discharges involving the amygdala and hippocampus which were recorded by telemetry and during which lever pressing was not inhibited and normal social relations were not disturbed.

The lasting inhibitory effects of reticular stimulation have also been demonstrated in the chimpanzee, in the experimental situation shown in Figure 2. The animals were trained to press a lever to obtain food, and from time to time they engaged in different types of social activities. Brief periods of reticular radio stimulation, at low intensity and only sparsely applied, were effective in completely inhibiting both instrumental responses and spontaneous social interactions.

TWO-WAY RADIOCOMMUNICATION WITH THE HUMAN BRAIN

In some patients with focal electrical dysfunction associated with behavioral abnormalities, the depth of the brain may be explored by means of indwelling electrodes (see review in Ramey and O'-Doherty, 1960). In these cases stimoceivers may be used to avoid the restrictions of the connecting leads and the stress imposed by the recording room. Cerebral electrical exploration may thus be performed for as long as necessary without disturbing the rest or spontaneous activities of the patients who are free to move about in the hospital ward. The procedure has important diagnostic applications, considerable scientific interest for the study of mechanisms of emotions, and therapeutic possibilities because it is conceivable that programmed stimulations of the brain may induce lasting beneficial modifications of emotional reactivity. While this last possibility requires further study, the clinical usefulness of stimoceivers has already been demonstrated (Delgado, Mark, Sweet, Ervin, Weiss, Bach-y-Rita, & Hagiwara, 1968):

In four patients suffering from psychomotor epilepsy and behavioral disorders, electrodes were implanted in the temporal lobe in order to identify sites of abnormal intracerebral activity, to determine brain excitability, and to evaluate the responses elicited by neuronal stimulation, in order to guide contemplated therapeutic surgery. One of the main advantages of telemetric methodology was the acquisition of many hours of EEG which was tape recorded and correlated with spontaneous behavior. In this way we could assess the frequency, duration, severity, propagation, and behavioral correlations of the spontaneous electrical afterdischarges and determine their pathological significance.

The stimoceiver is a small and light instrument which can be concealed within the head bandage, as shown in Figure 3, providing continuous day and night monitoring of depth EEG and the possibility to apply stimulations without touching or disturbing the subjects.

Tape-recorded interviews with each patient were structured to elicit free verbal expression without influencing its ideological content. During these conversations, two intracerebral points were chosen for study, to be stimulated according to a predetermined schedule at 3-5 min intervals, and each point was stimulated seven times during three 60-90 min sessions. In the four patients, telemetered EEG showed patterns of activity which were typical for each linkage and reliable on different days. In general, predominant pacemakers were absent and each area of the brain showed patterns which lacked synchrony among different channels, suggesting the

Fig. 3. Two patients equipped with stimoceivers for intracerebral stimulation and recording, placed under their head dressings. Monitoring of brain waves and application of programmed stimulations were thus performed for as long as necessary while the patients engaged in the activities of the psychiatric ward (*from* Delgado, *et al.*, 1968).

existence of autochthonous electrical generators. This electrical in-dependence of restricted areas of the brain has an important func-tional significance. It contrasted with the widespread uniformity of synchronous activity recorded during evoked afterdischarges, indi-cating that in this case there was a common driving force located in the artificially created focus. It was clear that while all areas pulsated at the same pace during evoked afterdischarges, each structure had its own rhythm during spontaneous activity. This increased the prob-ability of detecting possible behavioral-EEG correlations.

In one of the patients (JP), brief periods of aimless walking around the room coincided with a considerable increase in high-voltage sharp waves located in the posterior part of the optic radiation. This was accompanied by spontaneous inhibition of speech, lasting for several minutes and by bursts of spike activity in the same region. Psychological excitement was related with an increase in the number and duration of 16-Hz bursts localized in the amygdala. The signifi-cance of these correlations was increased by the fact that other be-havioral manifestations did not produce detectable EEG changes, and the patient walked around the room, went to the toilet, read papers, and conversed without visible changes in the telemetered depth activity.

In the same patient several crises of assaultive behavior similar to her spontaneous bursts of anger were elicited by radiostimulation of the right amygdala. About 7 sec after the onset of stimulation (50 Hz, 1.0 msec of pulse duration, 1.2 mA) the patient interrupted her spon-taneous activity and threw herself against the wall in a fit of rage, without directing her fury against the interviewer. Then she paced around the room for several minutes and gradually resumed her normal behavior. The fact that an aggressive response similar to the behavioral problem of the patient was elicited from only one of the contacts suggested that the surrounding neuronal field was involved in her aberrant conduct.

Radiostimulation of different points of the amygdala and hippo-campus in the four patients elicited a variety of responses including pleasant sensations, elation, deep thoughtful concentration, odd feel-ings, relaxation, and colored visions.

Discussion

Experimental studies in animals have demonstrated that long-term programmed stimulation of the brain is feasible, safe, and reliable, and that it can modulate emotional reactivity, introduce a functional bias, inhibit assaultive behavior, influence appetite, modify drives, and influence intracerebral mechanisms (Delgado, 1964b, 1967a, 1967b; Fonberg & Delgado, 1961; Delgado, *et al.*, 1968). Methodology is already available for the establishment of multichannel two-way radio communication with the depth of the brain in animals and man without restrictions in their mobility and social activities. It should therefore be expected that the interest of more investigators will be directed to this new field of research.

Repeated electrical stimulation of the brain has been proposed as a therapeutic procedure by Heath (1963), Sem-Jacobsen (1964), Walter and Crow (1964) and other authors who have reported that repeated excitation of positive reinforcing areas improved the mood and the well-being of patients. The use of stimoceivers may be advantageous in these cases because it permits radio stimulation of ambulatory patients and simultaneous monitoring of electrical activity. The main technical handicap at present is the existence of leads piercing the skin which represents a continuous threat of infection in addition to other medical and cosmetic problems. The development of a microminiaturized, totally subcutaneous instrument would offer obvious advantages, and preliminary studies in our laboratory indicate that reception and transmission of power and information through the intact skin is perfectly feasible. The effectiveness of cardiac pacemakers is well known and a similar principle could be used for the development of a cerebral pacemaker, although the problems are far more complex because of the requirements of many channels, the need for external control of the several parameters of stimulation, and especially because of the great functional complexity of the brain.

In spite of many difficulties, the principle of electrical modulation of emotions has been established, the feasibility of long-term stimulation demonstrated, and the clinical applications started. It may be predicted that this field of endeavor will expand quickly in the next few years, posing at the same time a new host of ethical and philosophical questions about the possibilities and limits for the intelligent control of emotional life.

SUMMARY

Study of the neurophysiological correlates of emotions requires the collection of data and the introduction of experimental variables without disturbing the phenomena under consideration. The newly developed methodology of stimoceivers is suitable for this purpose because it allows three channels of radiostimulation plus three channels of telemetric recording of EEG in completely free subjects while they are engaged in social relations or performing instrumental responses.

Experimental data show that in cats, monkeys, and chimpanzees, long-term modulation of functions is possible by programmed electrical stimulation of specific areas of the brain. This has been demonstrated for pupillary size, food intake, grooming, aggressive behavior, and instrumental responses.

Two-way communication with the brain of patients with temporal lobe disorders has been established by means of stimoceivers, allowing the continuous monitoring of EEG, the establishment of electrical-behavioral correlations, and the functional exploration of neuronal activity. This methodology may have further therapeutic use for the programmed stimulation of the brain in order to obtain beneficial modifications of emotional reactivity.

ACKNOWLEDGMENTS

The investigation described in this paper was supported by research grants from the U.S. Public Health Service, #5-R01-MH-02004, and the U.S. Navy, #ONR/Nonr 609(48).

REFERENCES

Delgado, J. Prolonged stimulation of brain in awake monkeys. *Journal of Neurophysiology, 1959,* **22**, 458-475.
Delgado, J. Telemetry and telestimulation of the brain. In L. Slater, (Ed.), *Bio-telemetry.* New York: Pergamon Press, 1963, pp. 231-249.
Delgado, J. Electrodes for extracellular recording and stimulation. *Physical Techniques in Biological Research, Part A*; 1964, **5**, 87-143. (a)
Delgado, J. Free behavior and brain stimulation. *International Review of Neurobiology,* 1964, **4**, 349-449. (b)
Delgado, J. Social rank and radiostimulated aggressiveness in monkeys. *Journal of Nervous and Mental Disease,* 1967, **144**, 383-390. (a)
Delgado, J. Man's intervention in intracerebral functions. *IEEE International Convention Record,* 1967, **9**, 143-150. (b)
Delgado, J., & Anand, B. Increase of food intake induced by electrical stimulation of the lateral hypothalamus. *American Journal of Physiology,* 1953, **172**, 162-168.
Delgado, J., Mark, V., Sweet, W., Ervin, F., Weiss, G., Bach-y-Rita, G., & Hagiwara, R. Intracerebral radio stimulation and recording in completely free patients. *Journal of Nervous and Mental Disease,* 1968, **147**, 329-340.
Fonberg, E. & Delgado, J. Avoidance and alimentary reactions during amygdala stimulation. *Journal of Neurophysiology,* 1961, **24**, 651-664.

Gellhorn, E. *Autonomic imbalance and the hypothalamus. Implications for physiology, medicine, psychology, and neuropsychiatry.* Minneapolis: University of Minnesota Press, 1957.

Heath, R. G. Electrical self-stimulation of the brain in man. *American Journal of Psychiatry*, 1963, **120**, 571–577.

Lilly, J. Learning motivated by subcortical stimulation: The start and stop patterns of behavior. In H. H. Jasper, L. D. Proctor, R. S. Knighton, W. C. Noshay, and R. T. Costello (Eds.), *Reticular Formation of the Brain, Henry Ford Hospital International Symposium.* Boston: Little Brown, 1958. Pp. 705–721.

Meehan, J. & Rader, R. Multiple channel physiological data acquisition system for restrained and mobile subjects. Report to Air Force Systems Command on Contract #AF 04 (695)-178, 1965.

Ramey, E. & O'Doherty, D. *Electrical studies on the unanesthetized brain.* New York: Harper (Hoeber), 1960.

Sem-Jacobsen, C. Electrical stimulation of the human brain. *Electroencephalography and Clinical Neurophysiology*, 1964, **17**, 211.

Sheer, D. *Electrical stimulation of the brain.* Austin, Texas: University of Texas Press, 1961.

Walter, W. & Crow, H. Depth recording from the human brain. *Electroencephalography and Clinical Neurophysiology*, 1964, **16**, 68–72.

5

PSYCHOPHYSIOLOGICAL CORRELATES

10

SOME AUTONOMIC-CENTRAL NERVOUS SYSTEM INTERRELATIONSHIPS

John I. Lacey and Beatrice C. Lacey

INTRODUCTION

THE "SEA OF SOMATIC RESPONSE"

That the functioning of autonomically innervated organs is intimately involved with affect or emotion is a matter of common knowledge — a knowledge embedded in sometimes surprisingly accurate form in the mythology and folklore of even very primitive peoples. Pounding hearts and sweating palms and churning stomachs are well celebrated in song, poetry, and prose. Davis (1955), moved by the ever-present minor ripples and major waves of bodily disturbance, spoke of a "sea of somatic response." Indeed, it is true that the organism, engaged in almost any nonhabituated task whatsoever or stimulated by almost any nonhabituated exteroceptive stimulus, reveals almost invariably a change in many vital functions such as blood pressure, heart rate, blood flow, sweat-gland activity, and pupillary activity, to name a few easily observable items in a long list.

The concept that is commonly used to integrate these phenomena is that of arousal or activation. Whether the investigator adopts the concepts of Cannon, Hess, Selye, Lindsley, Duffy, or Malmo, the implicit assumption he is likely to make is that these autonomic responses can be viewed as meter readings or indices of a complex called emotion or affect or arousal or activation.

THE AUTONOMIC NERVOUS SYSTEM IS NOT SOLELY AN EFFECTOR
SYSTEM

The ANS (autonomic nervous system) is commonly viewed solely
as an effector system. Although it is generally conceded that the autonomic responses can be controlled, integrated, and modified by
higher levels of the CNS (central nervous system), nevertheless,
these responses are usually regarded purely as effector events; they
are considered to be the end of a chain of events beginning with the
interaction of the organism with its environment.

That the ANS is considered to be only an effector system, however,
is purely an historical accident and a pedagogical convenience. Our
textbooks are full of illustrations and diagrams which show the nervous pathways downwards from the CNS to autonomically innervated organs, but commonly they omit entirely the vast systems of
visceral afferent fibers receiving messages from innervated receptors
within the body cavity and sending them forward to the CNS.

These systems have been known from the very beginning of research into the ANS, but because their study did not seem to show
anything new as opposed to the study of exteroceptive systems they
were not emphasized. In the past 25 years, however, the pace of research has accelerated, and the afferent input from the thoracic and
abdominal cavities back to the brain *and their effects on brain function* have become a matter of more intensive study.

CARDIOVASCULAR SYSTEM: A NEGATIVE FEEDBACK
PATHWAY TO THE BRAIN

In recent years in our laboratory, we have been concerned primarily with the possible role in behavior of the cardiovascular feedback system to the brain. We think that in the past 15 years a
revolution has been wrought in considerations of the cardiovascular
system. The evidence mounts steadily that the cardiovascular system
is the source of a negative feedback pathway to the CNS, by means
of which there is produced a number of electrophysiological effects
which can best be characterized by calling them *inhibitory*.

SOME INHIBITORY EFFECTS OF BAROCEPTOR STIMULATION

Early evidence dates back to 1929 when Tournade and Malméjac,
and Koch two years later (see Heymans & Neil, 1958), showed that
direct stimulation of Hering's nerve (the carotid sinus nerve, contributing afferent fibers to the glossopharyngeal nerve which enters the

brainstem at the bulbar level) or an increase in pressure within the carotid sinus itself, produced a decrease in muscle tone in anesthetized animals. Koch, in a hotly debated demonstration, also showed that he could inhibit motor activity and even produce prolonged sleep in dogs by sharply increasing the pressure within the carotid sinus.

Beginning about 15 years ago, French and Italian neurophysiologists, in particular, began a variety of experiments all of which have served to demonstrate that increases in heart rate and blood pressure (which effectively stimulate the so-called baroceptors that are found predominantly in the aortic arch and carotid sinus) cause many electrophysiological changes.

For example, Bonvallet, Dell, and Hiebel in 1954a showed in acute cat and dog studies that distention of the carotid sinus produced a marked change in cortical electrical activity: The electrocorticogram shifted from low-voltage fast activity to high-voltage slow activity. The frequency could drop to as low as 3 to 5 per sec. This is an accepted sign of a sleeping, inactivated, or inhibited cortex.

These findings have been confirmed in several ways, and a variety of control observations show that this effect is not secondary to a homeostatic reduction of blood pressure that would be produced by such massive inputs to the pressure-sensitive receptors.

Bonvallet, Dell, and Hugelin (1954b; Dell, Bonvallet, & Hugelin, 1954) showed that increased pressure within the carotid sinus resulted in a direct neural inhibitory effect on an evoked monosynaptic reflex; i.e. the threshold for this response was elevated.

The pathways mediating these effects have not been thoroughly studied, but sectioning at the pontomesencephalic level was shown to eliminate them.

An Ascending Bulbar Inhibitory Mechanism to Control Response Duration

Nine years later, in a most important paper, Bonvallet and Allen (1963) described an ascending bulbar inhibitory mechanism whose central locus was close to but separate from the classical, and more ventromedial, inhibitory reticular system. This newly described system exerts inhibitory control of the duration and course of cortical, autonomic, and muscular responses to internal and external stimulation. Precisely delimited coagulations of a minute area in the brainstem did not change the immediate cortical, autonomic or motor response to "activating stimuli," but resulted in a prolongation of the effects of the input stimuli.

Bonvallet and Allen in one demonstration in a cat preparation maintained on a paralyzing drug, showed that a 3-V stimulus to the mesencephalic reticular system resulted in a very prompt response — a decrease in tonic pupilloconstrictor activity, as seen in records of integrated activity from the short ciliary nerves. Upon cessation of the stimulus, the tonic pupilloconstrictor activity returned rapidly to baseline. After bilateral coagulation of this newly identified inhibitory area, the animal showed an equally prompt response to the same 3-V reticular stimulation, but the course of recovery was enormously different. Instead of a prompt return to the resting level after the cessation of the input stimulus, there was, instead, a long, rolling, physiologic instability; the effects of the input stimulus were sustained. In other words, a very small part of the nervous system has been found which has been demonstrated to account for what seem to be reverberatory effects within the CNS, a finding of profound implication for the student of the physiology of behavior who constantly is called upon to invent the notion of recirculating neural effects within the CNS.

This finding could be replicated in the Bonvallet and Allen (1963) and Bonvallet and Bloch (1961) studies, whether an artificial electrical stimulus or a normal exteroceptive stimulus was used. Furthermore, these effects could be found in electrocortical recordings, in autonomic recordings from the short ciliary nerves, and in skeletal recordings from the neck muscles.

This bulbar inhibitory area is localized at the head of the nucleus of the *tractus solitarius*, a major aggregate of cells concerned with autonomic function. This is the same area that is richly endowed with cardiovascular afferents. It is in or immediately proximal to this area that one can locate unit activity synchronous with the heart beat, activity which disappears when the glossopharyngeal and the vagus, the main lines of communication back to the CNS from the heart, are severed.

The facts so far presented obviously suggest that the cardiovascular system has some control over this bulbar inhibitory area. Bonvallet and Allen in fact did demonstrate that if the glossopharyngeal and vagus nerves were cut, poststimulatory cortical activation was prolonged. In other words, the elimination of glossopharyngeal and vagal input, the pathways by which blood-pressure and heart-rate activity are fed back to the CNS, resulted in a prolongation of an episode of cortical activation, and of pupilloconstrictor and skeletal muscle activity.

Inferentially, the increase of cardiovascular afferent traffic fed back to the central nervous system along these pathways will result in a prompter termination of an episode of cortical, motor, and autonomic activity.

Zanchetti and his collaborators in Italy have produced some dramatic evidence using sham rage in the acutely decorticated cat as a complex activity to be terminated by increase in cardiovascular feedback (Bartorelli, Bizzi, Libretti, & Zanchetti, 1960; Baccelli, Guazzi, Libretti, & Zanchetti, 1965). The acute preparation can easily be provoked to, and indeed, without external provocation, spontaneously will show, massive prolonged dramatic episodes of motor and autonomic upheaval: piloerection, pupillary dilatation, extended claws, changes in blood pressure and heart rate, and so on.

If at the height of one of these episodes of sham rage, one electrically stimulates the large pressoreceptive fibers (either aortic or carotid sinus) the stimulation dramatically and instantaneously aborts the episode of sham rage!

A Reinterpretation of Some Cardiovascular Responses

These neurophysiological findings have led us to some new interpretations of acute cardiovascular responses which we have presented elsewhere, along with the qualifications they require at this stage of our knowledge (Lacey, 1959, 1967; Lacey, Kagan, Lacey, & Moss, 1963). The temporary hypertension and tachycardia observable in acute emotional states and in "aroused" behaviors of all sorts may not be the direct index of so-called "arousal" or "activation" they are so often considered to be. Instead they may be a sign of the attempt of the organism instrumentally to constrain, to limit, and to terminate the turmoil produced inside the body by appropriate stimulating circumstances. Moreover, to quote from an earlier statement of ours,

. . . if increases in blood pressure and heart rate signal a physiological attempt to restrain excitatory processes, then it seems likely that their diminution, absence, or conversion to blood pressure and heart rate decrease signify an absence of this restraining process and, therefore, a net increase in excitation: a lowering of threshold, a prolongation of the impact of stimuli, an increase in spontaneous activity, and the like. [Lacey, 1967, p. 30].

It is this last interpretation, and derivatives from it, that appealed to us as indicating the most strategic and dramatic approach to demonstrating the role of cardiovascular activity in the behavior of intact humans, and to challenging current activation theory, which has long seemed to us to be a grossly oversimplified view of the role of autonomic and skeletal activity in behavior.

Two initial steps seemed to us to be required. We first had to spec-
ify, if we could, experimental conditions that reliably would produce, not the familiar elevations of heart rate and blood pressure, but
decreases in these variables, while other physiological variables
simultaneously were showing sympathetic-like changes. We then
had to demonstrate, if we could, that acutely produced decreases in
cardiovascular activity were correlated with increased behavioral
efficiency, a result that would be contrary to current views. Ultimately, of course, we would need to show that these facts — if they
could be demonstrated in intact human organisms — truly could be
explained by the operation of the negative feedback path from the
heart to the brain.

We have had some success in taking the first two steps. The rest of
this paper will be devoted to a brief review of the evidence that
leads us to suggest that one important effect of cardiovascular activity
on behavior is to gate environmental inputs and motor outputs into
and out of the CNS; that elevations in blood pressure and heart rate
may produce, under appropriate circumstances, a sort of "stimulus
barrier" (to use a picturesque term from psychoanalysis) and that
decreases in heart rate and blood pressure may produce a more per-
meable "stimulus barrier."

EXPERIMENTAL EVIDENCE FOR THE BEHAVIORAL
SIGNIFICANCE OF BRADYCARDIA AND HYPOTENSION

SITUATIONAL STEREOTYPY: DIFFERENT STRESSORS PRODUCE
DIFFERENT CHARACTERISTIC PATTERNS OF PHYSIOLOGICAL
RESPONSE

The first piece of evidence is from a previously reported experiment (Lacey *et al.*, 1963), in which three different groups of individuals were required to engage *seriatim* in a variety of tasks. In
Figures 1 and 2 these tasks are roughly arranged in order from those
in which the subject's primary task was to attend to environmental
inputs, like photic flashes [10 Hz] or white noise, or a dramatic recitation with which he was asked to empathize, to tasks like mental
arithmetic, reversed spelling, make up sentences, and noxious stimulation (the cold-pressor test), in which there is warrant for assuming
that external environmental inputs are disruptive to the organism in
the performance of the task. A subject does not want to pay attention
to external environmental events while doing mental arithmetic.

The task labeled "Rules" is one in which the subject must *both* attend to the external environment and simultaneously engage in internal cognitive elaboration and memorization in order to take a quiz immediately after the rules of a fictitious card game had been orally presented.

It is obvious from Figure 1 that all tasks resulted in increased palmar conductance. Conductance rose from base to alert and again from alert to stimulus.

Heart-rate changes from alert to stimulus, however, as shown in Figure 2, were bidirectional. Those tasks requiring internal cognitive elaboration of a problem-solving sort, or requiring exposure to noxious stimuli like the cold-pressor test, produce massive cardiac acceleration, both in minimum and maximum rates, and also an increase in variability (spread). Those tasks in which only simple environmental reception is required produce significant cardiac decelera-

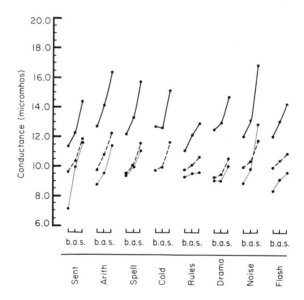

Fig. 1. Average palmar-conductance response curves for three groups of subjects: Group C1, N = 93-95 (—), Group C2, N = 29 (····), and Group F, N = 29-30 (----). Eight stimulus conditions were used and were presented in a different order to each group. The cold-pressor test, however, was not given to the C2 group. Each graph consists of three points: "b" for base level (the last minute of rest prior to an alerting announcement), "a" for alert level (a 1-min period subsequent to an announcement that the next task or stimulus would be presented in 1 min), and "s" for stimulus level. Shown are the highest conductance values obtained during the 1-min base or alert and the 1 or 2 min of stimulation or task-involvement.

tions and decreases in variability; indeed the heart rate drops significantly below the level found in the subjects at rest.

The task requiring combined activities of environmental reception and internal cognitive elaboration (Rules) produces intermediate results in the heart rate. Heart rate seems to be a sort of a vectorial resultant of at least these two apparently opposing demands on the cardiovascular system!

Figure 3 shows, for the three different groups of subjects, the percentage of individuals for whom the various physiological measures

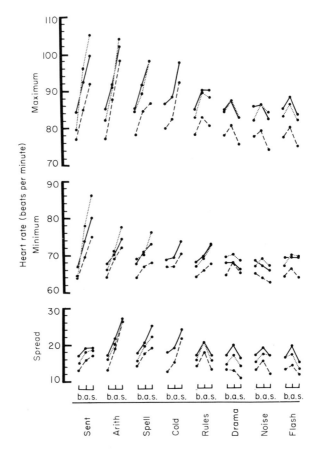

Fig. 2. Average cardiac response curves. Subjects, stimuli, and tasks are the same as in Figure 1. Maximum heart rates are averages of the 12 fastest beats for each subject in the period of observation; minimum heart rates, of the 12 slowest beats; and spread is the difference. All three measures differentiate between tasks which primarily require sustained attention to the external environment and those which do not.

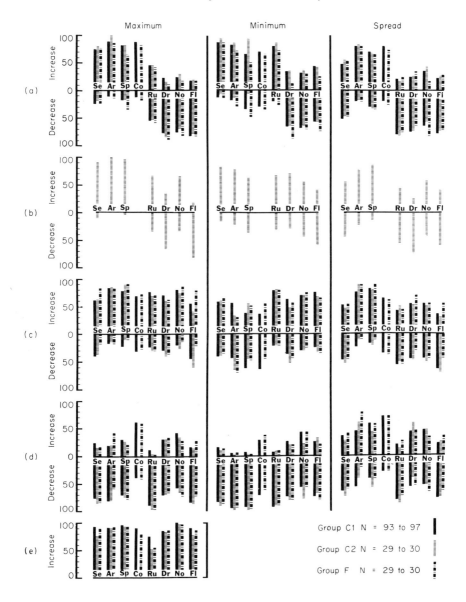

Fig. 3. Percentage of subjects showing increases and percentage showing decreases in (a) heart rate, (b) blood pressure, (c) I-fraction (ratio of inspiratory duration to total cycle time), (d) respiratory period, and (e) palmar conductance, between the alert and stimulus periods. Groups, stimuli, and tasks are as in Figures 1 and 2. Blood pressure was recorded for the C2 group only. *Se*, sentences; *Ar*, arithmetic; *Sp*, spelling; *Co*, cold-pressor test; *Ru*, "Rules," *Dr*, dramatic recitation; *No*, noise; *Fl*, Flash.

increased or decreased from alert to stimulus. For heart rate we see that the majority of subjects show increases during internal cognitive tasks and while withstanding noxious stimulation, that the majority of subjects decelerate during environmental intake, and that about half increase and half decrease in combined tasks. Blood pressure behaves similarly, except that the presumably noxious qualities of the intense white noise result in an equivocal response, neither hypotensive or hypertensive. Inspiratory fractions, however, do not distinguish between these two kinds of tasks; neither does respiratory period, nor palmar conductance. These three variables behave in the familiar way to "index" a state of "activation." Only heart rate and blood pressure differentiate the tasks. Why? The neurophysiological facts earlier reviewed, which imply to us modification of sensorimotor integration by cardiovascular activity, suggested the next steps in the development of our research to answer this and related questions. We needed to show (a) that the deceleration and hypotension occurred systematically in still other circumstances requiring vigilance and attention to environmental inputs, and (b) that these relatively unfamiliar responses (unfamiliar to behavioral physiologists) were correlated with improved sensorimotor performance. Both these demonstrations, of course, are practically heretical in the light of current arousal or activation theory.

CARDIAC RESPONSE IN REACTION TIME EXPERIMENTS

The reaction time experiment, dynamically rich and easily quantifiable, has served well to make both demonstrations. We have completed about 12 experiments in this area, but only a few of the major results will be mentioned here.

Figure 4 shows cardiotachometric records produced by on-line computation, cardiac cycle by cardiac cycle, of the heart rate in beats per minute. What is recorded is the envelope of cardiac activity beat by beat. Below each cardiotachometric record is the corresponding respiratory record. The records show two trials for each of three subjects. The ready signal (R in the graph) informs the subject that in an unannounced period—actually 4 sec—a signal will be presented (S in the graphs) to which he is to respond as rapidly as possible by raising his hand from a telegraph key. Characteristically, as in each trial in Figure 4, heart rate begins to decelerate 3 or 4 beats before the imperative stimulus, a nadir being reached with the onset of stimulation, which is followed by a recovery to base level. This decel-

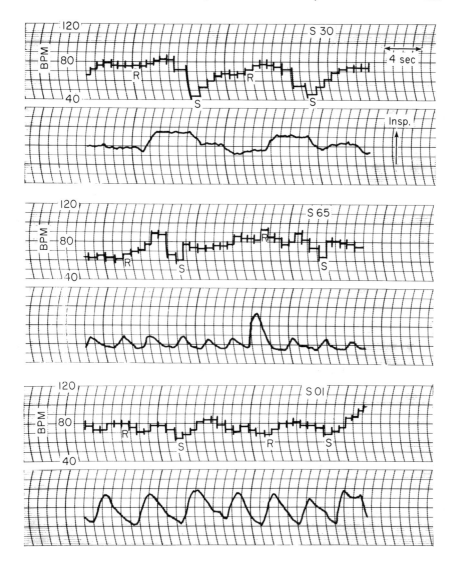

Fig. 4. Cardiotachometric recordings of heart rate and thoracic pneumograph recordings of respiration for three typical subjects (S30, S65, and S01) during a 30-sec period in which two reaction-time trials were presented. *R* identifies time of occurrence of ready signal; *S*, the "imperative" or "go" stimulus requiring rapid release of a telegraph key that had been depressed at *R*. BPM means beats per minute. Note that the anticipatory cardiac decelerations cannot be attributed to any consistent respiratory response.

eration can be very large: In the first illustrated trial for S 30 it is 40 beats/min. This systematic beat-by-beat deceleration during the preparatory interval in a simple reaction-time experiment is seen both early and late in an experiment; it is seen in an overwhelming majority of subjects and trials, and occurs with a wide variety of accompanying respiratory patterns. It is important to note that other data from our laboratory show that the deceleration is not a response secondary to a momentary hypertensive episode. The cardiac response to the ready signal, it should be noted, while more modest and much less consistent, is most frequently acceleratory.

Effect of Increased Motivation. If the subject is especially motivated to respond as quickly as possible, and shows this by highly significant decreases in reaction time, both the acceleratory components and the deceleratory components of the cardiac response are increased, as shown in Figure 5. Statistical analysis shows that the increase in the early acceleration is algebraically less than the increase in the later deceleration and is not as significant. So, in its response to motivation, the anticipatory cardiac deceleration appears to be eminently qualified as an "activation" response.

Effect of Stimulus Omission. What happens when the imperative stimulus, the stimulus which is to release the prepared motor response, is omitted?

The results seen in Figure 6 are from an experiment in which a number of so-called "catch trials" were included. Instead of presenting the imperative stimulus four seconds after the ready signal, the stimulus was omitted for these trials and the trials were then terminated by a special signal 1 sec later. For the catch trials, heart rate continued to decrease, past the point in time where the stimulus was expected, to the trial termination 1 sec later. The heart clearly reveals the organism's continued anticipatory search for the expected stimulus.

While the effect can be seen in both low and high heart-rate subjects, it is much more dramatic in the latter. A person with a low heart rate has time for only a single cardiac cycle in the additional one second, whereas subjects with high heart rates frequently had two or more heart beats in this period.

Effect of Foreperiod Duration. What happens when the foreperiod is increased from 4 sec to 10 sec? This question needed to be answered in order to insure that we were not seeing a response, evoked by the ready signal, with a time course adventitiously coincident with the 4 sec duration of the preparatory interval (PI) used. In

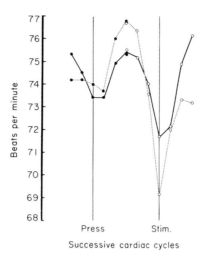

Fig. 5. Group averages of median cardiac response curves for 28 subjects to 20 "unmotivated" (—) and 20 "motivated" (····) trials. Motivation consisted of asking the subject to make a maximum effort to respond as quickly as possible, and of truthfully announcing each reaction time to him. Reaction times were uniformly speedier in the group motivated by this technique. Successive cardiac cycles were oriented with respect to the preparatory key press (closed circles) and the imperative stimulus (open circles). The vertical lines labeled Press and Stim. show the time of occurrence of these events, respectively. Both the acceleratory and deceleratory limbs of the response curve are enhanced with increased motivation, but the increase in the magnitude of the deceleration is greater and more reliable.

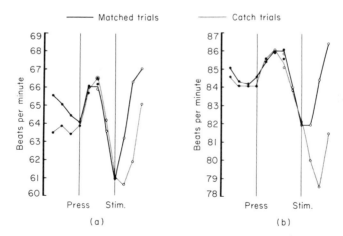

Fig. 6. Group averages of the median cardiac response curves of the 33 subjects with (a) lowest heart rates and of the 33 subjects with (b) highest heart rates in a reaction-time experiment. Results are shown for 12 regular trials and 12 temporally contiguous "catch trials" in which the stimulus was omitted. Successive cardiac cycles are oriented as in Figure 5. When the stimulus is omitted, the heart continues to decelerate until the trial is terminated.

such a case, the cardiac response would really have nothing to do with the preparation of a subject to make a given response.

Figure 7 is from an experiment conducted in collaboration with Dr. Jean-Marie Coquery. No preparatory key press was required; instead the response to the imperative stimulus was a key press. It shows most clearly that the development of the obtrusive deceleratory response is not restricted to a 4 sec PI; rather it is time-locked to the presentation of the imperative stimulus. Despite the 6-sec difference in duration of the two PIs, the heart decelerates to almost identical levels at the time of the imperative stimulus.

The 10-sec PI under the conditions of this experiment seems to provide time enough for the subject to elaborate a total response of early acceleration followed by a massive, longer-lasting, and algebraically greater deceleration. In the 4-sec PI, where time is not sufficient for the evolution of the full response, it is the early acceleration which is sacrificed, but the deceleration from the base level remains unchanged.

Relationship to Behavioral Efficiency. A persistent, although modest, correlation has emerged from all our experiments with simple reaction time. The greater the cardiac deceleration, the faster is the reaction time to the imperative stimulus. This has been demonstrated on both an intra- and intersubject basis. For intersubject

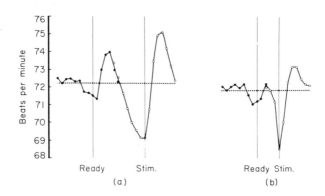

Fig. 7. Group averages of the median cardiac response curves for 26 subjects for 100 trials, half with a 10-sec (a) and half with a 4-sec (b) preparatory interval (P.I.). Two subgroups were used to counterbalance order of presentation of foreperiods. Successive cardiac cycles were oriented with respect to both ready signal (solid circles) and imperative stimulus (open circles). The heart reaches approximately the same level at the imperative stimulus despite differences in length of anticipatory periods. It is the early acceleratory phase of the response which is restricted when time is insufficient for development of the full response.

comparisons, the correlations seem to hover between values of .30 and .40. Concomitant blood-pressure changes are generally very small increases, the largest of which tend to result in a slowing of reaction time. The early acceleratory limb has been inconsistently related to speed of response in the various studies. In the one case where a significant relationship was found, acceleration resulted in a slowing of reaction time. All of these effects are inconsistent with current arousal theories, but consistent with the neurophysiological and psychophysiological effects earlier reviewed.

RELATIONSHIPS TO ELECTROENCEPHALOGRAPHIC ACTIVATION

We move now to studies relating the cardio-deceleratory response to EEG (electroencephalographic) "activation." W. Grey Walter and his collaborators (Walter, Cooper, Aldridge, McCallum, & Winter, 1964) investigated the behavioral significance of a slowly changing potential which, according to current interpretations, arises in non-specific frontal cortex, and can be easily recorded in a vertex-to-mastoid scalp derivation. It exhibits far less attenuation compared with direct cortical recordings than the normal EEG. Adequate recordings require the use of DC amplifiers or long time-constant AC amplifiers. The response is an increasing negativity of the vertex. They called the response the "contingent negative variation" (CNV), and it was said to reflect the readiness of the organism to respond (as measured by reaction time) and the organism's evaluation of the reinforcement contingencies provided by the experimental environment. Our prediction was clear: We should be able to relate the response of cardiac deceleration to this new measure of EEG "activation."

Averaged responses are necessary to clearly see the CNV. Figure 8 illustrates such averages secured by a Computer of Average Transients starting with different triggering points, that is, points at which the analysis is begun. *R* denotes the ready signal, *S* the stimulus, and *P* the preparatory press in a standard simple visual reaction time experiment. Briefly, the figure shows that at the ready signal there is a massive evoked complex in which the vertex becomes abruptly more negative with respect to the mastoid. There is then a slow minor change towards positivity, and then a steadily increasing negativity in anticipation of the imperative stimulus. This increased negativity is abruptly terminated at the onset of the imperative stimulus and the immediately subsequent motor response.

If we set our computer to begin averaging at the subject's preparatory press (which initiates the timing of the preparatory interval), we

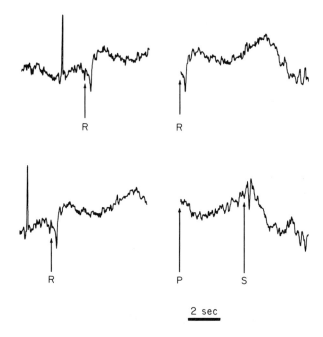

Fig. 8. Averaged vertex-to-mastoid DC potentials for 15 reaction-time trials in a single subject. Negativity of vertex produces an upward deflection. The spike appearing 2 sec before *R* is an in-series calibrating potential change of 50 μV. A TMC Model 400 Computer of Average Transients was used to analyze the EEG that had been recorded on magnetic tape. Considerable care was taken to avoid contamination by eye movements. Each graph starts with a different trigger point in order to show details of the total response. R stands for ready signal, S for stimulus, and P for the preparatory press that initiated the 4-sec foreperiod.

see clearly the steady increase in negativity that is sustained until the onset of the imperative stimulus.

Cardiac Deceleration and the CNV. Figure 9 shows the result which both neurophysiological evidence and our early psychophysiological evidence had led us to predict: the greater the cardiac deceleration the greater the CNV. In this experiment, each individual was his own control. Trials were segregated into those in which the subject had shown minimum cardiac deceleration (lower third of the distribution of decelerations) in anticipation of the imperative stimulus and those in which he demonstrated maximum deceleration (upper third). The solid line shows the results for minimal deceleration trials and the broken line maximum deceleration trials.

If the subject is engaged in trials in which he minimally decelerates, the early positivity is greater, and is followed by only a slight increased negativity prior to the imperative stimulus. For the trials with large anticipatory decelerations, however, there is a very prompt termination of the positive limb and then a marked increase in negativity. This relationship between cardiac deceleration and the CNV was statistically significant at below the 1% level of confidence.

Behavioral Efficiency and the CNV. The same experiment also showed a significant relationship between the CNV and speed of response (Figure 10). Subjects showed greater CNVs on those trials on which they responded most rapidly. Walter and his colleagues had reported a similar relationship in their 1964 article when they noted that "In most adult subjects the development of a consistent CNV with an abrupt termination is associated with a marked reduction in reaction time to the imperative stimulus."

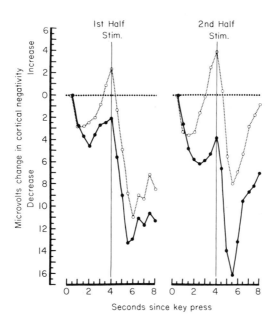

Fig. 9. Average group curves showing changes in cortical negativity by half-second intervals during the 4-sec foreperiod in a reaction-time experiment as a function of the magnitude of cardiac deceleration. The solid line shows results for the trials in which there was minimal cardiac deceleration (lower third of distribution for the individual subject) and the broken line shows results for trials with maximal cardiac deceleration (upper third of distribution). Increased negativity (CNV) prior to the imperative stimulus starts earlier and is greater in trials with maximal cardiac deceleration. The differences are enhanced rather than habituated in the second half of the experiment. The vertical line labeled Stim. shows the time of occurrence of the imperative stimulus.

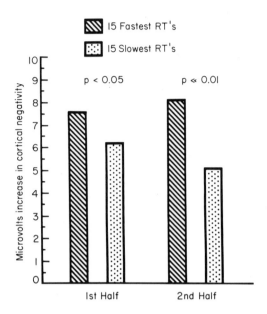

Fig. 10. Average group increases in cortical negativity (CNV) during the foreperiod for 15 fastest and 15 slowest reaction-time (RT) trials (of a total of 45 trials in each half of the experiment). The CNV was significantly greater when subjects' reaction times were fastest. Again the relationship is enhanced in the second half of the experiment.

CARDIAC AND CNV CHANGES WITH RESPONSE-INTENTION

We are currently involved in a series of experiments in which the subject performs, in operant conditioning terminology, on a DRL-LH schedule (differential reinforcement of low rates of responding, with a limited hold). These are very complex timing experiments in which the subject, with no external stimulation except his perception of the elapsed period since his last key press, decides when to press again. For purposes of analysis, the tape on which cortical activity is recorded is played backwards, so that we can see the development of response starting 8 sec prior to the press. Figure 11 contains averaged curves which show the gradual increase in negativity of vertex with respect to mastoid which develops prior to the subject's press. Note that the temporal orientation of these curves is reversed, the press being the left-most and press-minus-8-sec the right-most point on each curve.

Similar cardiac analysis shows marked heart-rate deceleration prior to the subject-initiated press, much the same as that found during the anticipatory period of the reaction-time experiment. Figure 12 is an example of such a response and shows a cardiac deceleration which

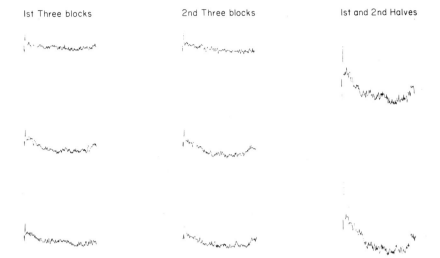

Fig. 11. Averaged curves of vertex-to-mastoid potentials for one subject in an operant conditioning experiment, by blocks of nine trials, and by first and second halves of the experiment. The subject must decide when to press a key. Presses that occur at no less than 15 sec or no more than 19 sec since the previous press are positively reinforced; all other presses are negatively reinforced. Reinforcements consist of visual signals indicating the gain or loss of small sums of money. Each graph is temporally oriented from right to left (see text) and covers an 8-sec period ending with the key press. The sharp spikes are 25 μV calibrating pulses. Negativity of the vertex is upwards. Increasing negativity is seen as the subject gets ready to press and simultaneously to attend to the resulting visual indication of monetary gain or loss.

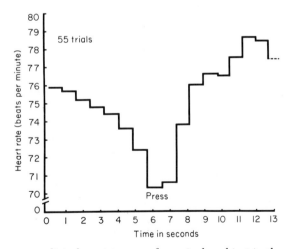

Fig. 12. Average cardiotachometric curve for a single subject in the operant conditioning experiment for which CNVs were shown in Figure 11. Heart rate decelerates markedly during the period of increased negativity of the vertex (CNV), in anticipation of the key press and simultaneous administration of the reinforcement.

increases exponentially to the press. It is our impression that the cardiac deceleration leads the CNV, i.e., starts prior to the electro-cortical response.

An experiment in which we are currently engaged is designed to study cardiac and EEG differentiation of attention and the response-intention emphasized in these DRL experiments, variables which are confounded both in the reaction-time experiments and in these DRL experiments. The experiments presented, however, do show that cardiac deceleration accompanies EEG activation.

CARDIAC DECELERATION AND COGNITIVE STYLE

There are two recent extensions of our work which come from other laboratories which are most relevant and should be mentioned here.

Dr. Nancy Israel of the Research Center for Mental Health at New York University has reported (Israel, 1968, 1969) an interesting link-age of the "bradycardia of attention" we have described here to the "cognitive style" of the organism. Cognitive style is defined as the enduring strategies (enduring over time and situations) which the individual employs in dealing with the stimuli of his external environ-ment.

Dr. Israel and her colleagues have been studying for some time a dimension of cognitive style called leveling–sharpening. Sharpeners are individuals whose characteristic style is to be attentive – perhaps overly attentive – to all kinds of external details. They tend to pay attention to everything, to focus on differences rather than similari-ties among stimuli. They do not habituate very readily in the (Soko-loff) habituation experiment. Levelers on the other hand are de-scribed as individuals who make global judgments, habituate quickly, and are inattentive to many details in the environment. We would expect, then, that sharpeners would show greater decelera-tions than levelers. This expectation was confirmed.

The subjects were classified as levelers or sharpeners on the basis of a laboratory perceptual test. They were then subjected to a series of geometric stimuli, each preceded by a preparatory period. The stimuli varied in complexity and the subjects knew whether they were going to be boring and monotonous, low- or high-preference stimuli, and so forth.

Dr. Israel found that skin conductance did not differentiate the two groups of subjects, but the cardiac response did. Both groups decel-erated, but the sharpener, the person acutely aware of and attentive to the details of his external environment, showed about the same decelerations no matter what the stimulus, whether it was low preference, high preference, or anxiety producing. He was characteristically equally attentive to everything, and this attentiveness was shown by cardiac deceleration of about the same degree to all stimuli. Levelers on the other hand did not decelerate as much, and the magnitude of the deceleration in anticipation of the visual stimulus depended upon whether it was a low-preferred or high-preferred or anxiety-producing stimulus. They could be said to have a physiological lability which paralleled the lability of their attitude toward the external environment.

CARDIAC DECELERATION AND VICARIOUS STRESS

Craig and Woods (1969) at the University of British Columbia have reported differences in the direction of the cardiac response, between directly experienced and vicariously experienced stress. Both experiences, however, produced increases in skin conductance. When subjects immersed their hand in water maintained at −4°C and were required to hold it there as long as possible (a modified cold-pressor test), a massive cardiac acceleration resulted. When they watched others do the same thing, the vicarious experience produced cardiac deceleration! The deceleration was enhanced in those subjects who had already had the direct experience and were no longer threatened by it.

SUMMARY AND CONCLUSIONS

In this chapter we have come from surgically manipulated, drugged cats and dogs, through simple laboratory studies of reaction time and operant responses, to the consideration of cognitive style and controlled social learning and empathy. It should be pointed out that so far there are only suggestive parallels between the neurophysiological and psychophysiological studies we have reported. The suggestion is that the key to the understanding of the psychophysiological results does indeed lie in the operation of visceral afferent feedback pathways which enable the heart to communicate with the brain.

We are doing chronic animal studies now to try to demonstrate that this visceral afferent feedback pathway does indeed operate in the way we think it does, in the experimental situations we have described. Many problems have yet to be solved and much work done before really effective demonstrations can be made.

In the meantime, the cardiovascular system commends itself to psychiatric study, not as a nonspecific index of arousal or emotion, but as a highly specific and apparently quite delicate response mechanism, integrated at the highest levels with the affective and cognitive variations among people, and revealing specific personal idiosyncrasies in the way people deal with their external world.

ACKNOWLEDGMENT

Preparation of this paper and the reported research originating in the Department of Psychophysiology-Neurophysiology, Fels Research Institute, were supported by grants MH-00623 and FR-00222 from the National Institutes of Health, United States Public Health Service.

REFERENCES

Baccelli, G., Guazzi, M., Libretti, A., & Zanchetti, A. Pressoceptive and chemoceptive aortic reflexes in decorticate and in decerebrate cats. *American Journal of Physiology*, 1965, **208**, 708-714.

Bartorelli, C., Bizzi, E., Libretti, A., & Zanchetti, A. Inhibitory control of sinocarotid pressoceptive afferents on hypothalamic autonomic activity and sham rage behavior. *Archives Italiennes de Biologie*, 1960, **98**, 308-326.

Bonvallet, M., & Allen, M. B. Prolonged spontaneous and evoked reticular activation following discrete bulbar lesions. *Electroencephalography and Clinical Neurophysiology*, 1963, **15**, 969-988.

Bonvallet, M., & Bloch, V. Bulbar control of cortical arousal. *Science*, 1961, **133**, 1133-1134.

Bonvallet, M., Dell, P., & Hiebel, G. Tonus sympathique et activité électrique corticale. *Electroencephalography and Clinical Neurophysiology*, 1954, **6**, 119-144. (a)

Bonvallet, M., Dell, P., & Hugelin, A. Influence de l'adrénaline sur le contrôle réticulaire des activités corticale et spinale. *Journal de Physiologie (Paris)*, 1954, **46**, 262-265. (b)

Craig, K., & Woods, K. Physiological differentiation of direct and vicarious affective arousal. *Canadian Journal of Behavioral Science*, 1969, **2**, 98-105.

Davis, R. C., Buchwald, A. M., & Frankmann, R. W. Autonomic and muscular responses, and their relation to simple stimuli. *Psychological Monographs*, 1955, No. 405, **69**, 20.

Dell, P., Bonvallet, M., & Hugelin, A. Tonus sympathique, adrénaline et contrôle réticulaire de la motricité spinale. *Electroencephalography and Clinical Neurophysiology*, 1954, **6**, 599-618.

Heymans, C., & Neil, E. *Reflexogenic areas of the cardiovascular system*. Boston: Little, Brown, 1958.

Israel, N. R. Cognitive control and pattern of autonomic response. Paper presented at meeting of the Eastern Psychological Association, Washington, D.C., April, 1968.

Israel, N. R. Leveling-sharpening and anticipatory cardiac response. *Psychosomatic Medicine*, 1969, **31**, 499-509.

Lacey, J. I. Psychophysiological approaches to the evaluation of psychotherapeutic process and outcome. In E. A. Rubinstein and M. B. Parloff (Eds.) *Research in Psychotherapy*, Washington, D.C., American Psychological Association, 1959.

Lacey, J. I. Somatic response patterning and stress: Some revisions of activation theory. In M. H. Appley and R. Trumbull (Eds.), *Psychological stress: Issues in research*, New York: Appleton, 1967.

Lacey, J. I., Kagan, J., Lacey, B. C., & Moss, H. A. The visceral level: Situational determinants and behavioral correlates of autonomic response patterns. In P. H. Knapp (Ed.), *Expression of the emotions in man.* New York: International Universities Press, 1963.

Walter, W. G., Cooper, R., Aldridge, V. J., McCallum, W. C., & Winter, A. L. Contingent negative variation: An electric sign of sensorimotor association and expectancy in the human brain. *Nature (London)*, 1964, **203**, 380-384.

THE PERCEPTION AND LABELING OF BODILY CHANGES AS DETERMINANTS OF EMOTIONAL BEHAVIOR

Stuart Valins

INTRODUCTION

When William James (1890) defined emotion as the perception of bodily changes he succeeded not only in arousing considerable disbelief but also a great deal of experimentation. James believed that perceptions of bodily changes were necessary and sufficient conditions for the arousal of emotion, yet the research stimulated by his argument seemed to support the conclusion that such perceptions are neither necessary nor sufficient. Cannon's (1915) objections to the James-Lange theory of emotion suggested that bodily changes have little importance as determinants of emotional experience. Nevertheless, the fact that Cannon addressed himself to the *occurrence* of bodily changes rather than to their *perception* reduces the impact of his critique. James believed that emotions could not be experienced without the perception of bodily changes. Cannon presumed to demonstrate that emotions could be experienced without the occurrence of bodily changes. Clearly, Cannon's critique is viable only if we equate occurrence with perception. To the degree that occurrence does not lead to perception, and to the degree that perception does not depend upon occurrence, Cannon's critique is irrelevant.

It is not the purpose of this paper, however, to defend James or to criticize Cannon. Our purpose in mentioning their work was solely intended to introduce a distinction which is necessary in the light of current research. When evaluating the relevance of bodily changes for emotional experience one should distinguish the perception of these changes from their actual occurrence. This distinction should not be interpreted as suggesting that perception and occurrence are completely orthogonal but rather as suggesting that there may be sufficient independence to warrant separate conceptualizations and investigations. Studies investigating the relationship between report of bodily change and actual change indicate that the distinction may be justified. Mandler and his associates (Mandler & Kremen, 1958; Mandler, Mandler, & Uviller, 1958) have subjected undergraduates to stressful intellectual tasks and related their verbal reports of perceived bodily changes to their actual bodily changes during the tasks. Although positive, these correlations were generally weak and leave considerable variance to be accounted for. The perception of bodily change is evidently not highly dependent upon actual bodily change. Furthermore, there is some indication that perception and occurrence may have different consequences for emotional behavior. Mandler and Kremen (1958) have found that the perception of bodily change is more highly related to performance on a stressful vocabulary test than is the occurrence of bodily change. Individuals who reported bodily changes performed poorly. The occurrence of bodily changes was not, however, related to performance.

Since occurrence and perception are obviously not identical variables we should separately assess their relevance for emotional behavior. Methods for assessing their relevance will, however, depend upon which variable is of interest. If we ignore the perception of bodily changes, as many with a neurophysiological bent do, then the relevance of bodily changes for emotional behavior will be investigated by a consideration of the anatomy and physiology of the nervous system. We will be particularly interested in internal receptors, afferent connections between the peripheral organs and the brain, and in those areas of the brain which are involved in emotional behavior. If we are interested in the perception of bodily changes, however, a different set of questions arises which lead us to areas other than the anatomy and physiology of the nervous system. We focus less on the physiological consequences of bodily changes and more on their cognitive consequences. What does an individual do when he perceives a bodily change? Do individuals differ in what they do? Does what they do have an effect on emotional behavior?

To answer these questions we have only to assume that emotional stimuli produce perceptions of bodily changes. It is with the consequences of these perceptions that we will be concerned.

A COGNITIVE AND PHYSIOLOGICAL APPROACH TO EMOTIONAL BEHAVIOR

MANIPULATION OF VERIDICAL BODILY PERCEPTIONS

Consider a person who is experiencing palpitations. He is aware that his body is reacting in an unusual manner. What does the person do with this information? Does he take note of it and disregard it or does he integrate it with whatever else he is experiencing at the moment? Common sense tells us that novel information about ourselves is not disregarded. We think about it and attempt to understand it. This evaluative process is the crucial element in Schachter's cognitive and physiological theory of emotion (1964). Bodily sensations represent information which must be processed. An individual feels a need to understand these sensations in the sense that he requires a label or explanation for their occurrence. Emotional behavior results to the extent that these sensations are attributed to emotional stimuli. In this way the perception and labeling of physiological changes influence subjective and behavioral reactions to emotional stimuli.

The evidence for these views is by now well known. Schachter and Singer (1962) manipulated the perception of bodily changes via actual occurrence by injecting subjects with epinephrine or placebo. They also manipulated a subject's need for an explanation for these sensations by correctly informing some epinephrine subjects what they might expect to experience, while not informing other epinephrine subjects. According to the theory, these uninformed subjects need an explanation for their bodily sensations and would be most likely to be affected if one were available in the form of an emotional situation. Such was the case. Uninformed subjects felt and acted more angry in an anger-inducing situation (and more euphoric in an euphoria-inducing situation) than did informed or placebo subjects. Informed and placebo subjects displayed an equivalently low level of emotional behavior. Thus, emotional behavior was jointly determined by the perception and labeling of bodily changes.

This experiment left two important questions unanswered. First, are Schachter and Singer's results specific to a situation in which there is an artificial and extreme induction of autonomic arousal? If this were so, the experiment, although interesting, would have fewer implications for the study of emotional behavior. Second, how is the crucial cognition, "That stimulus (emotional) has caused my body to react," translated into emotional behavior? This cognition presumably has an effect on emotional behavior through some intermediary process. Nisbett and Schachter (1966) conducted an experiment which gives reasonable answers to both questions. They used fearful and painful electric shocks, rather than a pharmacological manipulation, to induce bodily changes and perceptions. One group of subjects was led to attribute these shock-induced bodily sensations (palpitations, tremors, etc.) to a placebo capsule. A second group of subjects was allowed to correctly attribute their sensations to the shocks. These subjects received a placebo and were told that it produced sensations which are not likely to accompany the experience of shock. Nisbett and Schachter found that those subjects who attributed their shock-induced sensations to the placebo considered the electric shocks to be considerably less painful and withstood more of them than did subjects who attributed their sensations to the shocks. Subjective and behavioral reactions to electric shock were evidently affected by the perception and labeling of a naturally induced set of bodily sensations. These results indicate that the significance of Schachter's work is not restricted to a situation in which an extreme pharmacological manipulation is employed. It can also be concluded that the cognition, "That stimulus (emotional) has caused my body to react," results in a reevaluation of the emotional stimulus and that this reevaluation may be responsible for the effects of the cognition on emotional behavior. Since the stimulus is perceived as more intense, the subject's emotional reaction is heightened accordingly.

MANIPULATION OF NONVERIDICAL BODILY PERCEPTIONS

Although dealing with the perception of bodily changes, Schachter's experiments manipulated perceptions via actual occurrence. To demonstrate the importance of these perceptions and of the consequent evaluative process, he has induced bodily changes using drugs or emotional stimuli. The research that we shall now discuss is also concerned with the effects of bodily perceptions but these perceptions were manipulated in a different manner. Using a convincing deception, we provided subjects with false information about their bodily reactions and studied the effects of this information on their subjective reactions to emotional stimuli. These experiments were all introduced as studies of physiological reactions to emotional stimuli and the cover stories were variations of the following:

Most of our research is conducted over at the Bell Medical Research Building. We have all sorts of electronic wizardry and sound proof chambers over there. Right now there are several experiments being conducted and our facilities at Bell are too overcrowded. Because of this situation, we are doing this experiment here, and are forced to use a fairly crude but adequate measure of heart rate. In our other lab we record heart rate using electrodes which are taped to the chest. They pick up the electrical impulses from the heart which are then recorded on a polygraph. Here we are recording heart rate the way they used to do it 30 years ago. I will be taping this fairly sensitive microphone to your chest. It picks up each major heart sound which is amplified here, and initiates an audible signal on this signal tracer. This other microphone then picks up the signal and it is recorded on this tape recorder (the signal tracer, amplifier, and tape recorder were on a table next to the subject). By appropriately using a stop watch and this footage indicator, I can later determine exactly where each stimulus occurred and evaluate your heart rate reaction to it.

"Unfortunately, this recording method makes it necessary to have audible sounds. They would be a serious problem if we were employing a task which required concentration. Since our procedure does not require concentration, it won't be too much of a problem and it is not likely to affect the results. All that you will be required to do is sit here and look at the slides. Just try to ignore the heart sounds. I will be showing the slides from the next room through a one-way screen. I'll tape this microphone to your chest and after recording your resting heart rate for a while, I will present 10 slides to you at regular intervals. Then I will record your resting heart rate again for several minutes and I will repeat the same slides again in the same order.

Although the emotional stimuli varied, in all of these experiments the subjects heard heart-like sounds which were prerecorded. The presentation of the emotional stimuli was coordinated with a tape recording so that the experimenter controlled the subject's perceptions of the magnitude of his reactions to the different stimuli. In the first experiment of this series (Valins, 1966) subjects saw slides of female nudes. One group heard an increase in their heart rates (72-90 beats per minute, BPM) in reaction to five slides and no change in their heart rates (continuation of a 66-72 BPM variation) to five other slides. A second group heard a decrease (66-48 BPM) in response to five of the slides and no change to five others. Two control groups heard the same tape recordings and saw the same slides but knew beforehand that the sounds were tape recorded. The effects of the false heart-rate information were assessed using measures of the subjects' attraction for the slides. All subjects rated the attractiveness of each nude, chose copies of five of the nudes as a reward, and ranked the attractiveness of the nudes one month later during a disguised interview.

The data from these various measures were all quite similar. Nudes to which subjects heard their heart rates change, whether increased or decreased, were liked significantly more than nudes to which they heard no change in their heart rates. Control subjects showed no consistent preferences. These data are exactly what one would have expected had heart-rate changes and veridical perceptions of palpitation been pharmacologically induced to some slides but not to others. The mechanism operating to produce differential liking is presumably the same regardless of the veridicality of the perceptions. Individuals need to evaluate and understand their bodily changes. Our subjects could best evaluate their presumed bodily changes by reference to the series of nudes. Since all of the nudes were very attractive, the subjects could not interpret a change in their heart rates as indicating disgust. They had to interpret it as indicating greater attraction than no change. Subjects were thus oriented toward liking the nudes to which their hearts had reacted more than the other nudes.

Postexperimental interviews suggested that this orientation led subjects to attend more closely to the nudes in order to account for what their hearts were "telling" them. In effect, they liked the nudes which had affected their hearts because they looked for and found positive characteristics which could explain their reactions. Some support for this interpretation was found in a subsequent study (Valins, 1967a). When subjects were asked to rate specific features of the nudes (breasts, face, hair, general pose), they rated the features of the nudes to which they heard their hearts react as "nicer" than those of the nudes to which their hearts did not react. It seems reasonable, then, that subjects did selectively attend to various features of the nudes in order to explain their presumed heart-rate reactions and that the results of this process produced strong and relatively enduring changes in their attitudes toward the nudes.

This selective-attention hypothesis is of help in explaining the results of another experiment (Valins, 1968) in which subjects were debriefed about the deceptive nature of the feedback after they had seen the slides and heard their heart-rate reactions. In spite of the fact that they were shown the equipment and convinced that the feedback was false, subsequent assessments of their liking for the nudes revealed that these subjects continued to prefer those nudes to which they had heard their hearts react. These preferences were just as strong as those of subjects who were not debriefed. If we accept what our subjects have been telling us, namely, that the feedback directs their attention to positive or negative features of the nudes, then these results are reasonable. Convincing them that the feedback was false does not negate the fact that they have become aware of an objectively positive feature of a nude.

It should be clear from this discussion that we are emphasizing the cognitive consequences of perceptions of bodily change. Nevertheless, it may be asked whether the manipulation of these perceptions has physiological consequences and whether these physiological consequences are mediating differences in "liking" of the nudes. Available evidence suggests that our manipulation does not have important physiological effects. The actual heart rates of subjects exposed to the false feedback manipulation do not seem to differ from those of control subjects for the slides to which they hear a change in the rate of the sounds or for the slides to which they hear no change (Valins, 1966).[1] Furthermore, when queried about their actual feelings of palpitation or heart beating, experimental subjects report *fewer* palpitations than control subjects (Valins, 1966). These data suggest that the effects of the false feedback manipulation are primarily a result of cognitive factors and not physiological ones. Moreover, the feedback evidently masks actual physiological cues by diverting the subject's attention from his true internal reactions.

THE MODIFICATION OF ESTABLISHED EMOTIONAL BEHAVIOR

MANIPULATION OF VERIDICAL BODILY PERCEPTIONS

An obvious extension of these laboratory studies of emotional behavior is to the treatment of individuals whose emotional behavior is maladaptive. We should be able to modify well-established emotional behavior by manipulating the perception of bodily changes. Schachter and Latané (1964) conducted an experiment along these lines using epinephrine to arouse fear in the psychopath. The *primary* psychopath, as defined by Cleckley (1955) is an individual whose antisocial behavior seems to be caused by the absence of feel-

[1]Research recently reported by Botto and Stern (1968) seems to indicate that false heart-rate feedback may have relevant physiological effects. An adequate evaluation of this issue must await a more complete report of their data.

ings of fear or guilt. The absence of these feelings is considered not
to be symptomatic of any underlying neurotic processes.

Working with the assumption that the psychopath is emotionally
flat because of hyporeactivity of the sympathetic nervous system and
the resulting absence of physiological cues, Schachter and Latané
reasoned that the psychopath might be made to be emotional if he
was provided with these cues. A shock-avoidance learning task was
selected since Lykken (1957) had previously shown that psychopaths
learned this task poorly, relative to normals. Schachter and Latané
tested criminal psychopaths and normals in two conditions. In one
condition, subjects received injections of saline solution prior to the
beginning of the learning task. The results of this condition replicated Lykken's. Relative to the performance of the normals, the psychopaths did not learn to avoid the shock. In another condition, all
subjects received an injection of epinephrine (but remained ignorant
of its side-effects) before beginning the learning task. Psychopaths in
this condition learned significantly better than they did with placebo
and better than the normals. The epinephrine had presumably given
the psychopaths the bodily cues which they ordinarily do not experience but which are necessary for the arousal of fear. Fear then motivated them to learn to avoid the shock.

Although we shall later question the assumption that this study
was based on—that psychopaths are sympathetically hyporesponsive—the results do suggest that established emotional behavior can
be modified by manipulations involving bodily perceptions and labeling. The therapeutic potential of these manipulations becomes
most apparent when we consider systematic desensitization therapy.

MANIPULATION OF NONVERIDICAL BODILY PERCEPTIONS

Systematic desensitization is a therapeutic procedure developed
by Wolpe (1958) for the treatment of anxiety-based disorders. Wolpe
assumes that the experience of anxiety or fear to a stimulus is dependent upon the occurrence of certain autonomic response patterns and
that if these patterns are inhibited by antagonistic ones, the stimulus
will no longer evoke anxiety. In the most popular variation of this
procedure, clients are trained to relax their muscles while they are
thinking about items taken from a hierarchy of anxiety-arousing situations. The muscular relaxation is a response which is presumably
incompatible with and which inhibits the physiological correlates of
anxiety. This procedure has been shown to be clinically effective

(Wolpe, 1958) and laboratory studies indicate that its two major components, the muscular relaxation procedure and the gradual presentation of the anxiety stimulus, seem to be jointly necessary for the reduction of anxiety (Lang, Lazovik, & Reynolds, 1965; Davison, 1968).

Although the efficacy of systematic desensitization is usually explained by reference to neurophysiological concepts (reciprocal inhibition) or learning concepts (counterconditioning), we believe that a cognitive interpretation, based on the perception and labeling of bodily states, is equally plausible. According to this interpretation, an individual who was previously autonomically aroused when in an anxiety-provoking situation may have become anxious because of the cognition, "That stimulus has caused my body to react." By substituting muscular relaxation for autonomic arousal, desensitization leads to the cognition, "That stimulus no longer causes my body to react." It is this new cognition that may result in anxiety reduction.

To assess the effects of this cognition, we manipulated subjects' perceptions about their bodily reactions to electric shocks and snake stimuli (Valins & Ray, 1967). Since laboratory investigations of systematic desensitization frequently use avoidance of snakes as a dependent variable, we chose a similar one as a measure of the effects of "cognitive" desensitization. Subjects reported for an experiment investigating physiological reactions to frightening stimuli. We were presumably measuring the heart-rate reactions of the experimental subjects to slides of snakes and to slides consisting of the word "shock" (followed after seven seconds by an actual shock to the fingertips). These subjects heard what they thought were their heart-rate reactions, and heard their "heart rates" increase to the shock slides and actual shocks but heard no change in their "heart rates" to the snake slides. Since snake stimuli did not affect them internally, these subjects should consider any fear that they had of snakes to be unjustified. They should thus manifest more approach behavior when in the presence of a live snake than control subjects. Control subjects were equally frightened of snakes and went through the identical procedure as the experimental subjects. These control subjects, however, knew that the sounds that they were hearing were tape-recorded and that they were not their heart beats. After this procedure, all subjects were exposed to a live snake. They were asked to perform various behaviors in an adjoining room in which a small (30 in.), and allegedly harmless, boa constrictor was caged. Subjects were requested to:

1. Enter the room and look at the snake.
2. Take the cover off the cage and look down at the snake.
3. Reach into the cage and get your hand far enough in so that your wrist is below the top of the cage.
4. Touch the snake once.
5. Pick the snake up a few inches.
6. Pick the snake up and out of the cage, and hold it for as long as you can.

The hypothesis was supported by the results of this snake-approach test. Experimental subjects, whose heart rate reactions "told" them that their fear of snakes was not justified, approached significantly closer to the snake (Mean approach behavior 5.55, based on the 1-6 scale) than control subjects who were given no information about their heart rate reactions (Mean approach behavior 3.62). Moreover, significantly more of the experimental subjects (65%) completed the entire approach task than did the control subjects (25%). This experiment was replicated with slight modification using a selected sample of subjects who were more frightened of snakes than most undergraduates. The results of these experiments suggest that the false-feedback procedure and the muscle-relaxation procedure used in desensitization therapy may both be effective because they allow subjects to believe that a previously frightening stimulus is no longer having a physiological effect.

In support of this cognitive interpretation of systematic desensitization, it should be noted that there is little evidence that the commonly used version of the muscle-relaxation procedure has any physiological effects. That is, subjects are trained and instructed to relax their muscles but they have not been observed to be more somatically or autonomically relaxed during training than control subjects (e.g., Grossberg, 1965). More importantly, there is no evidence that subjects who are presumably relaxed during the presentation of an anxiety item are less physiologically reactive to that item than unrelaxed, control subjects. Since the relevant physiological effects have not been observed, it seems reasonable that the muscle-relaxation procedure may be important because of its cognitive effects. Just as the false-feedback procedure makes subjects believe incorrectly that their hearts are not reacting, the muscle-relaxation procedure, which involves self-instruction, and instruction from a prestigeful experimenter or therapist, may lead subjects to believe incorrectly that their efforts were successful and that they are relaxed. The cognitive evaluation of this nonveridical physiological state may thus be responsible for fear reduction.

INDIVIDUAL DIFFERENCES IN THE LABELING OF BODILY PERCEPTIONS

PSYCHOPATHY

In our discussion of the modification of established emotional behavior, we summarized the research of Schachter and Latané (1964) with the unemotional psychopath. In this section we shall question one of the basic assumptions of that research. Schachter and Latané assumed that the psychopath was unemotional because of the absence of bodily cues. Deprived of the necessary bodily cues, the psychopath would not have an internal state to label and would therefore not experience emotions in the appropriate situations. Although this assumption led to the interesting hypothesis that the psychopath could be made to be emotional via injections of epinephrine, subsequent research indicates that this assumption may be incorrect. It has been found, for example, that psychopathic individuals react with higher heart rates in stressful situations than do nonpsychopaths (Schachter & Latané, 1964; Valins, 1963, 1967b).

If we interpret these heart-rate data as suggesting that psychopaths may experience more bodily changes than do nonpsychopaths, it is clear that we must alter our explanation for the psychopath's lack of emotion. One reasonable explanation would be that although the psychopath experiences bodily changes, he does not perceive them. If he does not perceive them then he would have no cues to label. There is little evidence, however, supporting this explanation. For example, in response to a question about the perception of palpitations, psychopaths have been found to respond no differently than nonpsychopaths in both epinephrine and nondrug conditions (Schachter & Latané, 1964; Valins, 1967b).

Another explanation would be that although the psychopath experiences and perceives his bodily changes, he ignores them in the sense of not utilizing them as cues when evaluating emotional situations. This explanation does have some support (Valins, 1967a). Subjects who were psychometrically classified as psychopathic or nonpsychopathic (by means of a questionnaire developed by Lykken, 1957) were run through the false heart-rate feedback procedure. They heard their heart rates change in reaction to some photographs of nudes but not change to others. It was found that nonpsychopathic subjects were markedly affected by the false feedback, whereas psychopathic subjects were not. Nonpsychopaths labeled the nudes as attractive or unattractive depending upon whether they thought their hearts had reacted. Psychopaths labeled the nudes with little regard to their presumed heart-rate reactions.

Further indications of the psychopath's failure to use his bodily changes as cues are provided by a study conducted by Stern and Kaplan (1967). Undergraduate subjects were given veridical feedback about their GSR (galvanic skin response) performance by means of a microammeter, and were instructed to try to produce decreases in skin resistance (as indicated by movements of the needle on the GSR meter). A significant correlation was found between a subject's score on Lykken's questionnaire and his GSR reactions. When instructed to produce GSR, psychopathic-like subjects failed to do so, whereas nonpsychopathic subjects did. The data of another experimental condition, which permitted an assessment of spontaneous GSR responding, revealed no relationship between psychopathy and GSR responding. Thus, psychopaths do produce as many GSR responses as nonpsychopaths, but cannot do so when instructed, and when feedback is available. The data suggest, then, that knowledge of bodily responses may be of little interest or use to the psychopath.

These data indicate that bodily changes or the perception of bodily changes may be irrelevant variables as far as accounting for the absence of emotion in the psychopath. The psychopath's failure to utilize his bodily changes as cues may alone account for his diminutive emotional behavior. To the degree that this cognitive variable proves to be important we may place less emphasis on the psychopath's actual physiological reactions as determinants of his emotional behavior.

OBESITY

Investigating the determinants of obesity and eating behavior, Schachter (1967) found that the labeling of internal hunger cues plays a major role. The suggestion (discussed above) that the emotional behavior of the psychopath may be independent of his bodily changes is paralleled by Schachter's suggestion that the eating behavior of the obese may be independent of their hunger-induced bodily changes. Schachter, Goldman and Gordon (1968) and Nisbett (1968) found that when gastric contractions were inhibited (by manipulations involving fear or preloading with food) individuals of normal weight ate less than when contractions were not inhibited. Overweight individuals, however, ate the same regardless of whether they were experiencing gastric contractions.

Could these effects be a function of differential occurrence or perception of gastric contractions? Negative evidence has been presented (Stunkard & Koch, 1964; Griggs & Stunkard, 1964). Overweight and normal-weight individuals experience contractions, and can be trained to perceive them, to the same degree. They do differ, however, in the extent to which their statements of hunger correspond to the occurrence of contractions. Normal-weight individuals report hunger when their stomachs contract. Reports of hunger from the overweight tend not to correspond with contractions. These data, in conjunction with Schachter's, suggest that the overweight individual ignores his internal hunger cues in the sense of not using them to define hunger or to initiate eating.

The psychopathic and the obese individual thus seem to have one thing in common: they are both unresponsive to some aspect of their bodily state. The psychopath seems to ignore emotion-related bodily changes and the obese individual seems to ignore hunger-induced bodily changes. It is reasonable to inquire whether responsiveness to bodily changes can be considered a general dimension upon which individuals may differ. One initial step would be to investigate whether the psychopath ignores his hunger-induced bodily changes and whether the obese individual ignores his emotion-induced bodily changes. Available data would suggest that responsiveness to bodily changes is not a general dimension, and that individuals may be hyporesponsive or hyperresponsive to particular kinds of changes. The psychopathy and obesity variables do not seem to be correlated, nor do the obese seem to be hyporesponsive to the false heart-rate manipulation (Barefoot, 1967). An individual's responsiveness to one internal state may thus be independent of his responsiveness to other internal states.

SUMMARY

The research that has been presented indicates that peripheral bodily changes can be viewed as determinants as well as correlates of emotional behavior. Bodily changes instigate cognitive processes which influence our subjective and behavioral reactions to emotional stimuli. Manipulating the perception of bodily changes — pharmacologically, naturally, or by deception — has enabled us to arouse and inhibit emotion-like behavior and to predict individual differences in this behavior. It has been found, however, that bodily changes alone will have little effect on emotional behavior if an individual cannot attribute these changes to emotional stimuli. This emphasis on the relevance of cognitive processes for emotional behavior is probably the most important lesson to be learned from this research. To adequately study emotional behavior we must

... adopt a set of concepts with which most physiologically inclined scientists feel somewhat uncomfortable and ill-at-ease for they are concepts which are, at present, difficult to physiologize about or to reify. We will be forced to examine a subject's perception of his bodily state and his interpretation of it in terms of his immediate situation and his past experience. We will be forced to deal with concepts about perception, about cognition, about learning, and about the social situation, [Schachter, 1967, p. 119].

ACKNOWLEDGMENTS

The preparation of this paper and the author's research were facilitated by research grants from the Foundations' Fund for Research in Psychiatry, the University of North Carolina School of Medicine, and the National Institute of Mental Health (MH 12715 and MH 14557). Helpful comments on an initial draft of this chapter were provided by Gerald Davison, Harvey London, Richard Nisbett, and Jerome Singer.

REFERENCES

Barefoot, J. Individual differences in the use of cognitive and physiological cues. Unpublished doctoral dissertation, University of North Carolina, 1967.

Botto, R. W., & Stern, R. M., False heart-rate feedback: The relationship of choice behavior to true EKG and GSR. Paper presented at meetings of Society for Psychophysiological Research, Washington, D. C., 1968.

Cannon, W. B. *Bodily changes in pain, hunger, fear and rage.* New York: Appleton, 1915.

Cleckley, H. *The mask of sanity.* (3rd ed.) St. Louis: Mosby, 1955.

Davison, G. C. Systematic desensitization as a counterconditioning process. *Journal of Abnormal Psychology,* 1968, **73**, 91–99.

Griggs, R. C., & Stunkard, A. J. The interpretation of gastric motility: II. Sensitivity and bias in the perception of gastric motility. *Archives of General Psychiatry,* 1964, **11**, 82–89.

Grossberg, J. M. The physiological effectiveness of brief training in differential muscle relaxation. Unpublished manuscript, 1965.

James, W. *The principles of psychology.* New York: Holt, 1890.

Lang, P. J., Lazovik, A. D., & Reynolds, O. J. Desensitization, suggestibility and pseudotherapy. *Journal of Abnormal Psychology,* 1965, **70**, 395–402.

Lykken, D. T. A study of anxiety in the sociopathic personality. *Journal of Abnormal and Social Psychology,* 1957, **55**, 6–10.

Mandler, G., & Kremen, I. Autonomic feedback: A correlational study. *Journal of Personality,* 1958, **26**, 388–399.

Mandler, G., Mandler, J. M., & Uviller, E. T. Autonomic feedback: The perception of autonomic activity. *Journal of Abnormal and Social Psychology,* 1958, **56**, 367–373.

Nisbett, R. E. Taste, deprivation, and weight determinants of eating behavior. *Journal of Personality and Social Psychology*, 1968, **10**, 107-116.

Nisbett, R. E., & Schachter, S. Cognitive manipulation of pain. *Journal of Experimental Social Psychology*, 1966, **2**, 227-236.

Schachter, S. The interaction of cognitive and physiological determinants of emotional state. *Advances in Experimental Social Psychology*, 1964, **1**, 49-80.

Schachter, S. Cognitive effects on bodily functioning: Studies of obesity and eating. In D. Glass (Ed.), *Neurophysiology and Emotion.* New York: Rockefeller Univ. Press and Russel Sage Foundation, 1967.

Schachter, S., Goldman, R., & Gordon, A. The effects of fear, food deprivation and obesity on eating. *Journal of Personality and Social Psychology*, 1968, **10**, 91-97.

Schachter, S., & Latané, B. Crime, cognition, and the autonomic nervous system. In D. Levine (Ed.), *Nebraska symposium on motivation*, pp. 221-273. Lincoln: University of Nebraska Press, 1964.

Schachter, S., & Singer, J. E. Cognitive, social and physiological determinants of emotional state. *Psychological Review*, 1962, **69**, 379-399.

Stern, R. M., & Kaplan, B. E. Galvanic skin response: Voluntary control and externalization. *Journal of Psychosomatic Research*, 1967, **10**, 349-353.

Stunkard, A., & Koch, C. The interpretation of gastric motility: I. Apparent bias in the reports of hunger by obese persons. *Archives of General Psychiatry*, 1964, **11**, 74-82.

Valins, S. Psychopathy and physiological reactivity under stress. Unpublished master's thesis, Columbia University, 1963.

Valins, S. Cognitive effects of false heart-rate feedback. *Journal of Personality and Social Psychology*, 1966, **4**, 400-408.

Valins, S. Emotionality and information concerning internal reactions. *Journal of Personality and Social Psychology*, 1967, **6**, 458-463.(a)

Valins, S. Emotionality and autonomic reactivity. *Journal of Experimental Research in Personality*, 1967, **2**, 41-48.(b)

Valins, S. Persistent effects of information concerning internal reactions: Ineffectiveness of debriefing. Unpublished manuscript, 1968.

Valins, S. & Ray, A. A. Effects of cognitive desensitization on avoidance behavior. *Journal of Personality and Social Psychology*, 1967, **7**, 345-350.

Wolpe, J. *Psychotherapy by reciprocal inhibition.* Stanford: Stanford University Press, 1958.

CONDITIONED EMOTIONAL STATES

Lynn J. Hammond

INTRODUCTION

Although substantial advances have been made in unraveling the physiological correlates of emotion, the problems posed by this research area are not confined to biological–psychological correlations. Much of the research endeavor also involves purely psychological questions concerning the theoretical and empirical nature of emotion itself. And in fact, recent papers both in this volume and elsewhere often use entirely different psychological concepts of emotion. The present paper outlines a particular approach to the study of emotion which, the author proposes, will be of much potential usefulness to the physiological investigator.

CONDITIONED EMOTIONAL STATES (CES)

Emotion is conceived as a central state of the organism which is elicited by important learned and unlearned stimulus events. The unlearned events fall in the category of rewards, punishments, and the absence of these events. The learned stimulus events are signals which bear some predictive relationship to the occurrence of reward or punishment. Through the process of classical conditioning, these signals acquire the ability to elicit responses similar to those which are controlled by rewards and punishments (in particular the general approach and withdrawal responses of the organism).

This theory of emotion will be presented first as treated by Mowrer (1960) and then as it has been modified by Rescorla and Solomon (1967). Emotion is treated within a motivational framework, as can be seen from the emphasis upon reward and punishment and upon approach and withdrawal behavior.

One of the primary advantages of the present approach is that emotions can be defined by the same operations for human and animal behavior. CES have been used for some time in physiological research and, in fact, Brady's work in this volume on conditioned anxiety (see Chapter 6) is an outstanding example of this method. The unique advantage of the approach offered here is that it deals with a variety of CES which have been systematically interrelated by Mowrer and Rescorla and Solomon.

PHYSIOLOGICAL CORRELATES

The major emphasis in this paper is on behavior. However, it includes selected examples of the application of this behavioral theory to physiological research involving lesions of the limbic system. This represents an extension of the well-established Papez–MacLean interpretation of limbic function.

The concept of the limbic system as primarily mediating emotion has been challenged in recent years by several other interpretations including one which involves the response-modulating functions of the brain. An impressive amount of research has accumulated supporting this latter interpretation (McCleary, 1966; Douglas, 1967). These studies used highly sophisticated techniques which measured subtle aspects of behavior. In order to adequately assess the role of emotional function in such studies, we need measures of emotion with comparable sensitivity.

CES: MOWRER'S APPROACH

In 1960, Mowrer drastically revised existing theoretical views of learning (including his own) and, in the process, he created a theory of emotion based on classical conditioning. This theory is briefly described below.

UNLEARNED EMOTIONAL STATES

Rewarding events in the environment result in decremental processes (drive reduction); punishing events result in incremental processes (drive induction). These correlate with the hedonic or emotional states of "pleasure" and "pain," and they will be treated here as the basic unlearned emotional states. The major consequence of these states is to motivate the organism, *i.e.*, to elicit approach and withdrawal responses. All other emotional states involve some degree of learning, more specifically, Pavlovian or classical conditioning.

LEARNED EMOTIONAL STATES

When a formerly neutral stimulus is presented repeatedly just prior to an incremental event, then this stimulus is called a "danger" signal. Stimuli which signalize decremental events are called "safety" signals. For Mowrer, the nature of the emotional state produced by these two signals depends upon whether the signal is turned on or off. Turning a danger signal on produces a state of "fear"; turning a danger signal off produces a state of "relief." In contrast, turning a safety signal on produces "hope," while turning it off produces "disappointment." These are the four major learned emotional states which will be discussed in this paper. The CES are learned through the process of Pavlovian conditioning, when the signals occur in a predictive relationship to reward or punishment. Whether or not the manipulation of these signals produces a particular subjective state (e.g., relief) is a matter of personal interpretation. The terms will be used only as convenient labels for emotional states which are reflected in behavior.

Signal Development. The advantage of Mowrer's scheme is that the manner in which these signals are developed can be exactly specified. Furthermore, the behavioral outcomes resulting from turning the signals on or off can be specified in terms of measurable approach or withdrawal responses. Since the development of safety and danger signals involves the processes of Pavlovian conditioning, the extensive research on the parameters of this form of learning can be utilized to increase the likelihood that the stimuli will become conditioned signals. For example, it can be stated that an electric shock of a certain intensity is a punisher (or an aversive stimulus) by demonstrating, in an independent situation, that the organism will escape from this noxious stimulation (Church, 1963).

CES Measurement. It can be determined by observing motivational behavior in a test situation that the onset or termination of a danger or safety signal produces the appropriate emotional state. Hope and relief are conditioned decremental or "good" (i.e., positively reinforcing) states and therefore should elicit approach responses, whereas fear and disappointment are "bad" (i.e., negatively reinforcing) and should elicit withdrawal responses.

Brady's conditioned anxiety paradigm (see Chapter 6 in this volume) illustrates the conditioning of a danger signal. After conditioning, the onset (and duration) of the signal results in a state of "fear" which elicits withdrawal responses that are incompatible with the monkey's ongoing rewarded behavior, producing suppression of the rewarded or approach behavior. With this technique, often referred to as conditioned suppression, we obtain a quantitative measure of fear based on its motivational properties. Such effects of fear states were extensively documented before 1960.

Also in the case of hope states, the motivational effects were widely investigated before Mowrer presented his theory (Wike, 1966). However, these effects were usually labeled secondary reinforcement. Stimuli preceding reward increase the probability of new responses when the new response is followed by the onset of that stimulus (i.e., a secondary reinforcing effect occurs). In addition, the onset of such safety signals, as Mowrer calls them, can have a facilitating (motivational) effect upon on-going rewarded behavior. Mowrer's use of the label hope and the emotional connotation given to secondary reinforcing effects represented a new interpretation of this large body of literature. For fear and hope states then, Mowrer was discussing known empirical facts and only his interpretation could be contested.

On the other hand, interpretative problems arise when relief and disappointment are considered. These problems seem to stem from the assumption that turning a stimulus off produces a qualitatively different behavioral state than turning that same stimulus on. For example, turning a danger signal off should produce a good state of affairs (relief) and this should be positively reinforcing. And indeed experiments have shown that rats will learn a new response to terminate a danger signal (e.g., Brown & Jacobs, 1949). However, it is not clear that the introduction of the new construct, relief, is necessary to explain this fact, because, in these experiments the danger signal elicits fear and upon termination of the signal fear ceases. Is the secondary reinforcing effect produced by fear reduction or relief induction? Bolles has suggested that the concepts of ". . . relief and disappointment appear to be redundant . . ." [Bolles, 1967, p. 364] and therefore unnecessary since Mowrer's system already contains fear and hope.

However, when certain procedural modifications are made in the method of development and measurement, the concepts of relief and disappointment become much more meaningful.

CES: RESCORLA AND SOLOMON

THEORETICAL MODIFICATIONS

The 1967 paper by Rescorla and Solomon is mainly devoted to theoretical learning problems, but is highly relevant here because their approach is based on the motivational properties of stimuli which have been related to reward and punishment in a classical conditioning paradigm. Although they do not use the term CES, they are dealing with approach-eliciting and avoidance-eliciting properties of Pavlovian signals which exercise control over instrumental behavior. In this sense, they have borrowed heavily from Mowrer and other earlier two-process learning theorists.

INHIBITION AND EXCITATION

One of Rescorla and Solomon's major contributions to this theory of emotion is their reemphasis upon the Pavlovian concepts of inhibition and excitation. When these concepts are applied, stronger support can be found for Mowrer's four CES and their interrelationship.

For Pavlov, there were two kinds of conditioned reflexes: excitatory — when signals are followed by reinforcement, and inhibitory — when signals are not followed by reinforcement. It was the latter kind of reflex, inhibitory, that so many western psychologists found unpalatable. How can a reflex be formed as a consequence of "nothing" or how can the absence of reinforcement be a reinforcer?

CONDITIONING AND PREDICTIVITY

By utilizing a slightly different conceptualization of Pavlovian conditioning, Rescorla (1967) provides a plausible answer to this question. He suggests that the important relationship between a signal (conditioned stimulus, CS) and reinforcement (unconditioned stimulus, US — reward or punishment) is a *predictive* one. According to this view, the isolated pairings of CS and US do not determine conditioning as was formerly thought, but rather it is the value of the CS in predicting occurrence of the US that leads to conditioning.

If the likelihood of getting shocked in a situation is the same while a buzzer is presented and in its absence, then such pairings of buzzer and shock will not produce conditioned fear to the buzzer. Fear of the CS develops only when the likelihood of shock increases following or during the CS. This is the case in the typical fear conditioning experiment where shock occurs only following the CS, and illustrates excitatory Pavlovian conditioning. These suggestions have been directly confirmed by experiment (Rescorla, 1968). On the other hand, when the probability of shock decreases during or following the CS, then inhibitory Pavlovian conditioning can take place. Thus when the absence of reinforcement is considered in relation to the occurrence of reinforcement at other times, nothing (i.e., absence of shock) can readily be viewed as an important event capable of influencing the organism. The behavioral effect of a CS which predicts a decrease in shock occurrence is similar to the effects of relief (termination of a danger signal) hypothesized by Mowrer. During inhibitory conditioning with electric shock, the whole situation becomes, in effect, a danger signal. But if no shock ever occurs during a CS presentation in that situation, then all danger ceases whenever that inhibitory CS is turned on, thus meeting Mowrer's conditions for a state of relief.

If we apply the excitatory-inhibitory distinction to Mowrer's four CES, their meaning is basically unchanged but the *defining operations* for their development and measurement have changed such that considerable empirical evidence is now relevant to the concepts of relief and disappointment.

The conditions for developing the four CES are as follows: Stimuli which predict an increase in occurrence of an aversive event produce fear, stimuli which predict a decrease in occurrence of an aversive event produce relief; in the case of appetitive events (i.e., rewards), stimuli predicting an increase in their occurrence produce hope, those predicting a decrease produce disappointment. Since each CES is produced by stimulus onset (and duration), the difficulties arising from signal termination have been eliminated. In addition, fear and hope are now produced by Pavlovian excitatory stimuli, while relief and disappointment are produced by Pavlovian inhibitory stimuli.

EMPIRICAL STUDIES ON RELIEF

Rescorla and LoLordo (1965) have clearly shown that signals for the absence of shock become Pavlovian inhibitory stimuli and that furthermore, these signals produce behavioral changes consistent with the definition of relief presented here. These two investigators used dogs responding on a Sidman (unsignalized) avoidance schedule of the type described by Brady in this volume (Chapter 6). The dogs were trained to maintain a high rate of instrumental jumping between the two sides of a shuttle box in order to avoid shock. During different sessions, the dogs were penned up in one side of the shuttle box and given Pavlovian conditioning (presentation of tone signals and unavoidable shock). One frequency signaled shock (excitatory stimulus) and a different frequency signaled absence of shock (inhibitory stimulus). When the excitatory stimulus was presented (without shock) during later avoidance sessions, it produced a marked increase in jumping rate, while the inhibitory stimulus produced a marked decrease in the rate of jumping. The inhibitory stimulus had acquired its relief properties because it predicted the absence of shock.

Similar effects were found by the author using rats exposed to a conditioned suppression procedure, which permitted fear and relief to affect instrumental responding for reward. Stimuli signalizing the absence of shock produced increased rates of bar pressing for reward (Hammond, 1966). This finding occurred when an overall fear of the experimental situation produced a lower rate of responding during sessions, after shock was introduced. When baseline responding recovers from this initial depression, the inhibitory stimulus ceases to produce relief (i.e., increased responding).

However, an inhibitory stimulus, which no longer facilitates rewarded behavior, can still have relief properties which can be measured in other situations.

One method combined relief and fear signals during testing. This combination caused less conditioned suppression than did the fear stimulus presented alone (summation technique, Hammond, 1967). In a second method, the former relief stimulus (which had signaled no shock) was changed so that it now predicted shock. In this case, acquisition of fear to the CS was retarded compared to a control condition where the CS had no previous inhibitory history (reversal technique, Hammond, 1968). Both the summation and the reversal techniques are sensitive methods for measuring active inhibitory properties of a Pavlovian conditioned stimulus, even after these inhibitory properties are no longer observed in the ordinary conditioned suppression situation.

The earlier work on dogs involving Sidman avoidance responding has been replicated with rats by Grossen and Bolles (1968). Also, the summation and reversal techniques for measuring inhibition during conditioned suppression have been used successfully in a parametric study relating shock frequency to the development of inhibition (Rescorla, 1969). Thus, many studies have demonstrated that stimuli predicting the absence of a punishing stimulus (unavoidable shock) acquire conditioned properties very much like relief. This can be seen when these stimuli are pitted in various ways against the effects of fear stimuli upon motivated behavior.

DISAPPOINTMENT

Empirical Support. Many studies support the concept of disappointment, once it has been redefined as a state produced by stimuli which signal nonreward (absence of appetitive reinforcement). Such a signal should be aversive or punishing since it signals that no reward will occur in a situation where reward is expected. Wagner (1963) has demonstrated that rats will escape signals for nonreward when these signals are presented in a new situation. First he trained rats to run down an alley to a goal box containing food. On half the trials, the goal box was empty (nonrewarded trials) and a complex CS was presented 2 ft before the rat reached the goal box. The rats were then placed in shuttle box and the complex CS (signal for nonreward) was presented at regular intervals. When the rat jumped to the other side of the shuttle box during these presentations, the CS terminated. The experimental rats jumped much more rapidly than the control rats, demonstrating escape from the CS.

Wagner described this signal as a "stimulus eliciting anticipatory frustration" (rather than disappointment) since a large body of evidence and theory has been reported for the construct of conditioned frustration (Amsel, 1958, 1962). This construct is operationally identical to disappointment as described here, and therefore the evidence cited by Amsel for conditioned or anticipatory frustration supports this CES as well.

Facilitating Effects of Frustration. Stimuli which predict nonreward (absence of appetitive reinforcement) are, by definition, potential Pavlovian inhibitory stimuli. Therefore the properties of stimuli which produce conditioned or anticipatory frustration are based on Pavlovian inhibition. It was stated earlier that the reinforcing event (US) for the development of inhibition is a decrease in the probability of reward or punishment. This event also has unconditioned effects. Amsel refers to these effects as primary frustration.

In addition to acting as an agent for inhibitory conditioning, primary or unconditioned frustration has a direct effect upon ongoing behavior. This effect is an increase in the vigor of reinforced behavior which Amsel terms the frustration effect (FE). The FE is hypothesized to increase the general drive level of the organism (i.e., to increase his overall level of motivation). The FE was originally demonstrated by Amsel and Roussel (1952). They ran rats in a double (tandem) runway apparatus where the first goal box then led to the second alley and goal. After training in which the rat ran for food in one and then the other section of the apparatus, the omission of food in the first goal box produced an increase in the vigor of responding in the second alley.

Since conditioned frustration and disappointment are defined as equivalent here, FE effects should occur in the course of developing the CES of disappointment. The FE is a well-documented phenomenon that can be operationally defined and it has been used to explain some lesion-produced behavioral changes.

Frustration and Punishment. Amsel thinks that the theoretical work involving reward and frustration can also be extended to an analysis of punishment and relief (Amsel & Ward, 1965). Martin (1963) concurs in suggesting that when increased resistance to extinction occurs after mild punishment of a rewarded response, this is caused by frustration produced by punishment. Martin's theoretical suggestion is also very important for the interpretation of many lesion-produced effects which will be described below.

RELATIONSHIP TO INCENTIVE

Mowrer's theory of learning and motivation is customarily termed an *incentive* theory and the mechanisms which he uses for incentive are the CES. Incentive concepts of motivation were introduced into psychological theory because it has been demonstrated that the conditions of reinforcement have a motivational effect upon behavior rather than determining what is learned or how well it is learned (Bolles, 1967, p. 366). The major conditions of reinforcement which have been varied in studies of incentive are the delay, amount, and quality of reinforcement. Presumably these manipulations produce their effects by altering the nature of the CES. Incentive is discussed here because some highly relevant physiological studies involving incentive manipulations will be cited below.

PHYSIOLOGICAL CORRELATES

Emotion and the Limbic System

It was stated at the beginning of this paper that CES theory is a useful tool for the physiological investigator of emotion. This will be illustrated in relation to some recent studies dealing with lesions of the limbic system.

In the 1930s, converging theory and data resulted in an emotional interpretation of limbic function, the Papez-MacLean theory (see Grossman, 1967, Chapter 9). Much of the earlier evidence for this interpretation rested upon observations of behavior such as the septal rage syndrome. Rats with lesions in this area sometimes become extremely aggressive towards the experimenter and appear very sensitive to handling, among other behavioral changes. Thus, removal of the septal area increases emotionality when it is defined in terms of gross observations of the animal.

When more sophisticated measures of the behavior of septally damaged animals were obtained, the results sometimes supported an emotional interpretation but sometimes they did not. Although septal lesions facilitate shuttle box avoidance (e.g., King, 1958), they consistently produce a deficit in passive avoidance (learning to withhold a punished response, e.g., McCleary, 1961). The first finding could be explained by assuming that animals with septal lesions are more reactive to shock, but then such animals should also show enhanced rather than deficient passive-avoidance learning.

Response Perseveration

In addition to the opposite effects on passive and active avoidance, there are many other recent findings with limbic lesions that are difficult to interpret as enhanced reactivity to reward and punishment. Consequently, several investigators have suggested that the major result of many limbic lesions in these complex behavioral situations is response perseveration (Douglas, 1967; Gerbrant, 1965; McCleary, 1966).

For example, there is a rather consistent deficit in go-no-go (successive) discrimination behavior, but normal performance occurs in either-or (simultaneous) discrimination for animals with septal or hippocampal lesions. Some other areas of the limbic system also produce these results when lesioned.

This response-perseveration interpretation of limbic lesions reduces to a fairly empirical statement. That is, animals with these lesions will show a temporary inability to learn to withhold high-probability responses. There are various mechanisms proposed to account for response perseveration (Douglas, 1967), but none of these mechanisms involves changes in emotionality.

INCENTIVE

Recently, another line of research conducted by Schwartzbaum and his associates has shown that rats with septal lesions often overreact to the incentive quality of reinforcement. Beatty and Schwartzbaum (1967) measured daily water consumption in septally damaged rats. When their water was first adulterated with quinine (an aversive stimulus), the lesioned rats drank less than the controls but when their water was adulterated with saccharine (an appetitive stimulus), lesioned rats drank more than controls.

Other studies also indicate that the septally damaged subject is more reactive to the aversive and appetitive properties of stimuli. Beatty and Schwartzbaum (1968) found that lesioned subjects drank more sucrose water than normals when satiated but that this difference was, if anything, reduced when both groups were hungry. Thus, the lesion appeared to affect incentive rather than drive. Schwartzbaum, Green, Beatty, and Thompson (1967) found that septalectomized rats were much more responsive to a light stimulus than normals, showing considerable escape behavior where the normals did not. These studies support the earlier contention that limbic lesions can influence emotionality if we define emotion within the context of incentive motivation. These results are difficult to interpret in terms of response perseveration, particularly the overreactivity to quinine.

APPLICATION OF CES THEORY

Studies involving gross behavioral observations (e.g., septal rage syndrome) and changes in incentive behavior offer unequivocal evidence of emotional changes resulting from limbic lesions. But many lesion studies involving avoidance and discrimination behavior can be interpreted in terms of response perseveration. However, when emotion is more rigorously and systematically defined, most of the studies showing response perseveration may then be explained by changes in emotion.

When the deficits cited by McCleary (1966) in support of the response-perseveration explanation are examined closely, a common behavioral theme can be seen—the situations are usually frustrating ones. Even the empirical definition of response perseveration — inability to withhold a high-probability response — implies frustration. Typically, an organism engages in high-probability behavior because that response results in reward or avoids punishment. To demonstrate inability to withhold such responses requires the omission of reward or the addition of punishment when the response occurs. The latter consequences are frustrating and if we assume that the limbic lesion enhances emotional reactivity, then the subject with septal lesions will be more frustrated than the normal one.

A typical consequence of frustration is the FE which facilitates ongoing behavior, thus producing a "perseveration" of the high-probability, ongoing response. For example, passive-avoidance deficits in septally damaged animals are explained by McCleary (1966) in terms of response perseveration. During passive avoidance, the animals are shocked each time they attempt to get food. According to Martin (1963) this produces primary frustration which increases the vigor of approach responses, and the animal perseverates by continuing to approach and receive shock. If septal lesions enhance frustration, then the lesioned animal would show more persistence than the normal and therefore a deficit in passive avoidance.

The suggestion that limbic lesions enhance frustration responses was made by Swanson and Isaacson (1967) in a report describing lesion-produced deficits in successive discrimination. As is typical of such deficits, the animals showed great difficulty in withholding responses during the signalized periods when reinforcement was not available. Although such findings have previously been interpreted in terms of response perseveration, Swanson and Isaacson suggest that the deficits are the result of an enhanced frustration response, an interpretation which (as suggested here) could be applied to most limbic-lesion deficits of a perseverative nature.

Response perseveration and enhanced frustration are not necessarily contradictory explanations of these changes in behavior following limbic lesions. Actually, enhanced emotionality becomes a mechanism of explaining why the lesioned animal perseverates. However, it is a different mechanism than those suggested by Douglas (1967) and McCleary (1966).

If these lesions do produce an increase in emotionality, it cannot be an enhancement of all emotional responses to stimuli. Rather, it appears necessary to assume that the primary frustration response is differentially affected by these particular lesions. This would certainly be true with respect to fear. In the passive-avoidance experiments, the lesioned animal continues to approach food which always leads to shock. If the lesion produced an equal increase in both fear and frustration, then the greater fear should cancel the increase in frustration-produced persistence, and no deficit would occur. Since deficits are consistently found in passive avoidance, it is unlikely that the lesion results in greater fear. This is also true when an attempt is made to measure fear directly with the conditioned-suppression technique; septal lesions cause less suppression (Brady & Nauta, 1953). Therefore, these results require the assumption of greatly enhanced frustration, as compared to fear. Since suppression of bar pressing for reward results in lost reward, frustration would be a likely result.

One fortunate aspect of the enhanced-emotionality explanation of response perseveration is that it can be examined empirically, since there are situations where the FE can be measured independently of the usual measures of persistence. The double runway used by Amsel and Roussel (1952) was designed for just this purpose. Increased vigor of running in the second alley as a consequence of FE is not a perseveration of a response, but a measure of response enhancement.

The possible mechanisms of response perseveration could be clarified by examining the FE behavior of limbic-lesioned animals in the double runway. Swanson and Isaacson (1967) mention an incidental finding which appears very much like an FE. Upon introduction of discrimination conditions, hippocampally lesioned subjects responded at higher rates during the withdrawal of reinforcement than previously, when responses were rewarded. Control animals did not show such an increase.[1]

The literature on response perseveration is only one area in which

---

[1]Since the completion of this manuscript, a double-runway study such as the one proposed above has been reported for rats with hippocampal lesions (Swanson, A. M., & Isaacson, R. L. Hippocampal lesions and the frustration effect in rats. *Journal of Comparative and Physiological Psychology*, 1969, 68, 562-567.) They found no effect of the lesion upon the magnitude of the FE. Consequently, it does not appear that all response-perseveration deficits can be explained by reference to facilitating effects of frustration. However, the author is still impressed by the potential role of frustrating conditions in the many situations where lesion-produced response perseveration occurs. Recently Joseph Lambert, working in the author's laboratory, has been exploring the effects of frustration in other situations besides food-reward and has found that for shock-escape behavior, frustration does not lead to a facilitating effect upon consequent behavior; but instead it produces a decrease in the vigor of responding (Lambert, J. V., & Hammond, L. J. Effect of frustrative non-relief upon shock-escape behavior in the double runway. *Journal of Experimental Psychology*, in press). This latter study strongly emphasizes that the immediate effects of primary frustration are varied and poorly understood. As more behavioral information accumulates about frustration effects, perhaps a better understanding of the correlation between frustrating conditions and the effects of limbic lesions will arise.

the theory of emotion based on conditioned emotional states can be of substantial usefulness to the physiological investigator. It would be valuable to know the effects of limbic lesions upon the four CES defined in this paper. Such studies could be done since paradigms exist for measuring fear, hope, relief, and disappointment (conditioned frustration) which are not confounded by possible effects of response perseveration.

SUMMARY

Mowrer's (1960) theory of emotion was modified through the use of Pavlovian excitatory and inhibitory conditioning, as outlined by Rescorla and Solomon (1967). This results in four conditioned emotional states all of which are produced by the onset of conditioned stimuli. Evidence was cited supporting the less recognized states, "relief" and "disappointment." The usefulness of this theory of emotion for physiological psychology was illustrated in relation to behavioral studies of limbic lesions. It was suggested that lesion-produced changes in the perseverative behavior commonly produced by many limbic lesions could be attributed to enhanced frustration responses.

REFERENCES

Amsel, A. The role of frustrative nonreward in noncontinuous reward situations. *Psychological Bulletin*, 1958, **55**, 102-119.

Amsel, A. Frustrative nonreward in partial reinforcement and discrimination learning: Some recent history and a theoretical extension. *Psychological Review*, 1962, **69**, 306-328.

Amsel, A., & Roussel, J. Motivational properties of frustration: I. Effect on a running response of the addition of frustration to the motivational complex. *Journal of Experimental Psychology*, 1952, 43, 363-368.

Amsel, A., and Ward, J. S. Frustration and persistance: Resistance to discrimination following prior experience with the discriminanda. *Psychological Monographs*, 1965, **79**, (4, Whole No. 597).

Beatty, W. W., & Schwartzbaum, J. S. Enhanced reactivity to quinine and saccharine solutions following septal lesions in the rat. *Psychonomic Science*, 1967, **8**, 483-484.

Beatty, W. W., & Schwartzbaum, J. S. Consummatory behavior for sucrose following septal lesions in the rat. *Journal of Comparative and Physiological Psychology*, 1968, **65**, 93-102.

Bolles, R. C. *Theory of motivation*. New York: Harper, 1967.

Brady, J. V., & Nauta, W. J. H. Subcortical mechanisms in emotional behavior: Affective changes following septal forebrain lesions in the albino rat. *Journal of Comparative and Physiological Psychology*, 1953, **46**, 339-346.

Brown, J. S., & Jacobs, A. Role of fear in motivation and acquisition of responses. *Journal of Experimental Psychology*, 1949, **39**, 747-759.

Church, R. M. The varied effects of punishment on behavior. *Psychological Review*, 1963, **70**, 369-402.

Douglas, R. J. The hippocampus and behavior. *Psychological Bulletin*, 1967, **67**, 416-442.

Gerbrant, L. K. Neural systems of response release and control. *Psychological Bulletin*, 1965, **64**, 113-124.

Grossen, N. E., & Bolles, R. C. Effects of a classically conditioned 'fear signal' and 'safety signal' on nondiscriminated avoidance behavior. *Psychonomic Science*, 1968, **11**, 321-322.

Grossman, S. P. *A textbook of physiological psychology*. New York: Wiley, 1967.

Hammond, L. J. Increased responding to CS in differential CER. *Psychonomic Science*, 1966, **5**, 337-338.

Hammond, L. J. A traditional demonstration of the active properties of Pavlovian inhibition using differential CER. *Psychonomic Science*, 1967, **9**, 65-66.

Hammond, L. J. Retardation of fear acquisition by a previously inhibitory CS. *Journal of Comparative and Physiological Psychology*, 1968, **66**, 756-759.

King, F. A. Effects of septal and amygdaloid lesions on emotional behavior and conditioned avoidance responses in the rat. *Journal of Nervous and Mental Disease*, 1958, **126**, 57-63.

Martin, B. Reward and punishment associated with the same goal response: A factor in the learning of motives. *Psychological Bulletin*, 1963, **60**, 441-451.

McCleary, R. A. Response specificity in the behavioral effects of limbic system lesions in the cat. *Journal of Comparative and Physiological Psychology*, 1961, **54**, 605-613.

McCleary, R. A. Response-modulating functions of the limbic system: Initiation and suppression. *Progress in Physiological Psychology*, 1966, Volume 1, 209-272.

Mowrer, H. O. *Learning theory and behavior*. New York: Wiley, 1960.

Rescorla, R. A. Pavlovian conditioning and its proper control procedures. *Psychological Review*, 1967, **74**, 71-80.

Rescorla, R.A. Probability of shock in the presence and absence of CS in fear conditioning. *Journal of Comparative and Physiological Psychology*, 1968, **66**, 1-5.

Rescorla, R.A. Conditioned inhibition of fear resulting from negative CS-US contingencies. *Journal of Comparative and Physiological Psychology*, 1969, **67**, 504-509.

Rescorla, R.A., & LoLordo, V. M. Inhibition of avoidance behavior. *Journal of Comparative and Physiological Psychology*, 1965, **59**, 406-412.

Rescorla, R. A., & Solomon, R. L. Two-process learning: Relationships between Pavlovian conditioning and instrumental learning. *Psychological Review*, 1967, **74**, 151-182.

Schwartzbaum, J. S., Green, R. H., Beatty, W. W., & Thompson, J. B. Acquisition of avoidance behavior following septal lesions in the rat. *Journal of Comparative and Physiological Psychology*, 1967, **63**, 95-104.

Swanson, A. M., & Isaacson, R. L. Hippocampal ablation and performance during withdrawal of reinforcement. *Journal of Comparative and Physiological Psychology*, 1967, **64**, 30-35.

Wagner, A. R. Conditioned frustration as a learned drive. *Journal of Experimental Psychology*, 1963, **66**, 142-148.

Wike, E. L. *Secondary reinforcement: Selected experiments*. New York: Harper, 1966.

BRAIN FUNCTION IN EMOTION:
A PHENOMENOLOGICAL ANALYSIS

Magda B. Arnold

THEORETICAL CONSIDERATIONS

The only certain knowledge we have about brain function is based on brain stimulation and brain lesions that produce reportable effects. We know that stimulation of the visual areas produces flashes of light; of the auditory cortex, sounds; of the somesthetic area, indefinite somesthetic sensations described as prickling, tingling, numbness, etc. Lesions in these areas produce cortical blindness, deafness, anesthesia. We also know that stimulation of the motor cortex produces localized movement. But lesions or stimulation of other cortical areas has not produced such agreement: while visual agnosia has been reported from lesions of Areas 18 and 19, auditory agnosia from lesions of Areas 21 and 22, tactual agnosia from lesions of Area 7, opinions are still divided as to the psychological activities mediated by these "association" areas. As for the function of other areas, like limbic cortex, hippocampus, and amygdala, the vigorous research effort of the last three decades has posed more problems than it has solved.

It may be true that there are various levels of brain function or, as MacLean (see Chapter 7) so picturesquely expresses it, three different brains, reptilian, old mammalian, and new mammalian brain. It may also be true that emotional arousal is reflected on the cortical, diencephalic, and brainstem levels, as Lindsley says (see Chapter 8). But until it is possible to spell out just how these levels are interconnected, and describe just what relays are activated when a given object is perceived, interpreted, and so arouses emotion with its physiological changes, and how such emotion may lead to action, we really have no way of choosing between these hypotheses, or even to test them. To achieve solid knowledge of brain function, we must try to identify the relays that mediate the sequence of psychological activities from perception to emotion and action, and then devise experiments to test our tentative hypothesis, and, hopefully, to improve it.

Phenomenological Analysis

Such an undertaking necessarily implies a phenomenological analysis. What is going on, psychologically speaking, when we see or hear something, interpret it, and are moved to fear or anger? Once we are reasonably certain of the psychological sequence from perception to emotion and action, it will become possible to look for the structures that could mediate each type of activity. The necessity of finding definite pathways to relay neural excitation from one structure to the next one in the sequence should provide a check and perhaps a corrective for too-easy psychological theorizing. And the published results of brain lesions and brain stimulation can supply the guidelines for a theory of brain function. Such a theory cannot be based on armchair speculation, a vague notion like "mass action of the brain," or "cell assemblies and phase sequences." While it is true that a great many brain cells are active in any psychological process, it is much more likely that they are excited in a well-defined pattern rather than *en masse*; and though it is true that directly or indirectly every neuron is connected with every other, and there may be many reverberating circuits active at a given time, it is much more likely that there are definite activation patterns for definite psychological activities, rather than a maze of reverberating circuits dispersed randomly throughout the brain. Gastaut, Jus, and Morrell (1957) have found that electrical activity in the brain is patterned and changes its pattern from the beginning of learning to the point where the learned performance becomes automatic. To identify the pattern, it is imperative to try to describe the sequence of psychological activities, starting from sensory experience and ending with the chosen action, so as to locate their neural counterparts.

Appraisal. When something is perceived, remembered, or imagined, it never remains an isolated bit of knowledge. Rather, each object is immediately seen in relation to ourselves and is evaluated as good, bad, or indifferent for us. In everyday life, the appraisal of everything we encounter in its relation to ourselves is immediate, automatic, almost involuntary. What is "good" in some way (significant, useful, beneficial) is attended to and striven for; what is "bad" (harmful, annoying) is avoided or overcome; and what is indifferent (insignificant, unimportant, useless) is simply disregarded. What we call the "meaning" or "interpretation" of a situation is the product of such an evaluation in relation to us.

Action Tendency. Every appraisal of something as good, here and now, produces an impulse toward it which leads to action unless another evaluation interferes. Whether something is good to eat, good to possess and enjoy (as a garden or a swimming pool), whether someone is good to talk to, good to love, good to work with, we tend to acquire the good thing, to approach the good person. Of course, we may next decide that the food we like is fattening, the garden or swimming pool too expensive for our income, that the person we like does not return our feelings, and act accordingly. The human being, as distinct from the animal, experiences not only immediate likes and dislikes but can also make reflective value judgments. Whether intuitive, "unconscious" appraisal, or deliberate value judgment, this estimate sets the thing appraised in relation to the subject and gauges its effect on the subject here and now. Thus appraisal complements perception and produces a tendency to deal with the object in some way. When this tendency is strong, that is, when the object is appraised as highly desirable or most undesirable, it is called an emotion. But even the simple positive attitude toward something appraised as good is a feeling-like experience. We really like certain foods, and though we may not be willing to call this liking or similar positive attitudes an emotion, it is an affective experience rather than a cold perception.

Appraisal and Memory. With the exception of the simple enjoyment or dislike of somesthetic and taste experiences, ranging up to the extremes of pleasure and pain, and the anger produced by physical interference with action, all new experiences seem to require memory as the basis of appraisal. We cannot appraise something seen as good to eat unless it looks, smells, or feels like something we have enjoyed in the past. Indeed, even the taste of a new food is often judged pleasant or unpleasant if it resembles something we have liked or disliked before.

Whatever is experienced, in any sensory modality, arouses not only a memory of similar things seen, heard, or otherwise known (modality-specific memory) but also revives the corresponding affect. The liking or dislike once felt toward a person or a thing is felt again as soon as we encounter anything similar. In the same way, what we have once enjoyed doing, or what we have once done successfully, will leave an inclination to the same action. These positive or negative feelings about an object or an action are affective memories. They represent a reliving of past appraisals, though they are experienced neither as "past" nor as "appraisals" but merely as an immediate positive or negative attitude which obviously cannot be produced by something seen for the first time. Most of the things we see, hear, or read about are prejudged in this way, a fact of which we usually are completely unaware. It is "affective memory" that accounts for this inclination to judge the present in terms of the past, to expect what our imagination and emotion predispose us to expect. Such emotional attitudes stemming from past appraisals have to be corrected by deliberate design to safeguard our judgment, just as our memory of facts has to be checked by comparison with objective data.

Appraisal and Imagination. Before a preliminary appraisal leads us to engage in action, the present situation together with the relevant memories induce us to guess at the future: Will this hurt or benefit us here and now? Thus the appraisal of a situation is based not only on memory but also on the expectation of a similar effect. Next, the individual must make some plan, must imagine possible ways of coping with this situation; and these possibilities of action also must be evaluated. The choice of one alternative, appraised as best here and now, finally determines action. This sequence from perception to action may be run through almost instantly, ending in panic flight, or it may be repreated over and over as different aspects of a situation are remembered, imagined, and evaluated before the final choice of action (for instance, in difficult decisions). On the basis of this sequence, I will now try to identify the structures and pathways in the brain that might mediate it.

NEURAL MEDIATION

Brain Structures Mediating This Sequence

It seems certain that the experience of objects or auditory patterns of speech and melody is mediated by relays from sensory organs via thalamic sensory nuclei to sensory cortical areas. It also seems certain that the sheer experience of light and darkness, of unpatterned sound, touch, pressure, taste, is possible even when the cortical sensory areas are damaged. Thus the quality of experience depends on sensory thalamic nuclei while the experience of visual, auditory, and pressure patterns, and the experience of objects, requires both intact thalamic sensory nuclei and intact cortical receiving areas.

Cortical Areas Serving Modality-Specific Memory. It is known that the various cortical "association" areas are connected with the primary sensory areas and receive relays from the corresponding sensory thalamic nuclei. Nielsen (1943) has insisted that these association areas mediate memory in the corresponding sense modalities, so that the visual association area serves visual memory, the auditory association area auditory memory, etc. This opinion, by no means generally accepted, seems to be confirmed by recent animal experiments. Pribram and his group have shown that a learned visual-discrimination habit is lost after ablation of the inferior edge of the temporal lobe and the preoccipital cortex (Pribram & Barry, 1956; Pribram & Mishkin, 1955), a learned auditory discrimination habit, after removal of the posterior temporal cortex (Weiskrantz and Mishkin, 1958), a learned somesthetic discrimination (touch and weight) after loss of the parieto-occipital association area (Wilson, 1957), and conditioned taste discrimination after destruction of the somesthetic association area for the tongue (Bagshaw and Pribram, 1953). From Allen's (1940) report that olfactory discrimination was lost after excision of the frontal lobes, and from the known distribution of olfactory fibers we may conclude that the orbital rather than the temporal cortex is necessary for olfactory discrimination.

Sensory discrimination depends essentially on the ability to remember previous sensory cues and to react now in the same way. Accordingly, the impaired performance after lesions of the association cortex seems to show a genuine deficit in visual, auditory, somesthetic, gustatory, and olfactory memory; because the area serving the registration of sensory memories has been destroyed, the loss is permanent. In addition, there have been many reports that destruction of the lateral frontal cortex produces loss of an alternation habit. Correct right/left alternation seems to depend on remembering what was done before, and imagining on that basis what is to be done now. Consequently, the prefrontal cortical area seems to mediate motor memory. Broca's area, destruction of which makes it impossible to speak, is also located in the lateral prefrontal cortex. To make the correct sounds means to move speech muscles in a remembered pattern, that is, to draw on motor memory.

Appraisal Areas. Once we realize that appraisal completes sense experience, we would expect that this activity would have to be mediated by relays from the various sensory cortical areas to adjoining areas. These seem to be the limbic areas which stretch along the thalamus on the medial side of the hemispheres from the orbital to the occipital cortex and include the insula which borders on the lateral motor and somesthetic areas. The limbic cortex is part of Olds' (1956) "reward system." And "reward" is the behavioral term for something that satisfies, something that is liked. The reward is received when the animal presses a bar that turns on a current in electrodes implanted in the brain. A slightly different location or a slightly different intensity of stimulation may turn the reward into punishment—another indication that the limbic cortex and the subcortical structures connected with it, mediate appraisal experienced as liking or dislike, acceptance or rejection.

The limbic system, bordering on all sensory and motor areas, is ideally situated for mediating the appraisal of sensory impressions and movements. The subcallosal and anterior cingulate cortex and the anterior insula border on the motor, premotor, and prefrontal cortex, hence may serve the appraisal of movement and movement impulses. The posterior cingulate gyrus and posterior insula, bordering on the somesthetic and somesthetic association cortex, may serve the appraisal of somesthetic and taste experiences, the retrosplenial and part of the hippocampal gyrus the appraisal of what is seen, and other parts of the hippocampus the appraisal of what is heard.

Pathways Mediating Modality-Specific Recall. Since all action tendencies are initiated by an appraisal, even the impulse to recall or imagine should be mediated by relays from the areas serving appraisal.

To remember or recall anything at all, it would seem to be necessary to reactivate the engram-bearing cells in exactly the same spatial and temporal pattern: to recall a particular hit in a baseball game, we must remember the pitcher throwing the ball and the batter hitting it. If the temporal sequence were changed, we might remember the batter hitting the ball before the pitcher threw it. If the spatial relations were changed, we might remember the pitcher throwing anywhere or the batter swinging when the ball was nowhere near him. Accordingly, there must be a pathway that can reactivate the engrams in the right spatial and temporal order. In contrast, there is nothing to prevent us imagining things and events in any order we please: we restructure earlier impressions as the purpose of the moment dictates.

This psychological fact would suggest that remembering and imagining, while depending on the same engram-bearing areas, are mediated by different circuits. The recall circuit would have to retrace the path of the original impression, while imagination could be mediated by a circuit leading to the same association areas by entirely different pathways. However, recall is always accompanied by imagination, as Bartlett (1932) pointed out, so that we draw on imagination whenever memory fails us.

On the basis of the above analysis and the reported results of brain stimulation and brain lesions, it seems likely that modality-specific recall is mediated by a multichain pathway leading from sensory cortical association area via hippocampal rudiment and hippocampus to precommissural fornix, hypothalamus and midbrain, to return via sensory thalamic nuclei to sensory and association areas (Figure 1). There are many research reports showing that hippocampal lesions interfere with visual and auditory discrimination. Septal lesions, which always damage the precommissural fornix, have been found to impair discrimination in all sensory modalities and also impair motor memory (left/right alternation). The other links in the proposed memory circuit are more difficult to investigate. Lesions in the hypothalamus or midbrain would destroy not only modality-specific memory but the primary sensory projection. It is possible, however, to infer from reports such as De Valois, Smith, Karoly and Kitai (1958) that, e.g., in the lateral geniculate (thalamic) nucleus the different layers serve different functions, one of which would be visual projection, another could be visual recall (cf. Arnold, 1960, Vol. II, pp. 68-70).

Pathways Mediating Affective Memory. Affective memory, the revival of an earlier appraisal, is experienced as an immediate favorable or unfavorable disposition and seems to be mediated by a circuit starting from the limbic cortex (which serves the appraisal of the object experienced here and now) and running via the cingulum to the postcommissural fornix, mamillary body, and anterior thalamic nucleus back to the limbic system (Figure 2). When nerve impulses arrive in these limbic areas, we experience the revived negative or positive attitude.

Since the connections activated in affective memory are less numerous than those activated in modality-specific memory, affective memories may be revived even when the actual incident can no longer be recalled. This would account for the effect of "repression," of forgotten traumatic memories, but also for unreasonable or inexplicable likes or dislikes. Since ordinarily we are not aware that such

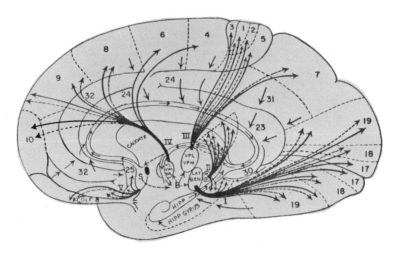

Fig. 1. Circuits mediating sensory experience and modality-specific memory. Sensory impulses travel via thalamic sensory nuclei to cortical sensory and association areas, mediating sensory experience. Associated impulses are relayed to limbic Areas (23, 24, 25, 30, 31, 32, and hippocampal gyrus), mediating appraisal. This appraisal of something seen, heard, felt, etc. initiates the spontaneous recall of similar things, via hippocampal rudiment, hippocampus, precommissural fornix, thalamic sensory nuclei, and the various cortical association areas. Motor impulses travel via ventral thalamic nuclei to frontal motor and association areas (see also Figure 3) and are similarly registered and recalled. ———— Reception and registration. - - - - - - Recall. Arrows indicate the direction of conduction. Short arrows indicate the connections for appraisal and recall.

I, visual system; II, auditory system; III, somesthetic system (including taste); IV, motor system; V, olfactory system. Arabic numerals represent Brodmann areas.

A, cortical auditory area; B, brainstem; HIPP, hippocampus; HIPP GYRUS, hippocampal gyrus; LAT GEN, lateral geniculate nucleus; MG, medial geniculate nucleus; OLF B, olfactory bulb; S septal area; VA, nucleus ventralis anterior; VM, nucleus ventralis medialis; VL, nucleus ventralis lateralis; VPL, nucleus ventralis posterior lateralis; VPM, nucleus ventralis posterior medialis.

"instinctive" likes or dislikes are derived from past appraisals, we take them at face value and let them influence our actions. Obviously, such emotional attitudes are important for all living beings. In fact, it is probably more helpful to feel an immediate reluctance or fear when encountering something that is actually dangerous than to remember exactly where or when we have been hurt by something similar. At the same time, these attitudes may lead to phobias and severely restrict a man's actions unless he is willing to expose himself to a corrective experience (in or out of psychotherapy), or pay less attention to his feelings than to his reflective judgment.

Pathways Mediating Emotion. When object or situation has been effectively identified (via modality-specific and affective memory circuits) it can be appraised as "good for action." Next, the possibilities of action will be evaluated by remembering past actions and their success or failure until the appropriate choice is made. Of course, when the object is evaluated as most desirable or very harmful, and produces a strong impulse to action (an emotion or an instinctive desire), the attraction of the object may outweigh the difficulty of reaching it. Thus the salmon fights its way upstream when the time has come to lay eggs, and the dog follows a bitch in heat no matter how often he is chased away. On the other hand, what is ap-

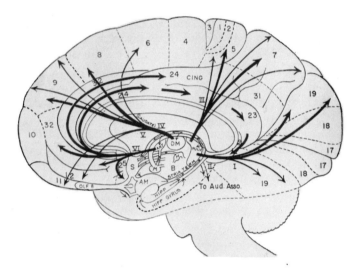

Fig. 2. Circuits mediating imagination and affective memory. Identification of an object by recalling similar things (relays from association cortex to limbic areas and via hippocampus-fornix to brainstem and thalamic sensory nuclei back to sensory association cortex), and reliving their effects on us (relays from limbic areas via cingulum, hippocampus, postcommissural fornix to anterior thalamic nuclei, limbic cortex) results in imagining possible effects of this thing on us and possible ways of coping with it (imagination circuit from limbic areas via amygdala to thalamic association nuclei and cortical association areas). Arrows indicate the direction of conduction.

I-V, circuits serving imagination: I visual, II auditory, III somesthetic, IV motor, V olfactory. VI, circuit serving affective memory. Arabic numerals represent Brodmann areas.

AM, amygdala; ANT, anterior thalamic nuclei; Aud. Asso., auditory association area; B, brainstem; CING, cingulate gyrus; DM, nucleus dorsalis medialis; HIPP, hippocampus; HIPP GYRUS, hippocampal gyrus; M, mammillary body; OLF B, olfactory bulb; PULV, pulvinar; S, septal area; STRIA TERM, stria terminalis.

praised as "bad, to be overcome" will be fought no matter how difficult. The snarling dog fighting a rival completely disregards blows
and won't stop fighting until he is dragged away bodily.

Since emotion is so closely connected with action and, indeed, as a
"felt tendency to action" directly leads to it, we would expect it to be
mediated by an "action circuit" connecting with the motor area.
When something is appraised as "good for a particular action," relays
from the limbic cortex seem to run to the hippocampus and connect
via fornix, hypothalamus, midbrain, and cerebellum with the anterior
ventral thalamic nuclei and the premotor and motor cortex (Figure
3). Stimulation of structures within this circuit (hippocampus, tegmentum, cerebellum, hypothalamus) has produced emotion in animals; and stimulation of the premotor cortex has produced a desire to
move in man (cf. Arnold, 1960, Vol. II, pp. 79–102). It seems reasonable to infer that the experience of emotion as a "felt tendency toward or away from something" is mediated by the premotor cortex.

This does not mean, of course, that stimulation of the premotor
cortex would produce the experience of emotion. In the first place,
the emotion absolutely depends on the appraisal that produces it and
gives it direction. In addition, the neural relays comprising the emotional pattern are concentrated in a comparatively narrow space in
the action circuit, particularly as it traverses the hypothalamus, but
disperse throughout the motor and premotor cortex to activate the
muscles and glands necessary for emotional expression and action.

It is also reported that emotion and imagination result in activation
of the amygdala (Lesse, Heath, Mickle, Monroe, and Miller, 1955),
and that bilaterally amygdalectomized animals showed more fear
than normals or sham-operated controls when put into the compartment in which they had been shocked; at the same time, they required many more trials to acquire an escape response ($p<.005$, Robinson, 1963). Both results can be explained by assuming that the
amygdala is a relay station in the "imagination" circuit. During emotion, the subject imagines possible actions, hence the activation of
the imagination circuit via the amygdala. With these structures removed but the memory circuit intact, the animals remember the
shock but cannot plan effective action: hence the increased fear
which slowly subsides as random attempts result in escape and are
gradually remembered and repeated.

To sum up: According to my theory, emotion proper is based on
appraisal mediated by the limbic system, and on *affective recall*
mediated by a circuit via cingulum, hippocampus, postcommissural

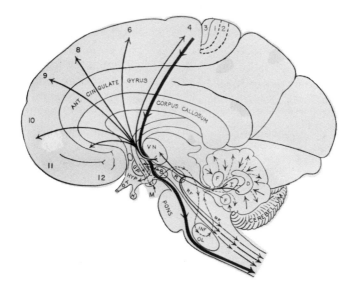

Fig. 3. Circuit mediating emotion and action. When something is appraised as good or bad (via relays to limbic cortex), a tendency to action is aroused which is mediated by relays via the hippocampus-fornix system to brainstem and cerebellum. From the cerebellar roof nuclei (dentate, D; fastigial, F; interpositus, I), the organized action pattern is relayed : (a) via ventral thalamic nuclei (VN) to the frontal lobe, connecting with corticobulbar and corticospinal tracts and mediating the felt tendency to action as well as the intended movement; (b) via the globus pallidus (GP) to extrapyramidal pathways, exciting the autonomic nervous system and organizing background motions; (c) via globus pallidus to hypothalamic (HYP) neurosecretory nuclei, initiating the secretion of appropriate hormones. ——— Relay from cerebellum to frontal lobe. - - - - - - Relay from hippocampus to cerebellum. ——— Corticospinal tract. ——— Relay from cerebellum to extrapyramidal and hypothalamic effectors.

Arabic numerals represent Brodmann areas.

D, dentate nucleus; F, fastigial nucleus; GP, globus pallidus; H, hypophysis; HYP, hypothalamus; I, nucleus interpositus; INF OL, inferior olive; M, mammillary body; OT, optic tract; R, red nucleus; RF, brainstem reticular formation; S, substantia nigra; VN, ventral thalamic nuclei.

fornix, anterior thalamic nuclei and back to various limbic areas. It is the limbic cortex that mediates the experience of liking or disliking, both as a new appraisal and as a favorable or unfavorable attitude produced by affective memory.

Each appraisal produces a felt tendency to action which either leads directly to appropriate behavior, or is modified by subsequent appraisals and subsequent action tendencies, all mediated via the action circuit connecting with the frontal lobe.

PROBLEMS OF EXPERIMENTAL VERIFICATION

Since we are not dealing with centers but rather with structures and pathways that connect sensory areas with motor areas and cannot be completely isolated from other pathways serving different functions, we must expect that experimental verification will be difficult and often ambiguous. Because an emotional action tendency includes not only the tendency to move in a particular direction but also a host of physiological and hormonal changes, only when the brain is stimulated within an area which includes relays initiating all these changes will recognizable "emotional" effects result. Stimulation of the cortical end station of the action circuit, the premotor cortex, could not be expected to yield emotional expression because such indiscriminate stimulation cannot be expected to reproduce the particular pattern of movement impulses or physiological changes that go with a given emotion. In contrast, stimulation of the subcortical relay stations (cerebellum, tegmentum, hypothalamus) has actually produced emotional effects.

LIMBIC SYSTEM

As for stimulation of limbic cortex and associated medial thalamic areas, the situation is more favorable. Olds and Milner (1954) and Olds (1955, 1956) have reported both "reward" and "punishment" effects from stimulating electrodes placed in these areas; Penfield and Jasper (1954) found that patients complained of an unpleasant taste when the border region between operculum and insula was stimulated electrically; and MacLean (1954) mentioned that electrical and chemical stimulation of the posterior cingulate gyrus has induced increased pleasure reactions to petting in cats.

Stimulation of the Anterior Limbic Cortex. This has given more ambiguous results—which is not surprising if this area mediates the appraisal of actions and action impulses, as I have suggested. Since action depends on the appraisal of action impulses, electrical stimulation of this area will interfere with action. Ward (1948) found that cats stopped walking when their anterior cingulate area was stimulated, and crouched when the current intensity was increased; and Kaada (1951) reported that such stimulation produced inhibition of cortically induced movements and autonomic responses, and also depressed spontaneous electrical activity in the motor cortex.

Lesions of the Limbic Cortex. These will give conflicting results, depending on the site of the lesion and on the extralimbic structures that may have been destroyed inadvertently. For instance, McCleary (1961) found that bilateral septal and precallosal lesions in cats produced a deficit in passive avoidance but did not interfere with active avoidance; in contrast, bilateral lesions of the cingulate gyrus impaired active avoidance but left passive avoidance intact. On the basis of his and Kaada's (1951) results, McCleary suggested that the subcallosal and precallosal cortex represent a motor inhibitory area while the cingulate gyrus represents a motor facilitatory area. If that were so, all responses should be inhibited after cingulate lesions and facilitated after septal lesions. My colleagues and I found, on the contrary, that bilateral septal lesions neither facilitated nor inhibited motor responses in rats; they merely increased errors in olfactory, visual, and auditory discrimination problems and in right/left alternation (Arnold, Fagot, Gavin, Planek, Driessen, & Snyder, in preparation). Instead of a simple motor facilitation after septal lesions, we found a severe deficit in four kinds of sensory discrimination. Considering that septal lesions always damage the precommissural and sometimes also the postcommissural fornix, this result is not difficult to explain. This is one instance where the destruction of different functional systems makes it impossible to explain the deficit without some theory of brain function. On the basis of the theory discussed above, it would seem that the septal lesions interrupted the modality-specific memory circuit by encroaching upon the precommissural fornix. This would explain the impairment in olfactory, visual, auditory discrimination and in motor memory (alternation problem).

The deficit in passive avoidance in animals with septal and precallosal lesions, as reported by McCleary, seems to stem from an interference with the appraisal of movement (precallosal cortex and anterior quarter of cingulate gyrus). When an animal is shocked in the foodbox, it will remember the shock (affective memory, via posterior cingulate) and will now appraise the impulse to approach the food as harmful and so inhibit it. After the lesion, this impulse can no longer be appraised and the cat will approach the food as before, i.e. show a passive-avoidance deficit.

Brady and Nauta's (1953, 1955) reports that rats with bilateral septal lesions showed "increased emotional reactivity" can also be explained: Since the interruption of the modality-specific memory circuit makes it impossible to identify their environment, everything is strange to these animals so that they expect harm from everywhere, hence their increased "emotional reactivity" — in other words, their increased fear and aggression.

Even if it is argued that the lack of discrimination found in rats

after septal lesions is the result of defective inhibition, we still do
not know how inhibition is achieved when the septal area is intact.
In this connection, it might be worthwhile to inquire whether a lesion of the "facilitatory" area would improve both inhibition and discrimination. According to McCleary (1961), bilateral lesions of the
(posterior) cingulate[1] gyrus impaired active avoidance and left passive avoidance intact, thus producing inhibition. But Thomas and
Slotnick found later (1962) that lesions severing projection fibers
from the anterior thalamic nucleus to the cingulate gyrus, thus producing active avoidance deficits, did not impair maze learning in
rats. Still later (1963), these investigators found that rats with cingulate lesions acquire active avoidance as easily as do intact rats, provided they are hungry. The deficit remains, however, when they are
sated. These rats also crossed over spontaneously to the compartment in which they had been shocked (passive avoidance deficit);
this happened more often when they were hungry than when they
were sated.

These findings cannot be easily explained as the result of damage
to a facilitatory system. But they can be explained on the basis of my
hypothesis that the limbic cortex bordering on the somesthetic association area mediates the appraisal of anything touched, and this
experienced liking or dislike is reexperienced when relays to the
cingulum, postcommissural fornix, and anterior thalamic nuclei return to the cingulate gyrus. When something touching the animal is
disliked and also when this dislike is reexperienced as a negative attitude, it produces an impulse to withdraw or escape. After a large
lesion of the posterior cingulate gyrus, somesthetic experiences from
body and hind legs can no longer be appraised as localized painful
touch nor can such experiences be revived. Hence pain will be felt
(via medial thalamic nuclei) but is no longer connected with a particular place or body part because the connection of the somesthetic
area with both the modality-specific and the affective memory circuit
is broken. As a result, there will be no impulse to avoid the shock
compartment, that is, no fear of the particular place where shock has
been experienced. Though rats with large posterior cingulate lesions
should no longer remember the pain of shock, they should still remember their response to the conditioned stimulus (light going out
in their home compartment and coming on in the "safe"

---

[1]McCleary calls his lesions "cingulate" lesions. However, he mentions (1961, p.
611) that the lesions producing impairment in active avoidance extended over the *posterior half of the cingulate gyrus* on both sides; in other words, they were posterior
cingulate lesions.

compartment), for the connection between the visual appraisal area (hippocampal gyrus) and the motor association area is still intact; but now they would have little motive for making the response. However, when they are hungry they want to find food. Recalling their previous response of jumping into the lighted compartment, they now repeat it *to look for food*—which the experimenter interprets as an intact "active avoidance" response. When sated, the animals have no drive toward food and the fear drive is eliminated: thus they stay in their home compartment, showing an "active avoidance" deficit. When hungry, they might cross over spontaneously because they have no fear of the dark compartment (passive avoidance deficit). When sated, nothing urges them toward that compartment (passive avoidance intact). As Thomas and Slotnick say, hunger "activated" the animals. But it restored active avoidance because hunger substituted for the defective fear drive; and hunger is a physiological appetite induced, it seems, by increased activity in the lateral hypothalamic nuclei, thus independent of the posterior cingulate gyrus.

EXPERIMENTS ON "AFFECTIVE MEMORY"

To test the notion of an affective memory circuit directly, we have conducted a series of experiments in which small electrolytic lesions were placed bilaterally at various points in the postulated circuit, namely the cingulum, the anterior and posterior insula, the fornix, hippocampus, and anterior thalamic nucleus. When this circuit is interrupted, the animal should have difficulty in reexperiencing a learned positive attitude toward a visual, olfactory, auditory, taste, touch stimulus, or toward a particular movement, depending on the site of the lesion. For instance, the affective memory of a pleasant or unpleasant taste, and of a pleasant or unpleasant touch to the face should be impaired by lesions of the posterior insula, of pleasant or painful touch to body and hindlegs by a lesion of the posterior cingulate gyrus.

This hypothesis can be tested by means of the active and passive avoidance reaction to electric shock (AAR and PAR) with shock applied either to face or hindlegs, but also by any other kind of learning problem, for the motivation to learn always implies affective memory. However, none of the results will be clearcut, whatever problem is chosen, because any learned performance is based on affective memory for more than one modality. For instance, anything seen or heard, when followed by reward, will facilitate the development of a positive attitude to the cue stimulus, which will lead to approach unless the movement toward it is appraised as undesirable because it has been punished. Accordingly, we have to consider the affective memory of the visual stimulus (sight of apparatus etc.) and also the affective memory of the appropriate approach movement. If the correct response demands approach (in AAR), the movement can be carried out without appraisal, and damage of the movement appraisal area (anterior cingulate or anterior insula) will not affect it. But if the correct response demands inhibition of approach movement, the impulse to this movement has to be appraised as inappropriate before it can be inhibited; as a result, damage of the movement-appraisal area will reveal a deficit.

Moreover, affective memory circuit lesions will be ambiguous because learning involves modality-specific memory in addition to affective memory. The animal must compare the present visual stimuli with the stimuli he has experienced in the past. Since hippocampus and fornix seem to participate in both circuits, as appears from their known connections, any deficits that result from lesions in these structures could derive from damage to either or both pathways. Finally, we must remember that appraisal of the present situation will initiate both modality-specific and affective recall. Consequently, a lesion anywhere in the cingulum, which necessarily also destroys cingulate cortex, and a lesion anywhere in the insula will also interfere with modality-specific (as well as affective) memory.

THE TASKS

Several groups of rats were trained in five successive[2] discriminations, one in each modality: visual, auditory, tactual, olfactory, and motor. The olfactory discrimination consisted of a box with a glass front. A moving tray with small cups of water appeared underneath the glass front, one cup at a time. The thirsty animal had to sniff the cup: when the odor was positive, the cup contained plain water; when negative, a quinine solution which the rat avoided. The motor problem was a single alternation T maze. Visual and auditory discrimination was tested in a Skinner box with flashing (versus steady) light as visual stimulus, a buzzer as auditory stimulus. For tactual discrimination the same box was employed; a slight shock was delivered to the grid as the only cue. The animal learned to press rapidly when it felt no shock, at which time each bar press produced a cup with a few drops of water; the rat learned to stop pressing as soon as

[2]Successive discrimination is a go-no-go type of task in which only the positive cue requires a response; to respond to the negative cue is counted an error.

it felt a shock to its feet, when bar presses brought no water. The shocks were delivered at variable intervals. The lesions were placed in some groups before learning, in others after learning and a pre-operative retention test.

Some of these experimental groups were also trained in passive avoidance in an apparatus similar to McCleary's (1961), except for its smaller size. They were trained successively (a) with shock to the face as soon as they touched the water in the drinking cup, and (b) shock to the hindlegs as soon as they started drinking (with forelegs resting on an insulated step). This variation was devised to see whether shock to the hindlegs would result in greater impairment after cingulate lesions, on the assumption that appraisal of foreleg touch or movement may be partly mediated by the anterior insula while movement of the hindlegs should be appraised totally via the cingulate. The active avoidance apparatus was a two-way shuttle box. Five seconds before the grid floor was electrified, the ceiling light in the home compartment went out, and the now safe compartment lighted up.

RESULTS

A preliminary analysis of the data showed the following results for the various lesions:

Cingulum Lesions at the Genu (Damage to Area 24, Bilaterally). Of 15 rats, all showed some retention deficit in the visual, auditory, tactual, and motor problems. When the retention scores of each animal before and after the lesion were compared separately, it was found that two animals showed significant impairment in olfactory discrimination, three in tactual, six in auditory, seven in the right/left alternation, and eight in visual discrimination (p between $<$ .05 and $<$ .01). Since all these tasks imply bodily movement, any impairment in affective memory for such movement will impair performance. Lesions at the genu should impair the ability of appraising a movement about to be made, and also to develop a positive or negative attitude toward a given movement. However, body movement is not decisive. Though the rat has to approach cup or bar, head and foreleg movements are also required. If head movements are appraised via the anterior insula and foreleg movements partly so, as I believe, only combined anterior cingulate and anterior insula lesions would show severe impairment.

Mid-Cingulum Lesions; Learning Studies. In a group of 17 rats with bilateral cingulum lesions and damage to Area 23, there was no deficit in postoperative learning of visual and olfactory discrimination. But in learning an active avoidance, the experimental group made significantly more spontaneous crossings ($p < .02$) and showed significantly fewer near-avoidances ($p < .002$), though there was no significant difference between the experimental group and intact controls in the time taken to reach criterion, or the mean number of avoidances. Like McCleary's (1961) cats with anterior limbic lesions, these rats showed intact active avoidance because their affective memory of pain (mediated via the posterior cingulate gyrus and cingulum) was intact and produced the impulse to jump into the safe compartment. The increased number of spontaneous crossings into the still "unsafe" compartment resembles a deficit in passive avoidance (cf. Pribram, Lim, Poppen, and Bagshaw, 1966) and suggests that the lesioned animals were not able to appraise their movements as inappropriate and so could not inhibit their impulse to move. On the other hand, the control animals were often prevented from correct avoidance because of their reluctance to enter a compartment in which they had been shocked. In learning *passive* avoidance, the lesioned rats were significantly inferior to intact controls, both after shock to the mouth and shock to the hind legs ($p < .02$ and $< .05$), which confirms that their appraisal of action impulses was impaired so that they could not withhold the response.

In a retention study, 11 animals with bilateral lesions of the cingulum, bilateral damage to Area 23, hippocampus, hippocampal rudiment, showed impaired retention of the auditory, tactual, and motor tasks ($p < .025$ to $< .005$) as compared with their own performance on a retention test before the lesions were inflicted; they remained stationary or improved in olfactory discrimination. However, since the hippocampal rudiment was transected and the hippocampus was damaged in those lesions, it is possible that the deficits were the result of such incidental damage which interfered with modality-specific memory.

In another experiment, 16 rats were trained preoperatively in visual and olfactory discrimination as well as in passive and active avoidance. According to histological evaluation, 11 of these animals had a complete bilateral transection of the cingulum, and bilateral destruction of Area 23, with some invasion of Area 24 in 6 rats, and of Area 29 in 3. This group of 11 improved both in visual and olfactory retention after the lesion, and showed no significant differences in active avoidance retention. In the passive avoidance task, their error scores (number of shocks received) actually improved when the aversive stimulus was shock to the face ($p < .05$). With shock to the feet, there was a slight (nonsignificant) deficit. However, they made significantly more erroneous approaches, both with shock to the feet and shock to the face, as compared with their preoperative performance ($p < .05$ and $< .01$).

In these approaches, the animals ran to the cup and then stopped with mouth 1-2 mm above it and forepaws resting on the electrifiable step. Then, instead of lapping the water, they would quickly withdraw, a type of behavior hardly ever observed in intact animals which usually stop before reaching the cup or never start at all. This curious behavior of the lesioned animals seems to have resulted from their inability to appraise body movement. Since they were thirsty, they approached the cup; but they did not begin to lap the water because the pain of electric shock, brought on by this movement in the past, was now revived (via the intact insula) and resulted in hasty retreat.

Eight rats out of the original group of 16 showed no deficit postoperatively; six of these were among the 11 animals with bilateral transection of the cingulum. After their postoperative retention tests were completed, they were given another lesion which bilaterally transected the cingulum at the genu and damaged Area 24 without encroaching on Area 23. After the second lesion, they showed improvement in the retention of olfactory discrimination and active avoidance, and no significant differences in visual discrimination; they did, however, show impaired retention in passive avoidance. They made more erroneous approaches both with shock to the face and shock to the feet ($p < .02$ and $< .05$). The number of shocks they received increased, both with shock to the face and shock to the feet. But only under the latter condition was the difference significant ($p < .01$). This seems to indicate that the additional lesions to the anterior cingulate further decreased their ability of appraising body movements.

Posterior Cingulum Lesions; Learning Studies. These lesions interrupted the cingulum bilaterally and destroyed Area 23 together with the anterior part of Areas 29b and 29c on both sides, without invading Area 24. Ten rats with such lesions showed a deficit in learning single alternation ($p < .01$) and avoided the electric shock in the two-way shuttle box significantly less often than sham-operated controls ($p < .01$; active avoidance deficit). Visual and olfactory discrimination learning showed no significant differences.

This experiment confirms earlier reports that active avoidance is impaired by posterior cingulate and cingulum lesions. In this situation, the animal is no longer able to relive the pain connected with shock and thus has no longer an immediate impulse to avoid it. However, the experimental animals made significantly fewer spontaneous crossings than the sham-operated controls ($p < .01$), which seems to contradict the results reported above, according to which 17 animals with Area 23 lesions made more spontaneous crossings into the "unsafe" compartment. Apparently, after bilateral damage of Area 29, the rats no longer had much incentive for moving out of their home compartment because the lesion interfered with their affective memory of pain. As a result, they made few spontaneous crossings because they were no longer afraid. According to my theory, damage to Area 23 alone is bound to produce effects different from those resulting from lesions of Area 23 plus 29.

The impairment in learning active avoidance and single alternation, as compared with the intact performance in visual and olfactory discrimination, can be explained on the basis of my theory which postulates that different pathways are involved in these performances. In active avoidance, the animal must remember the pain of shock and must have a revived positive attitude toward the lighted compartment. The affective memory for bodily pain requires an intact affective memory circuit via postcommissural fornix and anterior thalamic nuclei back to Area 29. Since this area is damaged together with the cingulum, both appraisal and affective memory of painful touch are impaired, so that there is no impulse to escape.

Similarly, in the single alternation problem the animal must remember what it has done before (modality-specific memory), but must also have a positive attitude toward turning now in a different direction. This requires an appraisal of the remembered action via a circuit from premotor area to anterior cingulate gyrus, and via cingulum to postcommissural fornix, anterior thalamic nucleus, and anterior cingulate gyrus. With a lesion in the posterior cingulum, this circuit is interrupted.[3]

---

[3]This explanation presupposes that relays from the anterior cingulum course around the corpus callosum to connect with hippocampus and fornix. Adey and Meyer (1952) and Adey, Sunderland, and Dunlop (1957) present evidence that most of the cingulum fibers dip into the subcortex a short distance from their point of entry, which would call this assumption in question. White, Nelson, and Foltz, (1960), however, reported that hippocampal potentials, evoked by a stimulating electrode placed in the midcingulum, were abolished by severing the cingulum posterior to the electrode, but were completely unaffected by a cingulum lesion anterior to the electrode. This would mean that there are enough long relays at least from midcingulum to hippocampus so that it can reasonably be inferred that some of these fibers are derived from more anterior parts.

On the other hand, in the visual discrimination problem the animal sees the bar together with the positive visual stimulus, remembers it as "good to press" via affective memory circuit running from hippocampal gyrus via hippocampus, postcommissural fornix, to anterior thalamic nucleus and anterior insula (appraisal of head and foreleg movements). Since there is no lesion in that circuit, this appraisal produces an impulse to the correct action. In olfactory discrimination, the positive odor recalls the "good" taste of water and strengthens the impulse to drink. In contrast, the negative odor recalls the "bad" taste of quinine (via posterior insula); thus the impulse to drink aroused by thirst is remembered as "bad" (via hippocampus to postcommissural fornix and anterior insula). Again, there is no lesion in these circuits and consequently no impairment.

Anterior Insula Lesions. The experimental group of 12 animals (5 with bilateral, 7 with unilateral lesions) showed significant impairment in *learning* the olfactory discrimination ($p < .01$), but no deficit in learning the visual discrimination problem and single alternation. Active avoidance also did not differ from that of sham-operated controls.

In the olfactory discrimination, the animals have to approach the cup and drink, if the cup has the remembered "good" odor. The rat remembers the water and approaches the cup. The intact animal then appraises the impulse to lap the water as either appropriate or inappropriate, and is able to inhibit drinking on detecting the negative odor. Since the anterior insula was damaged in the experimental animals, this appraisal of head movement was impaired; hence their inability to inhibit drinking. For the same reason, rats with such lesions have a passive-avoidance deficit, that is, they keep on drinking from a dish through which they have been shocked, as reported by Kaada, Rasmussen, and Kveim, (1962). In contrast, active avoidance is unimpaired because (a) no movement appraisal is necessary with approach as the correct movement, and (b) the area serving appraisal of bodily shock (Area 29) is intact.

Posterior Insula Lesions. The group of 12 experimental rats (3 with bilateral, 9 with unilateral lesions) showed a highly significant *learning* deficit in olfactory discrimination ($p < .001$) as compared with a group of sham-operated controls. Their performance on visual discrimination, single alternation, and active avoidance was unimpaired. The performance deficit in olfactory discrimination in this case seems to stem from the animals' inability to appraise the quinine solution as unpleasant, an appraisal mediated by the posterior insula, according to my theory. As a result, the rats did not avoid quinine and so never learned the discrimination. This interpretation is supported by Bagshaw and Pribram's (1953) findings that monkeys refuse quinine as long as the posterior insula is intact.

The intact performances on visual discrimination, single alternation, and active avoidance are explained similarly as the intact performance on these tasks after anterior insula lesions: the necessary modality-specific and affective memory circuits are intact.

Anterior Thalamic Nucleus Lesions. Fifteen out of 16 lesioned rats showed some impairment and all animals with bilateral lesions showed a significant deficit in *retaining* right/left alternation when compared with their own preoperative retention (p from $< .05$ to $<$ .00001). Fifteen animals had some deficit in postoperative retention of visual and tactual discrimination; this deficit was significant in 5 animals for visual, and in 4 animals for tactual discrimination. Eight rats had some retention deficit in auditory discrimination, which was significant in one animal. Only olfactory discrimination was retained perfectly by all rats.

This lesion seems to have produced a general impairment of affective memory in every modality except smell. Considering the very severe impairment in single alternation (which involves only motor and motor-affective memory), we could say that lesions of the anterior thalamic nucleus seem to affect primarily the affective memory for appropriate or inappropriate body movement; that is, the movements necessary for correct responses are no longer felt as clearly appropriate, and the erroneous responses are no longer felt as wrong. Consequently, incorrect responses can no longer be inhibited.

The intact olfactory discrimination in this group seems to suggest that the affective memory circuit for good/bad smell, starting from the subcallosal gyrus, and for good/bad taste, starting from the posterior insula, as well as the affective memory for appropriate/ inappropriate head movements, do not include the anterior thalamic nucleus; or rather, this circuit does not include the lesion sites.

Conclusions

Summing up, we can conclude that there is evidence for the theory that the anterior cingulate gyrus mediates the appraisal of body movement; the posterior cingulate gyrus, the appraisal of touch; and that such appraisals can be revived as positive or negative attitudes to similar things, via a circuit which runs from the above limbic areas via the cingulum to postcommissural fornix, anterior thalamic nucleus, and back to various limbic cortical regions. Moreover, the appraisal of head movements seems to be mediated by the anterior insula; the appraisal of taste, by the posterior insula; these appraisals also can be revived, but the corresponding affective memory circuit seems to run via the hippocampus and postcommissural fornix to the insula, avoiding the anterior thalamic nucleus.

Affective memory seems to be the basis on which new situations are appraised. Since every appraisal induces an impulse toward what is appraised as good, beneficial, and away from what is appraised as bad, harmful, it is the root of emotion. The kind of emotion aroused depends on the conditions of appraisal. Indeed, affective memory determines our emotional attitudes toward any situation we encounter. The hope for educating our emotions must rest on the possibility of correcting our present appraisal and through it our affective memory.

SUMMARY

A phenomenological analysis of the sequence of psychological activities from perception to emotion and action has suggested that emotion as a felt action tendency depends on the person's appraisal of the situation. Correct appraisal requires memory; and memory includes not only sensory and motor memory but the remembered positive or negative attitude to something (affective memory). In addition, the appropriate action must be rehearsed in imagination before it can be decided upon and executed. The large body of research reported in the literature allows the inference that appraisal, experienced as a positive or negative attitude, is mediated by limbic cortex (sub- and precallosal gyrus, cingulate, retrosplenial, and hippocampal gyrus, and insula) while affective recall (the reexperienced attitude) is mediated by relays that run from limbic cortex via cingulum and hippocampus to postcommissural fornix, mamillary body, anterior thalamic nucleus, and back to cortical limbic areas. Emotion as a felt tendency to action seems to be mediated by the "action circuit," via relays from limbic cortex to hippocampus, fornix, hypothalamus, midbrain, and cerebellum, connecting via anterior ventral thalamic nucleus with the premotor and motor area.

A series of small electrolytic lesions placed at various points of the proposed affective memory circuit in the brain of rats, either before or after they learned various tasks, has produced sufficient evidence to support the hypothesis that the anterior cingulate tyrus mediates the appraisal of body movements, the anterior insula the appraisal of head movements, the posterior cingulate the appraisal of touch, and the posterior insula the appraisal of taste; and that such appraisals are revived as positive or negative attitudes via the above circuit, and so contribute to learning.

REFERENCES

Adey, W. R., & Meyer, M. Hippocampal and hypothalamic connexions of the temporal lobe in the monkey. *Brain*, 1952, **75**, 358-384.

Adey, W. R., Sunderland, S. and Dunlop, C. W. The entorhinal area; electrophysiological studies of its interrelations with rhinencephalic structures and the brainstem. *EEG Clinical Neurophysiology* 1957, 9, 309-324.

Allen, W. F. Effect of ablating the frontal lobes, hippocampi, and occipitoparieto-temporal (excepting pyriform areas) lobes on positive and negative olfactory conditioned reflexes. *American Journal of Physiology*, 1940, **128**, 754-771.

Arnold, M. B. *Emotion and Personality.* 2 vols. New York: Columbia University Press, 1960.

Arnold, M. B., Fagot, H. J., Gavin, M. H., Planek, T. W., Driessen, G. J., & Snyder, J. F. The role of the hippocampal system in learning and retention. In preparation.

Bagshaw, M. H., & Pribram, K. H. Cortical organization in gustation (Macaca mulatta). *Journal of Neurophysiology*, 1953, **16**, 499-508.

Bartlett, F. C. *Remembering.* London and New York: Cambridge University Press, 1932.

Brady, J. V., & Nauta, W. J. H. Subcortical mechanisms in emotional behavior: affective changes following septal forebrain lesions in the albino rat. *Journal of Comparative and Physiological Psychology*, 1953, **46**, 339-346.

Brady, J. V., & Nauta, W. J. H. Subcortical mechanisms in emotional behavior: The duration of affective changes following septal and habenular lesions in the albino rat. *Journal of Comparative and Physiological Psychology*, 1955, **48**, 412-420.

De Valois, R. L., C. J. Smith, A. J. Karoly, and S. T. Kitai. 1958. Electrical responses of primate visual system. I. Different layers of macaque lateral geniculate nucleus. *Journal of Comparative Physiological Psychology*, **51**, 662-668.

Gastaut, H., Jus, A., Jus, C., Morrell, F., Storm van Leeuwen, W., Dongier, S., Naquet, R., Regis, H., Roger, A., Bekkering, D., Kamp, A., & Werre, J. Étude photographique des reactions électroencephalographiques conditionnées chez l'homme. *Electroencephalography and Clinical Neurophysiology*, 1957, 9, 1-34.

Kaada, B. R. Somato-motor, autonomic and electrographic responses to electrical stimulation of "rhinencephalic" and other forebrain structures in primates, cat and dog. *Acta Physiologica & Scandinavica Supplementum* 83, 1951, **24**, 1-285.

Kaada, B. R., Rasmussen, E. W., & Kveim, O. Impaired acquisition of passive avoidance behavior by subcallosal, septal, hypothalamic, and insular lesions in rats. *Journal of Comparative and Physiological Psychology*, 1962, **55**, 661-670.

Lesse, H., Heath, R. G., Mickle, W. A., Monroe, R. R., & Miller, W. Rhinencephalic activity during thought. *Journal of Nervous and Mental Disease*, 1955, **122**, 433-440.

MacLean, P. D. Personal communication, 1954.

McCleary, R. A. Response specificity in the behavioral effects of limbic system lesions in the cat. *Journal of Comparative and Physiological Psychology*, 1961, **54**, 606-613.

Nielsen, J. M. *Agnosia, apraxia, aphasia: Their value in cerebral localization.* (2d ed.) New York: Harper (Hoeber), 1943.

Olds, J. Physiological mechanisms of reward. In M. R. Jones (Ed.), *Nebraska symposium on motivation.* Lincoln: University of Nebraska Press, 1955.

Olds, J. A preliminary mapping of electrical reinforcing effects in the rat brain. *Journal of Comparative and Physiological Psychology,* 1956, **59**, 281-283.

Olds, J., & Milner, P. Positive reinforcement produced by electrical stimulation of septal area and other regions of rat brain. *Journal of Comparative and Physiological Psychology,* 1954, **47**, 419-427.

Penfield, W., & Jasper, H. H. *Epilepsy and the functional anatomy of the human brain.* Boston: Little, Brown, 1954.

Pribram, H. B., & Barry, J. Further behavioral analysis of the parieto-temporo-preoccipital cortex. *Journal of Neurophysiology,* 1956, **19**, 99-106.

Pribram, K. H., Lim, H., Poppen, R., & Bagshaw, M. Limbic lesions and the temporal structure of redundancy. *Journal of Comparative and Physiological Psychology,* 1966, **61**, 368-373.

Pribram, K. H., & Mishkin, M. Simultaneous and successive visual discrimination by monkeys with inferotemporal lesions. *Journal of Comparative and Physiological Psychology,* 1955, **48**, 198-202.

Robinson, E. Effect of amygdalectomy on fear-motivated behavior in rats. *Journal of Comparative and Physiological Psychology,* 1963, **56**, 814-820.

Thomas, G. J., & Slotnick, B. M. Effects of lesions in the cingulum on maze learning and avoidance conditioning in the rat. *Journal of Comparative and Physiological Psychology,* 1962, **55**, 1085-1091.

Thomas, G. J., & Slotnick, B. M. Impairment of avoidance responding by lesions in cingulate cortex in rats depends on food drive. *Journal of Comparative and Physiological Psychology,* 1963, **56**, 959-964.

Ward, A. A., Jr. The anterior cingulate gyrus and personality. *Research Publications Association for Research in Nervous and Mental Disease,* 1948, **27**, 438-445.

Weiskrantz, L., & Mishkin, M. Effects of temporal and frontal cortical lesions on auditory discrimination in monkey. *Brain,* 1958, **81**, 406-414.

White, L. E., Jr., Nelson, W. M., & Foltz, E. L. Cingulum fasciculus studied by evoked potentials. *Experimental Neurology,* 1960, **2**, 406-421.

Wilson, M. Effects of circumscribed cortical lesions upon somesthetic and visual discrimination in the monkey. *Journal of Comparative and Physiological Psychology,* 1957, **50**, 630-635.

Author Index

Numbers in italics refer to the pages on which the complete references are listed.

A

Ader, R., 98, *122*
Adey, W. R., 280, *284*
Ajmone-Marsan, C., 149, *186*
Aldridge, V. J., 219, *227*
Alexander, B. K., 40, 50, *57*
Allen, M. B., 207, 208, *226*
Allen, W. F., 265, *284*
Allikmets, L., 87, *89*
Altman, J., 136, *144*
Amsel, A., 252, 253, 257, *258*
Anand, B., 195, *201*
Andersson, B., 73, *89*
Andrew, R. J., 7, *18*
Aquinas, St. Thomas, 4, *18*
Aristotle, 4, *18*
Arana, R., 163, 164, *187*
Arduini, A., 149, 150, 158, *185*
Arnold, M. B., 6, 13, *18*, 267, 270, 273, *284*
Asaro, K. D., 154, 169, *188*
Ax, A. F., 6, *18*
Axelrod, J., 63, 66, *69*, 70

B

Baccelli, G., 209, *226*
Bach, L. M. N., 155, *184*
Bach-y-Rita, G., 197, 198, 200, *201*
Bagshaw, M. H., 265, 278, 282, *284*
Bak, I. J., 136, *146*
Baldessarini, R. J., 63, *69*
Bandura, A., 11, *18*
Bard, P., 12, *18*
Barefoot, J., 241, *242*
Barry, J., 265, *285*

Bartlett, F. C., 267, *284*
Bartorelli, C., 209, *226*
Bateman, D. E., 10, *19*
Bauer, J. A., 97, 114, 119, *124*
Baxter, B. L., 87, *89*
Beach, F. A., 12, *18*
Beatty, W. W., 255, *258*, 259
Beaulnes, A., 80, 86, 87, *89*
Beer, B., 96, *123*
Bekkering, D., *284*
Belluzzi, J. D., 75, *89*
Berger, H., *184*
Berlanger, D., 96, *122*
Bindra, D. A., 8, 15, *18*
Bizzi, E., 209, *226*
Black, A. H., 96, *123*
Black, W. C., 96, *124*
Bloch, V., 208, *226*
Bogacz, J., 175, *185*
Bolles, R. C., 248, 251, 253, *258*
Bondareff, W., 88, *92*
Bonvallet, M., 207, 208, *226*
Botto, R. W., 235, *242*
Bowden, J. W., 148, 153, 168, *186*
Bradley, P. B., 86, *89*
Brady, J. V., 76, *89*, 95, 96, 97, 99, 100, 101, 102, 103, 104, 105, 106, 107, 108, 109, 110, 111, 112, 113, 114, 115, 116, 117, 118, 119, 120, 121, *122*, *123*, *124*, *125*, 257, *258*, 273, *284*
Bragdon, H. R., 175, *184*
Bremer, F., 148, 149, *184*
Brill, N. Q., 98, *124*
Broadhurst, P. L., 10, *18*
Broca, P., 131, *144*
Bronson, G. W., 11, 12, *18*
Brown, J. S., 14, *18*, 248, *259*

287

Subject Index

A

Acetylcholine, 74
  diencephalon and, 79
  hypothalamus and, 79-80
  midbrain and, 86-87
  preoptic area and, 79
3-Acetylpyridine, hippocampus and, 136
ACTH, *see* Adrenocorticotropic hormone
Activation, *see* Arousal
Adrenocorticotropic hormone, conditioned anxiety and, 102, 103
Affection,
  maturation and,
    infant-mother and mother-infant, 37-40
    peer, 40-44
    social isolation and, 49, 53
Affective reactivity, *see also* Emotional reactivity
  amygdala and, 74
  hippocampus and, 76
  hypothalamus and, 78-79
  midbrain and, 83
Aggression, 150
  amygdala and, 74, 75, 76
  brain mechanisms and, 151
  carbachol and, 75
  caudate nucleus and, 82
  cerebral areas and self-stimulation of, 196
  direct stimulation of brain and, 190, 196, 199, 200, 201
  heritability of, 30, 31
  hippocampus and, 76-77
  hypothalamus and, 79
  limbic brain and, 134, 138
  maturation and, 37, 45-46
    social isolation and, 48-50, 54
  midbrain and, 84

modality-specific memory and, 273
  preoptic area and, 79
  septal lesions and, 254
Agnostic behavior, 30-31
  brain mechanisms and, 151
  electrical stimulation and, 196
Alcohol ingestion, avoidance conditioning and, 96
Alertness, 148, 154
  electrical stimulation and, 164
  electroencephalogram and, 161, 169
  evoked potentials and, 175-178
  hippocampus and, 150
  reticular formation and, 149, 153, 165-166, 183
Alimentary changes, 240-241
  avoidance conditioning and, 96-97
Amygdala, 151-152
  activation of, 270
  affective memory and, 269
  diencephalon and, 152
  drugs and, 74-76, 81
  limbic brain and, 133, 134
  radio stimulation of, 196-197, 199
Amygdaloid nucleus, 64
Anesthesia,
  cortex and, 172
  reticular formation and, 164-166
Anger, 263
  amygdala and, direct stimulation of, 199
  electroencephalogram and, 178
  perception of bodily changes and, 231
Antidepressants, *see* Drugs, antidepressant
Anxiety,
  conditioned, 98-102
  electroencephalogram and, 160, 161, 162
  heart rate and, 225

H